TYPHOON GIRL

TYPICAL GIRLS?

YOUNG WOMEN FROM SCHOOL TO THE JOB MARKET

CHRISTINE GRIFFIN

Routledge & Kegan Paul
London, Boston, Melbourne and Henley

First published in 1985
by Routledge & Kegan Paul plc

14 Leicester Square, London WC2H 7PH, England

9 Park Street, Boston, Mass. 02108, USA

464 St Kilda Road, Melbourne,
Victoria 3004, Australia and

Broadway House, Newtown Road,
Henley on Thames, Oxon RG9 1EN, England

Set in Journal 10/12pt
by Columns Ltd. Reading, Berks,
and printed in Great Britain
by T.J. Press (Padstow) Ltd.
Padstow, Cornwall

Library of Congress Cataloging in Publication Data

Griffin, Christine, 1953-

Typical girls?
Bibliography: p.
Includes index.
1. Young women—Employment—England—Birmingham
(West Midlands) 2. Young women—Education—England—
Birmingham (West Midlands) 3. Young women—England—
Birmingham (West Midlands) I. Title.
HD6055.6.G72B574   1985   331.3'4'0942496   84-18309

British Library CIP data also available

ISBN 0-7100-9881-2

Contents

Preface

Although there is only one name on the cover, this book would not have been possible without the cooperation and support of many other people. I am especially grateful to all those who took part in the research on which the book is based, and particularly to the young women I interviewed: *Typical Girls?* is written primarily for them. Any errors or omissions are entirely my responsibility, but I am especially indebted to the following people.

I was fortunate enough to be based at Birmingham University's Centre for Contemporary Cultural Studies during the research study. The commitment to collective work and discussion (however traumatic and time-consuming) and to radical political analysis, made 'the Centre' an interesting and challenging place to work. I am grateful to the numerous people with whom I discussed my work, especially the various members of Centre sub-groups on Work, Race and Politics, Sexuality and Education between 1979 and 1982.

I particularly valued the chance to exchange ideas with other women in an atmosphere where feminists (indeed women themselves) were not treated as unwelcome interlopers into the predominantly male world of academia. By no means all my ideas developed from academic analyses: I owe an enormous debt to the Women's Liberation Movement, and to other feminists with whom I discussed ideas, theories and strategies.

Liesel Rosindale, Mary Ballard, Ann Lane, Diedre Baker and Janet Warner carried out between them the invaluable work of transcribing tape interviews and typing manuscripts. I should also like to thank

Maureen McNeil, Dan Finn and Mick Billig, whose constructive comments on early drafts saved me from more than one writer's dilemma. Helen Armitage and Philippa Brewster, my editors at RKP, have both been patient and supportive as I struggled to cut a lengthy first draft into a more concise final manuscript.

Since late 1979 I have been working with a Girls' Group in a Birmingham youth centre. This work had no official connection with my research, but it taught me a great deal about the value of female friendship groups and the degree of (predominantly male) opposition to women meeting together. From discussions with other women and girls involved in similar work around Britain, I have come to appreciate the close links between academic research and 'practitioners' such as youth workers. Along with young women and their male peers, the latter must remain 'in the field' long after the researchers have departed.

Finally, I want to dedicate this book to my parents, to Anna McGuire, and to the Acocks Green Blossoms.

Christine Griffin
June 1984

Acknowledgments

The author and publishers are grateful to the following for permission to reproduce material: Virgin Music (Publishers) Ltd for kind permission to reproduce verses from the song 'Typical Girls' by the Slits; the author and publisher of *Gender and Schooling* by Michelle Stanworth, published by Hutchinson, 1983; Dan Finn for material from 'New deals and broken promises', Chapter 4, PhD thesis, Centre for Contemporary Cultural Studies, Birmingham, 1981; the Education Group, Centre for Contemporary Cultural Studies, for material from *Unpopular Education*, published by Hutchinson, 1981; the Department of Employment, Welsh Office, and Ann Loudoun for material from 'Guidance to Local Education Authorities on the 1973 Employment and Training Act', 1980 revision; Catherine A. MacKinnon for material from *Sexual Harassment of Working Women*, Yale University Press, 1979; Gage Publishing for material from *The Secret Oppression* by C. Backhouse and Leah Cohen, published by Macmillan of Canada Ltd, 1978; McGraw-Hill Book Company for material from *Sexual Shakedown* by Lin Farley, 1978; Sally Thorpe for material from 'Young women's employment: a survey in Birmingham', unpublished BSc dissertation, University of Aston, 1982; the authors and publishers for material from *Slump City* by A. Friend and A. Metcalf, Pluto Press, 1981; the author and publishers for material from Susan Griffin, *Pornography and Silence*, The Women's Press and Harper & Row, 1981; the Controller of Her Majesty's Stationery Office for tables from *Careers Bulletin*, Spring 1982; Birmingham Careers Service for statistics for 1979 school leavers.

Introduction

Typical girls are looking for something
Typical girls fall under a spell
Typical girls buy magazines
Typical girls feel like hell
Typical girls worry about spots, fat and natural smells.

Who invented typical girls?
Who's bringing out the new improved model?
Ah, that's another marketing ploy
Typical girl gets typical boy.

The Slits

Male pupil:	I don't really know those three well, but I think I'd put them all in the same bracket, they're typical girls.
Interviewer:	What's a typical girl then?
Male pupil:	Well, maybe they've all got the same attitude, like they don't want to be here . . . What I meant was they are all the same. They all sit down in the back corner, and they don't say much out loud, you hardly know they are there.

(Stanworth, 1981, p.43)

The above quotes are from the song 'Typical Girls' by all-female punk band the Slits, and from Michelle Stanworth's study of gender divisions in the classroom. In their different ways, they illustrate some of the reasons why this book is entitled *Typical Girls?* The book traces the experiences of a group of young women from leaving school in 1979 through their first two years in the full-time labour market. These experiences were shaped in part by assumptions about 'typical girls', whether these were reflected in the pages of girls' magazines, or in the behaviour of parents, teachers, employers, or their male peers.

I have tried to disentangle the various assumptions that are made about 'typical girls' in all their complexity and inconsistency. Such assumptions did not necessarily bear any close or direct correspondence to the lives of the young women I interviewed, so the central question was not whether they were 'true' or 'false'. When young women's own experiences were in direct contradiction to the notion of a 'typical girl' (for example those who moved into engineering jobs), they were discounted as unique exceptions. So the assumptions made about 'typical girls' sometimes denied or ignored the experiences of young women themselves, lumping them together into an amorphous and strangely anonymous mass (cf. Stanworth, 1981).

This book argues that there is no such person as a 'typical girl' (hence the question mark in the title), and shows how assumptions about such a being can affect young women's lives. Of course, I too had preconceived ideas and expectations about their lives: no one can be a totally objective and value-free research worker. *Typical Girls?* therefore includes those moments when my presence or my ideas affected the research on which the book is based. I would not dismiss these events as an unwelcome contamination of the research 'findings', since they usually helped me to understand particular aspects of young women's lives with greater clarity.

Typical Girls? had its origins in a research study of Young Women and Work which was funded by the Social Science Research Council, and based at Birmingham University's Centre for Contemporary Cultural Studies. The Young Women and Work project was set up as a sort of female version of Paul Willis's research on the school to work transition for young white working class 'lads' (Willis, 1977).[1] It aimed to follow a group of young working class women from school into the job market, looking at the influences of gender and family life on their experiences (see Griffin, 1984).

I visited six different Birmingham schools in the first six months of 1979, interviewing 180 students in groups and individually. I talked to fourth, fifth and sixth formers, middle and working class students, young Asian, Afro-Caribbean and white women — and some young men. Some students expected to leave the fifth form with few (or no) academic qualifications, to find a job or go to college; some were unsure about their futures; some hoped to stay on to the sixth form and take more exams. Most of the more 'academic' sixth formers were taking 'A' levels and expected to go to college or university, and (a minority) to get a job. I also interviewed headteachers, careers and form teachers, and careers officers.

These interviews in schools form the basis for Part I of the book. Chapter 1 outlines the very different positions of this diverse group of students in the education system, focusing on their last few months at school. Chapter 2 looks at their experiences of careers advice in school and the ambivalent relationship between the Careers Service and schools. Chapters 3 and 4 cover domestic work and family life, both of which had considerable influence on the young women as they moved from school into the full-time job market. Chapter 5 looks at leisure, the sphere in which social and economic pressures to get a boyfriend were especially crucial.

Chapter 6 examines the maintenance of gender differences and separate 'female' and 'male' spheres, looking at divisions between girls' and boys' subjects in school, women's and men's work in the home and the labour market, and the separation between female and male friendship groups in school. Chapter 7 covers young women's expectations of full-time employment and unemployment, after a brief look at their involvement in casual part-time jobs.

For most working class fifth formers, the distinction between office and factory work was particularly important; the former was seen as a 'good job for a girl', and the latter as far less desirable employment. Since this distinction crystallised so many ideas about 'typical girls' and women's work, I concentrated on those who moved into 'women's jobs' in offices and factories for the second stage of the research. Part II documents this work, as I followed twenty-five fifth formers from each of the schools into office and factory jobs, and into 'men's jobs' in the male world of engineering, as well as periods of unemployment. The nature of the research design and the limited time and resources available restricted this group to mainly young white working class women, who left school in 1979 with no qualifications, or up to four 'O' levels.

Although I followed a group of young white women from school,

I did interview young Asian and Afro-Caribbean women and men in schools and workplaces. As a white woman, I decided to concentrate on the influences of white racism, rather than try to give an account of young black women's lives which would be affected in part by my own ill-informed assumptions. I wanted to avoid the presentation of black people and black cultures as some sort of problem, a tendency which has been all too prevalent in social science research.[2]

I visited most of these twenty-five young women at home (at their invitation), in coffee bars and local pubs, and if possible in their workplaces. This stage of the research depended on the young women's cooperation, and they were all told from the outset what their participation would entail. The home visits usually took place in the 'best' front room or the kitchen, which was very much a female space. The young women's mothers and elder sisters were usually eager to talk, and were interested in the research. Fathers and elder brothers (if they were present) were more elusive. They showed a wary curiosity about my presence, popping their heads around the kitchen door before disappearing to the pub or to watch TV.

The most time-consuming — and exhausting — part of the research was the series of workplace case studies. I spent between five and ten working days in each of the ten companies visited. Part II is based on these case studies, and on young women's experiences after leaving school. Chapter 8 describes the twenty-five young women who were followed from school. Chapter 9 looks at those who went into office jobs, as office juniors, data processors, secretarial trainees and clerical workers in banking. Chapter 10 covers those in traditionally female factory work, including relatively skilled sewing machinists and those in monotonous assembly work in Birmingham's 'small metal trades'. Chapter 11 traces the experiences of those young women who moved into engineering as trainee technicians and operatives, working alongside men, or in the all-female Engineering Industry Training Board (EITB) schemes. Chapter 12 looks at young women's role in the Youth Opportunities Scheme (YOPS) and their experiences of unemployment.

Typical Girls? ends with a review of the changes in the youth labour market that have taken place since these young women left school in 1979, including the launch of the Youth Training Scheme (YTS). The concluding chapter summarises the 'results' of the research and the main arguments presented in the book. It also examines the practical implications of this analysis for young women themselves, and especially for those who work with young people.

Typical Girls? and the research on which it is based are unusual for a number of reasons. The Young Women and Work study was designed to rely mainly on qualitative research methods: loosely structured interviews and systematic observation. It had none of the traditional trappings of social science research: no surveys, no questionnaires and no computer programmes. So this book is not full of statistical tables and percentages, and it bears little resemblance to an academic report of research findings. It is structured by people's experiences, and especially those of the young women who took part in the study.[3]

My intention was not to find a group of young women who were strictly representative (i.e. 'typical') of all similar young women in Birmingham. *Typical Girls?* aims to present a picture of some young women's lives in all their complexity, putting their experiences into political and historical context. Most research work has tended to ignore women's experiences altogether, or to try and understand them using theories which were designed to explain men's position (Spender, 1980; Millman, 1975). So whilst young women's words are not taken at face value in any simplistic way, they *are* taken seriously.

The Young Women and Work study was also unusual because it focused on young *women's* lives and was carried out by a *female* researcher. The numerous male academics who have studied the position of (mainly white and working class) 'lads' pass without comment as perfectly normal, yet I was continually being asked why I was talking mainly to girls. I was assumed to be a feminist on several occasions before people had even seen me, because of the predominantly 'female' nature of the research. This assumption had positive connotations for women, and negative ones for men (see Griffin, in press, for a more detailed account of these events). The main point here is not whether my approach was biased, political or subjective, but that I was *seen* as biased regardless of my appearance or political perspective, whilst far larger and predominantly male studies are presented as objective and value-free (e.g. Halsey *et al.*, 1980).

There is now a fairly extensive research literature on youth subcultures and the transition from school to work (see Hall and Jefferson, 1975; Clarke, 1980). Most of these studies focus on the position of young white working class men, and theoretical approaches to this whole area reflect this imbalance. So whilst *Typical Girls?* does contribute towards this work, I found little in the existing studies that helped me to understand the important role that housework and childcare played in most young women's lives, for example (see Mc-Robbie, 1980, for a feminist critique of this research).

There is a recent and developing literature concerning gender differences in schooling and the labour market which has more to say about young women (e.g. Davies, 1979; McRobbie, 1978b, Deem, 1980; Pollert, 1981). Some of this work also looks at the way that race, age, class and gender interact for different groups of young women (e.g. Amos and Parmar, 1981; Jamdagni, 1981; Sharpe, 1976). Not all of these studies have much to say about one of the most crucial areas in young women's lives: sexuality and pressures to get a boyfriend. So *Typical Girls?* also draws on feminist analyses of the control of female and male sexuality and the social institution of compulsory heterosexuality (e.g. Barry, 1979; Rich, 1980; Rubin, 1975).

This book is not written primarily for young women: they are in the best position to write for each other (see Hemmings, 1982). *Typical Girlsl?* is written mainly for those who work with or 'study' young people as teachers, youth and community workers, careers advisers, social workers or researchers: for those who make decisions which affect young people's lives. Such people (and I include myself here) do not always take young people seriously or listen to what they have to say. Young women are particularly likely to be lumped together into a 'faceless bunch' of 'typical girls', rendered silent and invisible behind a haze of stereotypes and assumptions (Stanworth, 1981). *Typical Girls?* aims to make young women's voices heard, and to tell the stories of one group who entered Birmingham's job market in the early 1980s.

PART I

1
Education: the final years at school

The main move to comprehensive education in Birmingham's state schools took place in 1974, as Labour was returned to power under Harold Wilson.[1] Five of the six schools I visited in 1979 were comprehensives, although their fifth formers were the last year of the pre-comprehensive student intake. Teachers viewed the shift to comprehensive education with mixed feelings, mainly depending on whether their schools had initially been secondary modern or grammar. In the former cases, comprehensive schooling was usually welcomed as a positive change, and in the latter it was regretted as leading to a 'lowering of standards'. Despite the stress on mixed ability classes and de-streaming by advocates of comprehensive education, all of these schools retained some form of streaming system based on an assessment of 'ability levels'.

Woodborough Girls' School[2] was the only non-state school I visited. It had been direct grant until going independent after the changes brought by comprehensivisation. Woodborough then became primarily a fee-paying establishment with entrance exams and a few scholarship places. In 1979 it had about 700 students who were mainly white and middle class, and a sizeable sixth form of around seventy young women. Woodborough had a reputation as an elite academic establishment, and was sited alongside its 'brother' boys' school in one of Birmingham's more prosperous inner suburbs.

St Catherine's Girls' School had been a grammar until going comprehensive, and it had a reputation as a prestigious Roman Catholic girls' school. It had about 700 students, most of whom came from middle and lower middle class Irish, Polish and Southern European Catholic families. Since it turned comprehensive, a greater proportion of Asian, Afro-Caribbean and white working class students had entered the school. St Catherine's was in a quiet residential area close to one of the city's main trunk roads, and had a sixth form of around seventy students in 1979.

Tildesley School was a small mixed comprehensive which had a reputation as the roughest school in the area until losing its secondary modern status in 1974. The 500 students were mainly white working class young people from the surrounding council housing estates, with a small minority of Asian and Afro-Caribbean students. Tildesley was on the edge of one such council estate in an outer suburb of Birmingham. It had a small sixth form of ten students in 1973.[3]

Moorcroft Girls' School was a true comprehensive in the sense that it was an amalgamation of a grammar and a secondary modern on the same site. It had about 1600 students in 1979, who were an even mix of middle and working class girls, over two-thirds of whom were white and less than one-third Asian and Afro-Caribbean, reflecting the local population. Moorcroft was in an outer city suburb about a mile from Tildesley school, surrounded by a mixture of council housing, up-market private housing and low quality rented accommodation. It had eleven streams up to the fifth form, which comprised about 280 girls. The sixth form was around 100 students, most of whom were taking 'A' levels as in the sixth forms at Woodborough and St Catherine's.

Lodgehill School was a mixed Church of England comprehensive which had been a secondary modern. The 700 students were an even mix of Asian, Afro-Caribbean and white working class young people, reflecting the population of the nearby council housing estates. Lodge-hill was in a 'deprived' part of the city, in one of Birmingham's Social Priority Areas. It had a sixth form of about ten students in 1979.

St Martin's School was a mixed Roman Catholic comprehensive in another of the city's Social Priority Areas. It had been a secondary modern, and had about 700 students in 1979. It was in a deprived residential area on the edges of the city, with an even mix of Asian, Afro-Caribbean and white working class students, reflecting the local population. St Martin's had about twenty-five sixth formers who were mainly taking or retaking CSEs or 'O' levels, as in the sixth forms of Tildesley and Lodgehill.

I visited these schools in early 1979, interviewing a diverse group, of (mainly female) students as well as their teachers, careers officers and headteachers. The young women occupied very different positions on the academic scale. Most of the sixth formers at Woodborough, St Catherine's and Moorcroft were white and middle class, due to take between one and four 'A' levels before going on to university or college. Some of the fifth formers I interviewed were relatively 'academic',[4] taking six or more CSEs and/or 'O' levels, and hoping to stay on at school to take more exams. Most of the fifth formers were 'non-academic' students who were taking fewer than 4 'O' levels or CSEs or no exams at all, and hoping to leave school at 16 to find full-time jobs.[5] The majority of this group were working class: young white, Asian and Afro-Caribbean women.

This chapter compares the positions of female fifth and sixth form students in the six schools. It is not a comprehensive analysis of contemporary education for girls, since the emphasis is on the experiences of a particular group of young women.

The academic elite: sixth form students

Most of the sixth formers at Woodborough, St Catherine's and Moorcroft Schools were destined for college or university, followed by high status, well-paid 'careers'. The latter were seen as more than mere 'jobs', and ranged from a token female presence in professions like law and medicine (Woodborough), through to teaching and nursing at the lower end of the scale. These young women were well aware of the academic pressures that went with their academic privileges:

Gill: In this school, we're conditioned from the first year that you're gonna go to university. It's hard work.

Dianne: [leaving to get a job] I think it's 'cos we're scared of getting a job actually (laugh).

Anne-Marie: I don't think I've got the courage to go out and get a job, I'm scared of failing.

Dianne: Most people here will get a shock when they leave school and try to get a job. We've led sheltered lives and we *couldn't* leave at 16 and earn a living. We're too immature.

(St Catherine's)

Despite their air of apparent self-confidence and independence (a minority came to school in their own cars!), these young women saw themselves as 'immature' and 'sheltered from real life'. The benefits accruing from their position of relative privilege protected them from some of the harsher pressures of the labour market and sealed them in a predominantly white and middle class cocoon.

Julie: Although we have Saturday jobs, we don't really know what life's about really.

Liz: We *don't* know, we *are* very sheltered. I mean we've never come up against any sort of hostility in this school, not been beaten up (laughs). The one's who've come in now [since the school went comprehensive] they're more sort of working class and they all talk about boys. Mind you, you do tend to be a bit snobbish about these things.

(St Catherine's)

The main contact with their black and working class peers was through part-time Saturday jobs or the new comprehensive student intake. These girls were seen as trapped within 'deprived' cultures, so that the oppressive material conditions of black and working class life (i.e. poverty) were associated with the nature of black and working class *cultures*.[6]

Despite their very different experiences of education these sixth formers viewed the prospect of leaving school with a similar ambivalence to their fifth form peers. After almost thirteen years of schooling, it was hardly surprising that they were ready to leave.

Fiona: I hate school, it's boring and dead — no one has anything to say to each other. You really feel you've outgrown the system.

(Woodborough)

Typical girls? Fifth form students

The fifth formers I interviewed usually referred to their more academic sisters as 'snobs' or 'posh'; 'snooty types' who looked down on those whom they considered to be their inferiors. Non-academic fifth formers in particular felt that they had been defined as failures according to the schools' criteria of academic ability.

Sheila: I hate this school. Especially Miss Neville, she's so sarky. She says 'I can see what sort of home you're from, you'll never get anywhere.' Really gets at us about our homes.

(Moorcroft, white fifth former)

Sharon: Schools are awful. Ours is. They don't care about you. If you do exams they do. Otherwise they don't care, they don't push you or bother with you. It's OK in the first and second years, but after that if they don't think you're any good and you don't work they give up.

(Tildesley, Afro-Caribbean fifth former)

It would be simplistic to suggest that schools consigned certain groups of students to specific futures in an unambiguous manner, or that all teachers aimed to reinforce a sense of failure in their white working class or black students. Some teachers did appreciate the importance of class differences in the education system:

Ms Deakin: I went with a group of our lot to a big careers do for all sorts of schools in Birmingham. You could see real differences there between different groups of kids from different parts of the city. It wasn't so much clothes, I'm not talking about fashion, it was the *sort* of clothes: expensive. I'm not sure that it was such a good thing because our lot knew and they felt bad. I could see it. They could tell the others were *so* different: how they talked. They seemed older. But it was values and attitudes where the real difference was. Perhaps it's that I haven't been around middle class kids much and it struck me so strongly.

(Tildesley, fifth form teacher)

Some students had come into direct confrontation with the schools' criteria for determining academic ability. Brenda, for example, was a white working class fifth former at Tildesley school. She had started her secondary schooling at Moorcroft, but was transferred to Tildesley when her family moved house. She saw this as a definite move down the academic scale, but felt more at ease in the less 'snooty' atmosphere at Tildesley.

Contemporary education encourages students to work hard academ-ically in order to 'get on' and 'better themselves' in the labour market (see Education group, 1981; Byrne, 1978). So Brenda wanted to go on to the sixth form, take 'O' and 'A' levels after her CSEs (and one 'O' level), and go on to university or college to do teacher training. To her teachers, Brenda's aspirations were seen as 'unrealistic', partly because they felt that she lacked the academic ability, and also because she refused to accept her destiny as 'factory material'. Despite the promise of equal opportunities in education and the job market, the best places were still reserved for the academic elite, who are predomin-antly white, male and middle class.[7]

Brenda: The last school [Moorcroft] messed me about, kept on say-ing I was remedial, and I'd never be any good at this and that. It sort of disheartened me a bit. . . I didn't want to come here [Tildesley] but they've never cried me down and I've done extremely well. The last one they said I was just factory material. They had streams and I kept coming top in exams but they never put me up. This school's not as modern and posh as Moorcroft, but there was *no* way there I would have done an 'O' level English. . . 'cos they press on you the attitude like you're low class, you'll never do anything like this, you're too low down the school like.

Brenda disliked the 'snooty' atmosphere at Moorcroft because the girls were expected to be 'ladies' and preferred Tildesley despite the presence of boys (cf. Chapter 6).

CG: And what about that this school is mixed and the other was girls?
Brenda: Well boys have their bad points too they always call you names but you're always gonna get that. It's just a better atmosphere you don't feel so *pressed* on all the while. As girls at Moorcroft they expect you to be ladies and all you know. They pressurise you to be something that you're not really.

(Tildesley)

Conformity and deviance in school: 'good girls' and 'trouble-makers'

A number of studies have looked at the differences between the meanings of female and male deviance and conformity (e.g. Davies, 1979; Shaw, 1978; Millman, 1975; Casburn, 1979). Boys are expected to be disruptive and aggressive in more visible and vocal ways, and are more likely to be the focus of teachers' attention than their female peers (Stanworth, 1981; Spender, 1982). Girls' deviance in school does not always take different forms to the boys, but it is treated and perceived differently by teachers and other students. Young women's deviance is often seen in relation to their sexuality (Griffin, 1982b).

Most female teachers saw girls as being less trouble than boys, and this was usually in relation to non-attendance, problems with probation officers or the police. They went on to admit that girls could and did cause as much (if not more) trouble than boys in school, but that this disruption took different forms, and was seen to pose less of an acute discipline problem. 'Good girls' were those who caused minimal disruption in class, and were relatively quiet. These same students were not necessarily more academic or pro-school than their 'deviant' peers. Some were simply 'keeping their heads down', and resisting teachers' demands in more subtle, but less obvious ways (cf. Griffin, 1982a).

CG: What about the teachers then?
Cathy: I think they should be stricter. . .they just can't cope with
         us most of them. Mind you I can't bear it when they get
         clever. Mr Jones can be so *cruel*, and he makes you feel such
         a fool. It's a good idea to keep your head down in his class
         I can tell you.

                                   (Lodgehill, white fifth former)

Studies of white working class 'lads' in school have identified a specific counter-school culture which acts as a bridge into manual labouring jobs (e.g. Willis, 1977; Corrigan, 1979). I began this research expecting that I would find female equivalents to the pro- and anti-school cultures of the 'earoles' and the 'lads' which Willis (1977) has described, but no such female cultures emerged.

It was not always possible to identify a particular group of girls as 'deviants' or troublemakers who were also opposed to school and academic work, *and* destined for factory jobs. It was equally difficult to find 'good girls' who were pro-school *and* hoped to go on to college or office jobs. The situation was far more complex than analyses of male counter-school cultures might lead one to expect.[8]

Berni, for example, saw herself as a troublemaker, and when I talked to her in the fifth year, she was hanging around with a group of other white working class girls: all of whom saw themselves as troublemakers. Berni was taking four CSEs, and her friends were taking fewer exams, or no exams whatsoever. Her form teacher described the gang as 'a bit of a handful'. They distanced themselves from the 'swots' and 'pets' who wanted to stay on, and had a low opinion of the 'snobs' who wanted to get office jobs. Berni and her friends talked about these distinctions:

CG: So do you think you've changed as you've gone up the school?
Berni: Yeh, we've gone madder (laugh).
CG: Like who isn't mad in your form?
Berni: Everybody is just as stupid.
Shelly: Well there's three that usually don't laugh or mess around.
Jenny: Three at the front you know, very serious.
Shelly: Oh pets, (laugh) don't tell them Jenny, you're supposed to be a friend.
Berni: They don't laugh. I've never seen 'em laugh. They take life too serious, they should be laughing like us (laugh).
CG: Are they going to stay on?
Shelly: Yeh a lot of them stop on, I can't wait to get away though, I'm bored me.
Berni: They're posh too, snobs wanna do office jobs. We're the troublemakers (laugh).

(St Martin's, white fifth formers)

Yet Berni went straight into an office job immediately after she left school. It seemed there was no clear link between pro- and anti-school attitudes, friendship groups in school, and young women's subsequent jobs. It was less important to identify particular girls as 'good girls' or 'troublemakers', than to understand the meanings associated with these categories, and the ways that they were used to distinguish between groups of students by teachers and by the young women themselves.

Some of those young women who were seen as 'conformists' rejected the school's stress on the value of academic work, and had a low opinion of their own particular school. They had an eminently practical approach to their position, hoping to leave school and find a good full-time job. They valued only information and skills which might be useful to them in the labour market. They also rejected their child-like status in school, in preference for the adult status and independence which full-time employment was expected to bring. Academic knowledge 'for it's own sake' was seen as a complete waste of time. These young women recognised that there would be even less space for them in tertiary education or higher status 'careers' than their male peers. This group was closest to the 'earoles' described in Paul Willis's study (1977), and were mainly white working class fifth formers in the less academic schools, who were referred to by teachers as 'good girls' or 'bright girls' (e.g. Cathy and Jeanette at Lodgehill).

The 'troublemakers' were those who were more disruptive, the less academic students, or those who were seen to be heading for factory work, unemployment, or even prostitution (see Griffin, 1982b). These labels were not necessarily associated with a given group of students throughout their time at school. Young women's friendship groups were smaller than the larger 'gangs' of their male peers, so there were no equivalent female groups which could be identified as pro- or anti-school cultures. This is not to imply that Willis's analysis was mistaken, simply that it had no direct relevance to these young women's lives.

In all of the schools I visited, I only met one black teacher, an Afro-Caribbean woman who worked at St Martin's School. Most of the white teachers operated with generalised stereotypes of black students. Asian girls were often seen as passive and acquiescent, with a tendency to 'overaspire' and aim for 'unrealistic' jobs. Their Afro-Caribbean peers were more likely to be viewed as loud and aggressive. Teachers differentiated between white girls who were the 'good girls' and the 'troublemakers', but tended to lump Asian girls together as 'good girls', and Afro-Caribbean girls as 'troublemakers'. Black students were aware of this process.[9]

Azima: I want to be a lawyer, me. But the teachers said no I'd better try for a legal assistant's job. They think I can't do it, that I'm just a good little Asian girl, but I *can* do it.

(Moorcroft, Asian fifth former)

CG:	And what about the teachers?
All:	Oh God!! Hate the teachers.
Penny:	They're all horrible. None of them are interested in us, they've got no respect for us.
Jacinta:	True. And they say we should respect them.
Penny:	This school is backwards. It's the most backwards school I've ever been to. I only come 'cos my friends are here.

(Lodgehill, Afro-Caribbean fifth formers)

Carol:	They don't teach you nothing here.
Sonia:	It's better to get out, get a job and earn money.
Peach:	Mmm, go out and enjoy yourself. You only live once.
Sonia:	That's true, they just say we're trouble, can't wait for us to leave.

(St Martin's, Afro-Caribbean fifth formers)

Discipline and control in school

One other factor distinguished between 'good girls' and 'troublemakers': the teachers' ability to control students and maintain discipline in class.

Vanessa:	Half the teachers they don't teach you anything 'cos the kids in the class they tell the teachers what to do. They should just show them who's boss and not just stand there and take it all the time.
Jacinta:	They ought to but they don't.
Vanessa:	Like us, right, if we do something they tell us off 'cos they know we won't do anything, but the ones that make trouble, they won't tell them off 'cos they'll make trouble. They're frightened of the others and that leaves us out 'cos they take up most of the time.

(Lodgehill, Afro-Caribbean fifth formers)

Other students took a pride in 'cheeking' and 'winding up' particular teachers, whilst simultaneously bemoaning the fact that some teachers could not control them or make them work: 'there's just no challenge at this school.'

Sue: Everyone is soft ain't they, you can cheek them and everything and they don't say much (yeah). They just laugh you
know (yeah). Join in with ya.

Liz: It's like talking to mates most of 'em.

Sue: Mind you you get a few don't ya? Look at Mr Moss, he's terrible. We just sit there and throw rubbers and rulers at him,
don't we? They do honest, there's nothing else you can do in
that lesson.

(Tildesley, white fifth formers)

These students came into school expecting to be faced with a
strict and authoritarian form of control, but both teachers and students were caught in a no-win situation. Authoritarian forms of control were usually based on a mutual lack of respect, but teachers'
attempts at more progressive methods (e.g. leniency, friendliness)
often aroused students' suspicions.

CG: Would you like it then more if the school sort of made you
work more, was stricter?

Carol: No, nor if it was less stricter.

Peach: Still wouldn't like it either way. They try to be friendly,
but they don't mean it.

(St Martin's, Afro-Caribbean fifth formers)

Resistances in school: making spaces for girls

Maintaining discipline in schools depended partly on monitoring every
aspect of students' activities during (and even after) school hours.
Young women tried to avoid teachers' control by making their own
'leisure' in school. This ranged from not going to school at all (i.e.
'wagging it' or 'nicking off'), 'skiving off' lessons for a smoke or a
chat; reading girls' magazines or passing notes in class; through to
daydreaming or 'cutting off' when teachers were present. For example,
I was interviewing a group of six fifth form girls in Lodgehill School
when the deputy headmistress came in suddenly. From talking ani-
matedly, laughing and joking, the group became silent and motionless
in a second (Griffin, 1982a).

In mixed schools, girls also found ways of avoiding their male peers, and the girls' toilets or cloakrooms provided an ideal refuge from teachers and the boys. During one visit to Tildesley school, the fourth and fifth year girls were summoned to a special girls-only morning assembly. The deputy headmistress reprimanded them over 'a very unpleasant matter'. Since the toilets were a favourite place for skiving off lessons, they were kept locked throughout all lesson times, and students had to ask permission to have the toilets unlocked. A group of girls had gone into the girls' toilets when they were open, and smeared menstrual blood over the walls and floors, blocking the toilets with sanitary towels. Their male peers were particularly horrified by the girls' behaviour:

Mick: Did you hear about what the girls did? It's disgusting. They ought to be ashamed. It's worse than smearing shit on the walls. Ugh.

CG: Why?

Mick: I dunno, it just is.

(Tildesley, white fifth former)

Young women spent most of their time in mixed schools in female friendship groups, and many of their resistances to teachers' authority involved 'all us girls together'. The most exciting part of nicking off school was the collective act of sneaking from the school grounds or avoiding the Education Welfare Officer.[10]

Mary: The trouble with wagging it is you get so bored. I mean I never came in all last week but in the end I got so bored that I had to. If you stay off too long the inspector gets you anyway. All your mates are at school too.

(Moorcroft, white fifth former)

Maintaining some control over students' appearance was another aspect of the school's authority, and this was especially focused on young women. Resistances to these constraints included ignoring the school uniform altogether, or wearing a rough approximation of it; wearing clear nail varnish and barely detectable make-up; and interminable struggles over skirt length, hairstyles and shoes.

Jan: What gets me is that some of the girls are sixteen or seventeen, and they don't let you wear a bit of make up, if you get copped with it you have to take it off, and nail varnish.

(Lodgehill, white fifth former)

Jan's form teacher was more lenient than most, but her view of 'proper make-up' did not correspond with young women's ideas.

Ms Morgan: Well I've never minded the girls wearing a bit of make-up. Why should we try to force 15- or 16-year-olds not to? You just can't get away with it nowadays. But they turn up with make-up all over their faces. Great dark lines over their eyes and halfway round to their ears. Purple lipstick, green nails and I don't know what else (laugh). So I just tell them to wash it all off. If only they'd come with proper make-up, some nice blue eye-shadow, a bit of mascara, lipstick.

This was in 1979, some three years after the advent of punk in Britain, so purple lipstick and green nails formed part of a punk girl's style.[11]

There was also some concern about boys' appearance, as teachers objected to the styles adopted by punks, skinheads and Rastas.

Cathy: Andy came in to school the other day. It was a right laugh. He had a mohican cut [longer hair from the centre of the brow to the nape of the neck: bald everywhere else]. The head couldn't send him home to get it cut, 'cos then he'd have been bald all over: a *really* good skin cut (laugh).

(Lodgehill, white fifth former)

In another Birmingham school, the headmaster suspended a Sikh student for refusing to take off his turban. Two Appeal courts upheld this decision until March 1983, when the Law Lords found the headmaster guilty of racial discrimination. So struggles over appearance were an importance part of most students' experiences in school.

Mixed feelings: the prospect of leaving school

Almost all of the fifth formers complained about the tedium and monotony of school.

Penny: School's boring. I've never known anything so boring.

(Lodgehill, Afro-Caribbean fifth former)

CG: Have you noticed changes as you've gone through school?
Clare: Yeh (laugh) Yeh. I never wanna go to no lessons now! (laugh)
. . . especially since the exams were on. The revision lessons
are dead boring.

(St Martin's, white fifth former)

For the more academic fifth formers, this process of 'going off
school' was associated with anxiety and pre-exam nerves. Even those
who expected to stay on were affected by their final months of compulsory education.

Louise: Everyone is being put off school at the moment. You notice
a lot of fifth formers playing truant and that. They keep on
having to do checks on us. . . . They are really getting tired of
school, spending five years here, especially when the exams
are coming up now.

(Moorcroft, white fifth former)

For those who expected to leave at 16, the thought of entering
the full-time labour market was a simultaneously frightening and
exciting prospect. One headmistress saw this process in relation to
changes in the school leaving age (cf. Ariés, 1962).

Ms Evans: I remember when they left school at 14 and in the third
year we hated to teach them, they were a problem. They
seemed so old, mature and confident and then look at
the 14-year-olds now, they are like children. When they
left at 15 they seemed old. The present fourth year are
very young and school forces them to stay young. It keeps
them young. Just before leaving they get very cheeky and
boisterous and then they go quiet. They are aware of the
important change and they're frightened.

(Moorcroft)

However much young women were looking forward to leaving school, they still felt ambivalent about leaving their girlfriends and 'the laughs'.

Sheila: I won't miss the lessons (laugh).

Mary: You might, you never know. You might think of all the larks that you had at school and you might be sitting at home just watching telly or summat, and you'd think 'ooh it was good at school' but you didn't think it when you was at school. You might even miss some teachers (laugh).

Lorraine: You won't have as many friends as you did at school anyway.

Mary: Yeh, and some of them you never see again.

(Moorcroft, white fifth formers)

Elaine: I won't miss the actual school. Perhaps some of the people. But not the school itself as an institute (laugh).

(St Catherine's, white fifth former)

There was one point on which all students were agreed, even if they were staying on to the sixth form. They objected to being treated like children in school, and to the lack of respect and responsibility accorded to school students.

CG: Do you think it'll be different when you leave school?

Elaine: I think people will treat you a bit more grown up (Hmm) when you say 'school' and everybody thinks you're sort of behind a desk with a pen in your hand (yes) or in a school uniform, but ah, if you're working they think of you more as a grown-up, and adult. But school seems to paint an image of a school, and you always associate school with that. It doesn't make sense really 'cos I'm still the same person, I'm just gonna be paid more in my wage packet at the end of the week.

(St Catherine's, white fifth former)

So leaving school was not necessarily a smooth process and even those who were 'desperate to leave' had some regrets. Careers advisers in schools and in the careers service are officially required to smooth and monitor the move from school to college or the labour market, and the following chapter looks at their work in more detail.

2

Careers advice

Most of the young women had received some form of careers advice in school, and had been interviewed by a careers officer. The form and content of this advice varied considerably in different schools, depending on the available resources, and the enthusiasm and training of the careers teachers. One school (Moorcroft) had a large and well-stocked careers department, which was run by a committed senior careers mistress. Most schools had to contend with out-of-date books and films, with careers teachers who were either ill-equipped, overworked, or uninterested in fulfilling their role.

The usual practice in Birmingham was for each careers officer (CO) to work with a given caseload of schools and students. They would then go into the schools to interview fourth and fifth formers individually for about 20-30 minutes each, as well as giving general talks to larger groups of students. Since 1975, when school leavers ceased to have their National Insurance numbers allocated at the local careers office, they have been under no obligation to visit career centres. This has made it even more difficult for the careers service to keep in contact with young people after they have left school.

Contemporary careers advice is intended to meet the provisions of the 1973 Employment and Training Act, which placed a duty on Local Education Authorities in England and Wales to:

provide a vocational guidance service for people attending educational institutions other than universities and an employment service for people leaving them. . . . The intention is that young people who wish to continue to use these services after they have left education should be able to do so and that authorities should be able to keep in touch with those whom they have helped. (Guidance to LEAs, 1980 revision, Department of Employment)

Under the Youth Employment Service, which operated until 1973, careers advice aimed to fit students to the jobs available in the local labour market. There was an emphasis on the use of 'objective' psychometric tests to measure individuals' aptitudes and abilities, in order to 'fit the man to the job' (Roberts, 1972).

With the introduction of the careers service in 1973, a more humanist client-centred approach prevailed, which aimed to 'fit the job to the man'. Careers advice became less like a series of IQ tests and closer to counselling, as young people were encouraged to make 'occupational choices' through 'vocational guidance' (Roberts, 1980). The most radical approaches suggested that careers advisers' first duties were not to employers, but to the 'clients' (e.g. Hayes and Hopson, 1971). By the end of the 1970s, careers advice was promising young people equal opportunities in a declining job market that now included the various government training schemes (Knasel et al., 1982). The careers service was put into an increasingly difficult position as the youth labour market contracted and employers' needs began to take first priority once again.

Schools and the careers service

The careers service is concerned mainly with *placing* young people in the labour market and the tertiary education system. Careers education in schools focuses on *preparation* for that transition. However, there has always been some uncertainty about the respective roles of the careers service and careers teachers in schools, which has been attributed to the vague wording of the 1973 Employment and Training Act (see Roberts, 1976).[1]

Careers advice operates across the boundary between the school and the outside world: particularly the youth labour market. The official role of the careers service is clearer than that of careers education in schools, but there is considerable regional and even local variation. Both areas have their own jealously guarded professional skills, with careers officers usually coming into schools 'from the outside':

literally on to teachers' terrain. COs and careers teachers sometimes met with a degree of wary apprehension:

CG: What about the careers service?

Ms Haden: The careers service? (wry smile) I don't know how critical to be. There is an antagonism there especially when they come in and try to tell us what to do. Birmingham is behind the times though. There's no stress on social and personal development.

(Moorcroft careers mistress)

Ms Morgan, with far more limited resources, was equally committed to her work and was involved in in-service training for careers teachers. Her view of the careers service was more positive.

Ms Morgan: To me the careers interviews are a good thing. It's good when real people from outside come into school to talk to individuals and careers teachers like me shouldn't sit in on them. It's good to have someone adult from outside to come in and talk to them. It's all 'us and them' and distrust of organisations and the world outside.[2]

(Lodgehill careers mistress)

Part of Ms Haden's distrust stemmed from her view that several students' decisions had undergone fundamental transformations during the careers interview. She was critical of the careers service for disturbing what she saw as *her* work:

Ms Haden: The girls go into a careers interview and come out with another idea. Twenty minutes is not enough. It's not always what they say but what you don't hear that's important − it's how it's said.

(Moorcroft)

The CO with a responsibility for St Martin's school was aware of the constraints on her work:

Ms Preedy: I see 450 kids in a caseload of two schools on my own and two others I share. I don't liaise with careers teachers,

> I don't have time. The careers service gives information
> and advice, but has little real influence. We are limited by
> too little contact with the schools and the kids and too
> little time with them and that's what's needed: *time*.

Those careers teachers with more limited resources, and who were
less able (or willing) to be fully involved in careers advice, did express
some uneasiness about their role:

CG: And what about careers — is there a careers department?
Ms Ryman: Well the careers master is no help. Each form teacher
             from the fourth and fifth takes careers [lessons].
             It's difficult because we're not trained. Fourth years
             have no idea at all, or else they know exactly what they
             want to do and shut off. I feel that I can't teach careers
             — the kids get bored.

                                        (St Martin's, fifth form tutor)

One school (Tildesley) treated careers advice as a relatively low
priority. The headmaster and deputy headmistress justified this decision
on the grounds that students would survive in the job market regardless of the school's intervention: even if this meant prostitution for the
young women (see Chapter 7, and Griffin, 1982b).

Ms Barnes: Our kids will look after themselves. Some of them won't
             get jobs, but they're all survivors. They'll manage all
             right. Most of them will find jobs and if they can keep
             them they'll do OK. Mode 3 CSE doesn't mean anything
             much out there now. So what can you tell them?
Ms Hughes: And the girls will be all right. If they can't find work
             they'll go on the streets.

                                                           (Tildesley)

Whilst Ms Haden distrusted the persuasive techniques of careers
officers, other teachers welcomed the latter's apparent ability to
dissuade school leavers from undesirable or 'unrealistic' aspirations.

Ms Ryman: They think that if you just apply to college then you've
             automatically got in. They think they can walk out and

be offered jobs. They don't realise they have to compete in jobs with other kids with more qualifications and
that. It's difficult to teach that in careers. I think the
careers officer uses persuasion.

(St Martin's)

Careers advice as persuasion: pressures to be realistic

An important part of careers advisers' work involved providing young
people with relevant and up-to-date information on the schemes,
courses and jobs available, and on the qualifications necessary for
various occupations. The assumption that young people could make
real job *choices* was continually being undermined by the pressures
of the local youth labour market. Despite the superficial promise of
equal opportunities, employers' demands were often gender, race
and class specific (cf. Ashton *et al.*, 1982).

Ms Preedy: There is race discrimination and sex discrimination
from employers, but what can we do? If we don't send
them the sort of young person they want, they'll just
stop using us.

Apart from the academic elite in the sixth forms, who stood a
better chance of making a real career choice, most prospective school
leavers had to consider the demands of the education system and
the job market. The former urged students to 'get on' by working
hard, whilst the latter required that they should be 'realistic' about
their futures. In the more academic comprehensives such as Moorcroft and St Catherine's, which had been grammar schools until 1974,
some fifth formers were in extremely difficult positions. Young working class women who wanted to leave at 16 and look for office jobs
or clerical jobs were seen as academic failures.

Ms Haden: We have a lot of trouble with girls who leave at 16 to go
into banking and office work. Then at 18 they realise
their mistakes. With no 'O' or 'A' levels they're stuck.

(Moorcroft)

These school leavers were at a real disadvantage relative to their counterparts from less academic schools, since they had no commercial qualifications. Typing and other commercial subjects were only available in the sixth form at Moorcroft and St Catherine's, and some fifth formers preferred to go to college or straight into the job market rather than stay on at school. Whilst these students' aspirations were treated as evidence of failure or under-achievement, their peers at Tildesley, Lodgehill and St Martin's were seen as successful students if they aimed to go into office work: 'a good job for a girl'.

Pressures to be 'realistic' and move into appropriate jobs took different forms for young Asian and Afro-Caribbean women. White teachers and careers officers often referred to Asian students as 'very quiet, with language difficulties', or as 'unrealistic' or 'aiming too high'. Afro-Caribbean students tended to be seen as 'troublemakers' or 'layabouts', who were destined for menial factory jobs. There was little appreciation of the high value placed on education and gaining qualifications in some Asian and Afro-Caribbean cultures, nor of black families' concern for their children's education.[3]

Asian students were frequently labelled as 'over-aspirers', and their Afro-Caribbean peers as 'under-achievers'. The Rampton Committee's report on the 'under-achievement' of Afro-Caribbean students in British schools concluded that teachers' low expecations of black students, combined with personal and institutional racism, were the main causes of these students' poor performance in school (Rampton Committee report, 1981). According to Birmingham careers service statistics, the majority of black school students were born and brought up in Britain, so few would be likely to have 'language problems'. Asian students were often criticised for having 'unrealistic ambitions' which teachers would probably applaud in white middle class students. Black students were effectively being blamed for the racism of the education system and the labour market which prevented them from gaining equal opportunities (see Brooks and Singh, 1978; Stone, 1981; Brah and Golding, 1983).

Charno: I want to go on to do medicine. My brother knows all about it, he's a lot of help to me. He's a doctor so he's done it. I'll stay on here to do more exams, but then I'll leave and go to college for 'A' levels and that. They don't really help me here, they don't think I'll ever do it. But why shouldn't I try?

(Lodgehill, Asian fifth former)

Most young women appreciated the potential value of careers advice, but they were critical of the persuasive techniques used by some careers officers:

Mandy: She didn't even know what she [CO] was on about really, she tried giving me different jobs. She tried to make me join the navy to become a cook (all laugh). First she gave me some addresses about the navy, she'd got it into her head that I wanted to become a caterer just because I said I liked cooking.

Shelly: It all depends what you want information on. Like if you wanted addresses of colleges, she got us them, and that was helpful.

(St Martin's, white fifth formers)

Female students felt that they were channelled into suitably female jobs (cf. Benett and Carter, 1983; and Chapter 6).

CG: Did the careers officer give you any information on what you wanted to do, the ambulance driving?

Sue: No, what they told me, I already knew from the school. They told me to stay on in school and do a secretarial course (laugh). The CO was trying to put me off the idea of the ambulance service because he said it's mostly all men, but I'm not worried (laugh).

(Moorcroft, white fifth former)

CG: Have you ever thought of jobs like engineering, mechanics, that sort of thing?

Lorna: I thought of mechanics (laugh). You have to train for four years, if you do it wrong you're out.

CG: Have you seen the careers officer?

Lorna: Yes but they said they don't think I'd got much chance because there's lots of boys going for the job but I'd rather do mechanics anyway (laugh).

(Moorcroft, Afro-Caribbean fifth former)

Differences between women's and men's work were also reflected in careers or social education lessons:

CG:	I mean do you have any films or anything about different jobs?
Satyinder:	No we don't.
Jasbinder:	Well we had one about an electrician it was.
Satyinder:	They was all men though: he had to go into hospital hurt. There was somethin' with his eyes. It was a safety film.
Jasbinder:	There was a woman — her washing machine plug broke!
Cathy:	We talk about *Sid* and his engineering job too.

(Lodgehill, Asian and white fifth formers)

Careers advice: young women's experiences

Most careers advice is aimed at less academic working class students, designed to help them find a suitable job, training scheme or college course. Those students taking several 'O' or 'A' levels were expected to go on to university or polytechnic after the sixth form, only entering full-time employment at 21 or over. At school, their main 'careers' decision concerned which exams to take and which courses to aim for when completing their UCCA forms.[4] Yet even this privileged group could not forget their expected future roles as wives and mothers:

Fiona:	It's assumed that all the girls will go to university. There's no mention of jobs, 'cos it's assumed that we'll all be married by then.

(Woodborough, sixth former)

Most of the less academic fifth formers who hoped to leave school at 16 and look for jobs approached their careers interview with mixed feelings. Those who were interested in specific jobs or courses were more likely to find the interview useful. For those with no definite ideas about their future (a significant proportion), the interview was less likely to be a fruitful encounter.

CG:	Was the careers interview any use to you?
Claire:	Well no not really. They just sort of wrote on a piece of paper the addresses of the Job Centres near, and they just put down in notes what you talked about at the interview,

didn't do nothing extra. So I can't really say what that
was for.

Cheryl: And yet I found mine useful 'cos I told her which sort of
jobs I wanted and she put me towards the college.

Claire: It wasn't for me 'cos I couldn't decide what to do that
soon (laugh).

(St Martin's, white fifth formers)

CG: D'you think most people have any idea what they're going
to do when they're interviewed?

Vicky: I think most people say what they're going to do, what they
sort of like to do, but they don't really know . . . if they're
going to be that, 'cos you might end up with no exams . . .
or they might change their minds about it, find out what it's
really like and go 'Oh no'.

Kathy: It does give you an idea of how many jobs there are really.
What range of jobs you've got. I didn't know that there was
egg packing and all that till I came here (laugh).

(Moorcroft, white fifth former)

Careers advisers complained that some students viewed the careers
interview as an automatic route into particular jobs or college places.
A minority did expect to move straight into college with no selection
procedure, but this was because they assumed that tertiary education
was similar to primary and secondary schools, with an open access
policy. Most students had a clear idea of the potential value of the
careers interview.

Berni: They just give you addresses to write to. They don't do that
much good for you, it's you that has to get the job in the end,
it's not them.

(St Martin's, white fifth former)

For those who were seen as 'troublemakers', the careers interview
and careers advice was a worthless charade which simply reinforced
the school's view of them as failures:

CG: Have you had the careers woman come and talk to you?

Marjory: Yeah but they wouldn't let her talk to me. They said there's no use her talking to me about leaving school 'cos I wouldn't be able to find a job: two-faced ain't they?

(Lodgehill, Afro-Caribbean fifth former)

Careers education placed a heavy emphasis on job applications and interview techniques. This was seen as irrelevant by most non-exam students who expected to use informal family contacts and move into factory or shop work. One group of Afro-Caribbean fifth formers were particularly dismissive of the 'nice' feminine behaviour which was presented as an ideal interview technique — presumably with a male interviewer. They recognised this technique as little more than a form of flirting.

Marjory: They say when you go in you must smile, you must talk to the man. You can't smile *all* the time though — like a Cheshire cat (mock smile).

Vanessa: Bow in your hair and all this — sitting with your legs crossed! That's what you're meant to do. Look right in his eyes and if you're not looking in the eyes, you must look up (laugh).

CG: And you think that's not much use?

Penny: I think it's exaggerating. I do what I wanna when I go. When I went for a job the other week I never smiled like that.

Marjory: You smile too much they might think you're in love with them (laugh). If that's what they really interview you for I wouldn't smile.

Penny: Wouldn't ya?

Jacinta: She'd laugh in his face (laugh). If he was lucky.

(Lodgehill)

I almost always talked to students out of careers or social education lessons, because these classes were viewed as less important than the academic exam subjects. This reflected the priorities of an education system which placed a high value on the acquisition of academic qualifications. The relatively low priority given to careers and social education classes in some schools had been transmitted to students through the teachers' use of the lessons:

CG: I mean is careers any good, any use to you?

All: No [loud].

Penny: They don't tell you nothing. Mr Jones chats too much man, he just talks about his family.

Peach: He tells us about his daughters wearing contax lens (laugh).

Marjory: They're no good you know [to me].

(Lodgehill, Afro-Caribbean fifth formers)

Careers education at Lodgehill, Tildesley and St Martin's (the ex-secondary moderns) was provided with inadequate resources, and by untrained, uninterested or overworked staff. However committed they were to the value of good careers advice, these schools faced considerable problems as government education cuts and falling rolls combined to place academic resources at a premium. As the local youth labour market declined in the 1980s, it became even more difficult to present school leavers with real 'occupational choices' (Roberts, 1980).

Elaine: Most people who leave at our age gonna probably do something clerical anyway. They don't really have much choice what to do.

(St Catherine's, white fifth former)

As female students pondered on their futures in the job market, they also had to consider their possible roles in marriage and family life, as well as any current housework and childcare commitments. Chapters 3 and 4 deal with the influence of domestic work and family life on the move from school to waged work for these young women.

3

Domestic responsibilities: housework and childcare

Domestic work is the baseline against which all women's work is judged. Housework and childcare are vital tasks, but because they are mainly women's responsibility, these jobs pass mainly unnoticed: undervalued and unpaid (Oakley, 1974; Hobson 1978a).[1] There is a complex academic debate about whether domestic work can be viewed as productive in terms of Marx's theory of value (Seccombe, 1974; Gardiner, 1976), but most research has tended to ignore women's domestic commitments. Studies of youth cultures and the transition from school to work (e.g. Ashton and Field, 1976; Brannen, 1975) have also ignored or minimised the importance of young women's domestic work (cf. Griffin *et al.*, 1980).

Given the pervasiveness of the assumption that domestic work is not *real* work, it is hardly surprising that young women also talked about housework in these terms:

Gill: My mum doesn't work — stays at home and does housework (laugh).

(Woodborough, sixth former)

Marie: Only me dad works, me mum doesn't.
CG: So who does most of the housework?
Marie: Me mum and me sister.

(St Martin's, white fifth former)

Real work was paid, it took place outside of the home, and it conjured up images of hard manual labour: 'men's work'. Even when women were employed as childminders, this seldom reached the status of *real* work (see Chapter 7).

Ann: My mum hasn't got a job, she looks after children, she's a babysitter, a childminder.

(Moorcroft, white fifth former)

Who does the housework?

I asked school students who did most of the housework in their families, and whether they helped or did any particular chores. Their responses are given in Table A, and although I had no means of checking their accuracy, some definite patterns emerged.[2] The most obvious point is that housework and childcare was overwhelmingly women's responsibility. Overall, only about 8 per cent of fathers did any domestic work, compared to 45 per cent of the young women, 75 per cent of their mothers, 19 per cent of their sisters, and none of their brothers.

CG: So who helps out with the housework?
Doreen: There is sort of half between me and my mum. I do all the cleaning up and she does the cooking, or some of it.
CG: And do your dad and brother do . . .?
Doreen: Well me dad's not there.
CG: So your brother doesn't?
Doreen: No (laugh). He just lies around doing nothing, watching the tele all day.

(Lodgehill, white fifth former)

Karen: My dad won't help, he just sits there and if he has to do one thing he'll moan, but my sister and me do most of it.
Lorna: My dad usually goes out.
Monica: Mine doesn't like doing it.

(Lodgehill, white fifth formers)

Although I hardly expected that male members of households would be weighed down with domestic chores, I was surprised at their almost negligible involvement. Young women's uneasy laughter indicated that they too recognised the discrepancy between those who did and did not do domestic work. Several felt that it was particularly unfair when their brothers failed to do their share, but raised their eyebrows and shrugged their shoulders at the monumental effort involved in getting brothers — or fathers — to do any housework.

When boys and men did 'help out' in the home, their activities were judged against an assumed baseline of nothing. Since women were expected to do most of the domestic chores, their actual work was less surprising and less visible. Women's work in the home was taken for granted as 'normal'. It was their avoidance of, or refusal to do housework which was more noticeable.

Of the 104 young women that I asked about domestic work, only eight said that their fathers did any housework or childcare. This was mostly through force of circumstances, due to their mothers' absence, illness or employment (e.g. on late shifts or full-time jobs), or because of their fathers' own unemployment or shiftwork. This did not mean that mothers in full-time employment could necessarily count on their families' help with domestic work:

Juliet: My mother's a district nursing sister and works full time, but she does all the housework as well, 'cos we're lazy (laugh).

(Woodborough, sixth former)

Of these 104 young women, it was the white middle class students who were least likely to have domestic responsibilities (20.6 per cent as compared to 51 per cent of white working class, and 52 per cent of black working class girls). This was partly because a (female) daily help was employed to do most of the housework in a minority (5.9 per cent) of white middle class households, if the mothers had full-time jobs. In addition, these young women were not expected to do domestic work because of their relatively heavy load of academic school work:

Andrea: Well, I don't do much, it's not expected of me. My mother likes to see me working. I do some. I wash up and things but I don't really count that. It's not vacuuming and that sort of thing, I don't do that.

Sue: I'm not expected to . . . they [parents] want me to work.

(Woodborough, sixth formers)

These young women did not always do less housework because they were not expected to help out, since several mothers had clearly tried to make their daughters do more. The school work excuse was often used to avoid domestic work, although some young women did feel guilty about not doing enough housework.

CG: Who does most of the housework at home?

Sue: I've got a younger sister, she'll be leaving school same time as me. She's doing 'O' levels. She's a bit more handy around the house than I am 'cos I'm hopeless. We're meant to do a bit to help and we do help with the washing up, things like that, but we really don't help as much as we should do (laugh), and me dad doesn't do anything.

CG: Does your mum say anything?

June: Mine does say a lot of times she says why have kids and she's brought us up we've got to work. So I go upstairs and listen to the radio (laugh) . . . pretend to do my homework (laugh).

Fiona: I don't do anything (laugh), I know I should do more but I'm lazy.

(Woodborough, sixth formers)

Some social scientists have heralded the development of a new 'symmetrical' family form, based on a more egalitarian distribution of domestic work, and a new 'companionate' marriage relationship (see Newson and Newson, 1965; Young and Willmott, 1973).[3] This new family form has been presented as a product of more 'liberated' white middle class households (Rapoport and Rapoport, 1976). Of all the young women I interviewed, only one seemed to be part of such a symmetrical nuclear family, but this turned out to be a temporary arrangement:

Di: My mother works now. We live in the country 'cos my father gave up work. They swapped roles and he does a lot of house-work. Well he did, he's in London a lot now. When they both worked full-time we had a home help. I don't help much. I drive around on errands.

(Woodborough, sixth former)

Overall, domestic work was the most unequally distributed in white middle class families, and most evenly divided amongst the members of Afro-Caribbean households. Although the fathers (or stepfathers) of Afro-Caribbean students were less likely to live at home (see Table B and Chapter 4), a greater proportion did some domestic work as compared to their white counterparts (see Table A). The mothers of these young Afro-Caribbean women were more likely to have full-time paid work (see Table B), and there was also a more even distribution of domestic work between the female family members than in white middle and working class households (cf. Foner, 1978).

During one group discussion about housework, the Afro-Caribbean fifth formers (Vanessa, Jacinta and Penny) found that Sue (a white student) had few domestic commitments. This was seen as clear evidence that Sue was 'spoilt':

Vanessa: My sister and I do most of the housework. Our mum makes us do it most of the time, and then says we don't do anything.

Jacinta: Still you can't expect her to do it all.

Vanessa: She's at home every day!

CG: She's not got a job then?

Vanessa: She has yeah, from seven till eight, and then she comes home and waits for us to get in. She does cook and that but we do the washing. But most of the cleaning up you know we have to do.

Penny: So you should.

Sue: All we do is wash up after meals that's all. We might do the ironing sometimes.

Vanessa: Are you spoilt?

Sue: No (the others laugh).

(Lodgehill, fifth formers)

I interviewed about ten male fifth formers at Lodgehill school.[4] Only one Afro-Caribbean student (Morris) said that he did any housework, and even admitted that he liked it. His male peers were quick to deride this response as 'cissy'. One white fifth former in the group referred to Morris's position as the only male in an all-female household disparagingly as 'like Cinderella and the sisters' (cf. Chapter 4). So housework was very much women's work: but how did the young women feel about this?

Young women's experiences of domestic work

Young working class women had definite views about domestic work, and the various ways of avoiding it. Even if they did not object strongly to doing the work, what particularly rankled was being *told* to do it:

Vanessa: I don't mind doing the odd bits of housework.

Jacinta: The trouble is if you're at someone else's house and they tell you to do something you do it and enjoy it, but in your own house you know you've got to do it, you know even if you don't mind you still moan and say 'Oh I don't want to do it'.

         (Lodgehill, Afro-Caribbean fifth formers)

Young women's domestic responsibilities affected their schooling, and the move from school to college or the job market. Their non-attendance at school was often due to housework and childcare commitments, and this was treated less seriously than the 'truancy' of their male peers (see Shaw, 1978; and Chapter 1). Young women had a ready excuse for 'wagging it' which they could use to their advantage.

Since brothers rarely did any domestic work, responsibilities passed 'down' from the eldest daughter. The main lever which could exempt young women from these commitments was waged work. School students watched their elder sisters in eager anticipation of the day when they too would be in a position to avoid some of the housework.

CG: D'you think when you get a job you'll do the same housework or what?

Pippa: Oh less, 'cos you are out of the house, you know, and all my sisters now they're right scivers, you know. 'Oh I'm tired, I think I'll go and have a lie down.' And they're watching you do the rest of the housework and they go and have a lie down, and watch the tele and listen to the radio.

Kathy: My mum says it's 'Come on Kathy, you do the housework and when you'll be at work your little sister'll be doing it all.'

         (Moorcroft, white fifth formers)

CG: D'you think when you get a job it'll change, that you'll
do less?

Berni: It will yeh, 'cos I'll make it change. It'll have to — I won't
have time.

CG: So who do you think will do it then?

Berni: My sister will, she's 9 now (laugh). I can't wait, me.

(St Martin's, white fifth formers)

Despite her determination, Berni was still doing some housework
six months later, when she had a full-time job.

A few young women were paid for doing housework or childcare:
usually around 50 pence per task. A possible extension of this arrangement was to exempt young women from paying for their 'keep' once
they were full-time wage earners in exchange for their domestic work.
Since young women were less likely to be paid for doing housework
than their brothers or their male peers, this arrangement was relatively
unusual.

The most direct way of avoiding domestic work was to refuse to
do it, although young women were hardly arguing from a powerful
position in the household.

Viv: I'm going up town Saturday afternoon.

Loz: But I thought you helped your mum with the shopping then?

Viv: Oh well she'll have to lump it. She can piss off.

(Tildesley, white fifth formers)

Domestic skills formed a significant part of the curriculum for
non-academic working class girls, via lessons on cookery, needlework
and childcare.[5] Whether in the guise of domestic science or home
economics, housework and childcare were certainly expected to play
an important role in these young women's future lives (cf. Chapter
6).

Domestic commitments affected one young woman's move from
school to college with disastrous results. Sandra was a white working
class fifth former at St Martin's school who was taking four CSEs. She
had applied to a local college for a place on a full-time hairdressing
course before she was due to leave school in June 1979. Sandra was
from an Irish Catholic family and, like many of her peers, she stayed
with relatives in Ireland in July 1979 for a holiday.

While Sandra was away, the college wrote to her at home offering her a place, and asked her to return an acceptance form by September. Sandra's mother needed her at home to look after her elder sister's 2-year-old daughter, so she intercepted the letter and kept it from Sandra until it was too late. Both her mother and her sister had full-time jobs (the sister was separated from her husband) and Sandra's college place would not have brought in even a local authority grant. Only Sandra could have done the childcare, so she returned home to find that she had lost her college place, and had to go on the dole.

Sandra was only able to look for a job six months later, after her mother had changed shifts at the nearby car components factory, and was able to look after the child herself. By that time (March 1980) the local youth labour market had shrunk considerably, but Sandra did manage to find a job in a city centre hairdressing salon. Three months later, she was unemployed again, after a serious bout of dermatitis on her hands, arms and face, which was caused by using the shampoos with continually wet hands (Chapter 12).

Sandra's experience is quoted in some detail as one example of the way in which domestic commitments can shape young women's entry to college and the job market. A young man in an equivalent position would simply not have been expected to sacrifice his college place or a job for childcare responsibilities. If Sandra had been male, either her mother or her sister would have had to give up their job to do the childcare.

Women's primary responsibility is expected to be the home, and domestic work. This means working for others without pay, servicing the household, and dealing with their emotional and (in the husband or partner's case) their sexual needs. The art of sacrifice, and of minimising one's own needs, forms an important part of the female role in the home. Domestic work was only one of the ways through which young women learnt about their present and future positions in family life and the labour market.

4

Family life: present and future

The nuclear family form of father in a full-time job, mother as a full-time housewife, and an average of two children is frequently assumed to be a normal, even universal phenomenon. This 'normal' family form is a fairly recent development which is most common amongst the white Protestant middle classes in the industrialised West (see Coussins and Coote, 1981; Leonard, 1980; Carby, 1982). Margaret Thatcher's Conservative government has repeatedly stressed the importance — even the sanctity — of nuclear family life as the key to stability in British society.[1]

In post-war Britain, concern about the decline of nuclear family life has focused on the increasing divorce rate and the impact of the Welfare State (e.g. Fletcher, 1962), especially with regard to white working class families. Irish Catholic families in particular have been seen as irresponsible for producing 'too many children' (Humphries, 1977). Since the early 1970s, moral panics about the so-called sexual revolution and the influences of the second wave of twentieth-century Western feminism have been additional objects of concern (Barret and McIntosh, 1982).

With the immigration of people from parts of the New Commonwealth in the 1950s and 1960s, Britain has become an increasingly multi-cultural society. Black people from the Caribbean and parts of Africa and Asia have their own cultural traditions and family structures, which the British establishment has treated as 'backward', deviant, and even pathological (Lawrence, 1981; Race and Politics group, 1982; Brent CHC, 1981).

This image of the 'normal' nuclear family pervades the British education system as well as other state institutions. Most of the students I interviewed lived in households based around a nuclear family, particularly the young white women. Of the 106 young women I asked about their families of origin, 72 per cent at the very most lived in households with both parents present and their fathers in full-time jobs. This figure was 88 per cent for white middle class sixth formers, 79 per cent for white working class fifth formers, and 36 per cent for young black women (see Table B).[2] The whole area of family life and family size was an extremely sensitive issue. The idealised model of the cosy nuclear family shaped young women's views of their own family backgrounds, and teachers' perceptions of their 'problems'.

Considerable social stigma was attached to coming from a 'big family', even in Catholic schools:[3]

Shelly: I come from a small family, there's eight of us (laugh).

(St Martin's, white fifth former)

This was most marked in Church of England schools:

CG: Have you got brothers and sisters?
Marie: Yes (all others laugh).
Sue: How many is it? There's twenty-two of you ain't there?

(Lodgehill, white fifth formers)

Most of the teachers I spoke to were white and middle class, and women teachers distinguished between their own position and that of non-academic working class fifth formers:

Ms Haden: The ones you talked to, the lower streams, the lower ability girls, they'll be supermums. Unlike us, professional women who shove kids out all over the place and aren't particularly good mums. But *they'll* be there.

(Moorcroft, head of careers department)

Ms Haden praised the dependability of these 'supermums', and saw young working class women as naturally suited for motherhood and family life. Paradoxically, these young women also had to be *trained* to be good wives and mothers, in the idealised nuclear family mould (see Dyhouse, 1977; Whitfield, 1980).

Teachers tended to attribute the problems of working class students to their supposedly 'deviant' families, rather than to material conditions such as unemployment or poverty (cf. Stone, 1981). Catholic families were particularly likely to be seen as problems. 'They shouldn't have so many children if they can't afford it,' as Ms Ryman told me.

Ms Ryman: It's a real shame about Mary. She's had to leave school early. Her parents can't support her, it's sad. She has to go to work. Her dad's gone, so her stepfather lives there now. There's a social worker dealing with the family, and there's been trouble.

(St Martin's, fifth form tutor)

White teachers also referred to black students' family lives as a potential source of 'problems'. Even those who were involved in multi-cultural education programmes shared these views.

Ms Evans: Two West Indians and two white girls have had kids already. I tried to persuade one West Indian girl to have an abortion but she wouldn't. West Indian mothers are disciplinarians, though, so I couldn't do much. And Asian girls, I feel sorry for a lot of them. They have it very hard, especially in families.

Ms Haden: Well the Asian and West Indian girls as well as the Catholic girls all have problems. The Asian ones are under a lot of pressure but they cope. Which is proof that it's a strong culture.

Ms Evans was the headmistress and Ms Haden a senior mistress at Moorcroft school, which was introducing a multi-cultural curriculum in 1979. Such programmes have been presented as radical and progressive, but they do not always confront one of the main sources of black students' problems: the racism of white teachers and students (Carby, 1980; Stone, 1981).

Ms Evans and Ms Haden saw themselves as sympathetic to black students, but their views followed the pattern which Errol Lawrence (1981) has described in his analysis of 'common-sense' racism. Afro-

Caribbean students were seen to live in 'deviant' one-parent families if their mothers were unmarried, separated or divorced, and were the main breadwinners (cf. Pryce, 1979). Young Asian women were assumed to be forced into arranged marriages, or caught between two opposing cultures (cf. Watson, 1977).

These assumptions about Asian and Afro-Caribbean families ignored the historical reasons for the development of different family forms and cultural traditions (Foner, 1978; Wilson, 1978). They seldom acknowledged the potentially positive and supportive nature of family life for young black women, especially in the face of increasingly violent racist insults and attacks (see CRE, 1979; *Race and Class*, 1981).

Young women's experience of family life

The apparently innocuous process of asking young women about their families, which would be sectioned off as 'biographical details' on a questionnaire, was fraught with tension. This was partly because the model of the ideal nuclear family loomed over the young women's responses. It was also due to their experiences of family life, which sometimes seemed to be a continual battle. This was one of the main reasons why so many young women dreamt of leaving home.

Ten of the 176 students I interviewed admitted to having left home at some stage, usually to live with female relatives (usually older sisters). They were all white, working class, 'non-academic' students who were under 16 at the time, and most had been forced to return home by their parents. With no money and few legal rights, they had little choice in the matter.[4] Their main reasons for leaving were arguments with parents (especially fathers and stepfathers) and siblings, and unwanted restrictions on their leisure time.

Other young, white, working class women who had not actually left home made similar complaints about their family lives, and looked forward to leaving home sometime in the future. This was partly because leaving home was seen as a mark of financial and social independence, but it also reflected real dissatisfactions with family life.

CG: How do you get on with your parents?
Berni: Ooo (groan), terrible. They just keep me in all the time.
CG: Do you think that will change when you leave school?

Berni: Yes it will. Next Thursday's my *birthday.* I'll be 16 and I'll be able to do what I want to do. No it's not fair 'cos they think you're a baby and they don't trust you that's all it is. They just don't trust you. I keep saying 'I'm gonna leave home when I'm 16'. She goes 'you can't, you can't, you have to stay at home'.

CG: I mean do you think you'll leave or. . .?

Berni: No I won't, not till I get married I suppose (laugh).

(St Martin's, white fifth former)

Some young women had more urgent reasons for wanting to leave home: male domestic violence. Although accurate statistics are difficult to come by, those that are available suggest that such events occur with horrifying frequency in many homes, irrespective of class, race, religion or locality. The Home Office only asked police to keep records of 'indictable crimes of violence within marriage' in 1980. One national survey has estimated that about 8,000 such cases were reported in 1980, although this would represent only 2 per cent of the total number of cases (Dobash and Dobash, 1980). This survey found that wife-beating accounted for 25 per cent of all assaults in one year in Edinburgh and part of Glasgow. If this figure reflects a national trend, a conservative estimate would indicate that there are over 20,000 such cases each year in England and Wales alone (cf. Binney *et al.*, 1981).

Most young women were reluctant to discuss domestic violence with a research worker, or even with their peers. As I talked to young women after they had left school, a degree of mutual trust developed, and some groups felt more able to discuss their experiences:

Deb: Did you see that film about battered women on the tele the other night?

El: Yeh, it's terrible. She could have fought back like my mam does. *She* hits him back.

Penny: Don't you think she might get beat up worse then?

Sue: When my dad hits my mum and we think he shouldn't, we have a go at him and stop him. But sometimes when she goes on and on at him we don't 'cos she deserves it.

CG: You mean she deserves to get beaten up for just talking to him?

Sue: Yeh, well not really I suppose.

Sally: Well my mum left him and took us too. She had to.

Cathy: I'd just leave if I was being treated like that. I'd even leave the kids.

CG: Would you?

Sally: I bet when it came to it you wouldn't. You'd be frightened that he'd batter them.

El: What about if you have a daughter and she looks like you? If you go and leave her he'll take it out on her 'cos she reminds him of you.

Sue: If he beats you up does it means he loves yer?

Deb: When I first went with blokes I thought that getting beat up was just normal 'cos it happens all the time. I thought I had to put up with it 'cos that was what women was supposed to expect. Then I realised that it was wrong to have to put up with it.

> (Tildesley, white fifth formers; Deb was 17
> and had left the year before)

I am not suggesting that all of the young women who had left home or wanted to leave home had been beated up, but the figures do indicate that such assaults are disturbingly common, and that they affect young women to a disproportionate extent.[5]

Career women or supermums? Young women's expectations about their future position in family life

When I first interviewed these young women, I expected to find considerable differences between the experiences of the more academic middle class sixth formers and their working class peers. The former occupied more privileged positions in the education system and the labour market than the latter, partly as a result of women's struggles during the first half of the twentieth century (Delamont, 1980; Deem, 1978). By the late 1970s, I anticipated that these privileges combined with the impact of the 'second wave' of twentieth-century feminism would enable young middle class women to avoid some of the worst inequalities of married life. They at least stood some chance of earning a reasonable wage and living as independent women.

The full picture was, of course, far more complicated. I had underestimated the force of social (i.e. cultural and ideological) pressures to get a boyfriend and to marry. Alternatives to traditional marriage such as cohabitation (living together) were more acceptable to some sixth formers and to Afro-Caribbean students than to their white working class peers, but heterosexuality, marriage and motherhood were seen as inevitable 'facts of life' for most young women.

I asked all the young women about their expected future position in family life, and the potential effects on their employment prospects. Most students saw marriage and motherhood as distant if inevitable events, and found it difficult to think so far ahead (cf. Roberts and Sharpe, 1982).

CG: Do you think you'll get married ever or not?

Gill: I can't think about marriage yet I'm too young [17] I can't face it. If I did I'd go back to work when the kids were 5.

(Woodborough, white sixth former)

CG: So do you think in the future, you'll get married or have children or not?

Linda: Later on I suppose I will. Not until I'm in my late twenties though 'cos I'd like a nice career first.

CG: How do you think your job will fit in with marriage, perhaps kids?

Linda: I don't think it will (laugh). I'll definitely give up my job if I have children, 'cos I think all your time should be for your children until they're school age, and I'd probably try and get another job then. But then my mum's got a friend that tried that and she found it difficult to get a job afterwards, so. . . .

(Tildesley, white fifth former, staying on)

The majority of those sixth formers who expected to marry and have children anticipated that the latter event would lead them to give up their jobs. Most expected to return to the labour market (on a part-time basis) once the children were of school age (about 5) and some even expected to wait until they were 11 or 12. No white or black working class students expected to stay out of waged work for so long, mainly because they thought that they would need the money, or due to more established cultural traditions of women's employment.

All of the young women expected that they would have to manage some sort of conflict between their jobs or careers and their family commitments. Both young working class women and their more academic middle class peers saw their future employment being shaped by childcare and domestic responsibilities.

CG: Do you think about that [future family life] when you think about a job as well?

Tracey: Yeh, 'cos I was going to be an air hostess (laugh) and then I thought no, if I wanted to settle down I wouldn't have another career to fall back on. 'Cos I'm doing secretarial work. If I wanted to go on and do air hostessing I could do that and then I've got another career to fall back on.

(St Catherine's, white fifth former, leaving school)

Andrea: I don't want to get married until quite late, but if I get married I want to carry on with my job, perhaps have children towards my thirties, when I've been in a job quite a long time. And then I'd give up my job to have kids.

Julia: I want to get married and have children. I want to have them when I'm about 28. I don't think I'd go back to work afterwards, unless I felt that I really did miss my job and really enjoyed it and then I felt it was worth going back. But even so I wouldn't go back till the kids were at grammar school.

(Woodborough, white sixth formers)

What is striking here is the degree of fairly specific forward planning involved. These sixth formers had been encouraged to think ahead throughout their schooling, and to choose subjects and courses with a view to their future careers. They had also applied this principle to their anticipated future family lives. Ironically, their considerable domestic commitments would involve literally casting aside their careful academic and career planning. Childcare was viewed as valuable work which could not easily be combined with a full-time job.

CG: So what puts you off combining family with a job — is it that your job would mean travelling a lot?

Ann: Not really, I just don't think it's fair on any child — if I did have children — to work. I just want to bring it up, live with it completely. I just couldn't do that with my job.

(Woodborough, white sixth former)

Childcare is one of the few areas of women's work which is accorded some value, even though it is seen as a 'natural' feminine ability rather than a skill. Most young women did not expect men to do much childcare, and some saw this work as too important to be left to men alone, but there was no easy consensus on this issue (cf. Prendergast and Prout, 1980).

Marie: You have to give work up once you get married.

CG: Do you think that women should give up work to look after children?

Marie: Oh yes, you couldn't trust men to do it.

Sally: Oh no, God, you'd think that's all women were made for.

Marie: No I don't, but I think that if you've had a child you shouldn't not commit yourself and put it in a nursery and not have any interest in it yourself.

Sally: For a few years, but not for the rest of your life! I mean we went on this trip to Oxford and this woman gave a talk. She'd applied to a course on probation work or something, and she was pregnant. And they said 'what are you gonna do about the baby when the course starts?' and she said 'well I don't think that's any of your business. If I was a man and my wife was having a baby you wouldn't ask my husband what he was going to do with the baby! I think that's taking it a bit too far — but it's true I could see her point. But these days though, you *have* to work when you get married.

Marie: Yeh and I wouldn't do that (laugh) get a nice rich bloke to pay for me (laugh).

(St Catherine's, white sixth formers)

Young white and black working class women were not so cushioned from the harsher conditions of the local labour market as their white middle class peers. More immediate anxieties often prevented them from looking too far ahead:

Jane: I might get married, have kids, yeh. I haven't thought about that much at the moment . . . . Just worried about getting a job.

Clare: You don't really know what the future holds, not unless you're the sort of girl who's sort of planned it out (laugh).

(St Martin's, white fifth formers)

Many young women had some definite reservations about marriage and motherhood, although it was less controversial to criticise motherhood than marriage for young white women in particular.

Mary: When you've got kids you've got to stop home and look after them and I don't wanna do that (laugh).

Sue: Get married? You must be joking. I wouldn't get married. I wouldn't want children. Oh, I like 'em, but I wouldn't like them round me — nor a husband either (laugh).

CG: Why's that?

Sue: I dunno, I don't like getting tied to one person, I like to get out, and with a husband you couldn't — and kids round you.

Sheila: I never knew you thought that (surprise). *No* you don't *really* think that.

Sue: I do. I read in *Woman's Own* that lots of women don't have kids. The choice is between a career or a family.

June: I'd never get married.

Pippa: You've got to.

(Moorcroft, white fifth formers)

For one group of working class fifth formers at a Catholic school, social pressures to get married had taken a more tangible form in an RE (religious education) class for those not taking exams. This lesson did not necessarily have the intended effects:

CG: So do you think you'll get married or. . .?

Marie: After going through what we did yesterday. I got married yesterday (all laugh).

CG: Really?

Marie: We went through the wedding ceremony.

Shelly: It put her off (laugh). All the things you had to do. It's not for me.

Jenny: All the papers.

CG: Where did you get married?

Marie: Oh it was only in the library (laugh).

Shelly: And after we'd finished he told us how much the divorce would be! (laugh)

Jenny: What's the one you got married to?

Marie: I was gonna get married to one and he didn't turn up (laugh).

Jenny: I started to laugh when David was saying, to love and to cherish . . . it's a laugh, 'cos he's a real tough guy and he don't usually say things like that.

CG: So do you think you'll get married ever really? (Silence — laughter defused)

Jenny: Dunno.

Marie: Hopefully.

Shelly: Probably.

CG: What about kids?

Jenny: Help!

Shelly: Oh God.

(St Martin's, white fifth formers)

Marriage was hardly a positive choice, since no socially acceptable alternatives were available. It was expected to be an event over which young women would have negligible control: a spontaneous love relationship based on 'true romance' (cf. Leonard, 1980).

This stress on love and romance was most marked for young white women. Their Asian and Afro-Caribbean peers experienced pressures to conform to future domestic roles in different ways. Some studies have presented young black women, and especially Asian girls, as more restricted than their white peers in this respect (e.g. Khan, 1976; CRE, 1976; cf. Lawrence, 1981 for a critique of this approach). Asian students themselves did not view their situation in such negative terms. Young Asian and Afro-Caribbean women tended to be more critical of the mythical ideal of romantic love and marriage than their white peers.

Jasbinder: They [teachers] expect all us Asians to be having arranged marrriages. Well it's not true that.

Dalbiro: And anyway, what's the big problem? I know lots of English people that get into a mess with their marriages, worse even. I do have trouble with my family sometimes, but nothing like what they say.

(St Martin's, Asian fifth formers)

Carol: I don't believe in marriage me. Waste of time.

Sonia: Nor me.

CG: What about you? [to Clare and Jane] Do you think you might?

Clare: ⎫
Jane: ⎬ Yeh.
Carol: I knew *they* would (laugh).

> (St Martin's, Clare and Jane are white
> girls, and Carol and Sonia are Afro-
> Caribbean fifth formers)

CG: In the future do you think you'll get married?

Marjory: No no no. Definitely not. Not marriage. You just suffer man. You've got to rush home from work and cook and tidy up and. . . .

Babs: You want a good time first before you get married. You get tied down.

Marjory: Enjoy yourself yeh. I'd live in sin really. And you have to do everything. You're fighting, arguing. I'd live with my man, yeh, but not marry him, I can chuck him out when I like.

Babs: What about kids then?

Marjory: I'd keep it, yeh, treasure it (laugh).

Jan: I'd get married but not till I'm about 30 (all laugh). I wanna enjoy myself, I don't wanna get bored. Get married when I meet the right one.

Marjory: Oh no, it'd be really horrible looking at the same person every day. You come in to the same old thing. I'd want a change me, I don't want to keep him forever.

> (Lodgehill; Marjory is Afro-Caribbean,
> Babs and Jan are white fifth formers)

Of course, young men also faced pressures to marry and become fathers, but these events had a very different significance for them. Marriage would not place them in an unpaid servicing role, and fatherhood would not involve twenty-four-hour childcare responsibilities, but these events might also bring pressures to prove themselves as 'real men' by supporting a family on a full-time wage (cf. Tolson, 1977; Willis, 1979).

I talked to one group of white and black working class 'lads' about their future positions in family life:

CG: Do you think you'll get married in the future, have kids?

Abdul: I don't want to. It's a waste of time.
Brian: You lose your freedom.
CG: What about you?
Morris: I will, I like kids (laugh).
Abdul: I don't like the idea of marriage. It's too much (laugh).
CG: Too much what?
Brian: You can't have your freedom with something like a dozen
           kids running around.

(Lodgehill; Morris is Afro-Caribbean,
Abdul is Asian, and Brian is white)

The 'weight' of family life referred partly to a restriction of their freedom, as well as to the pressure to bring home a 'family wage'. Morris, who had earlier been dismissed as a 'cissy' for living in an all-female household and doing some housework (see Chapter 3), was seen as 'strange' for admitting that he actually welcomed some of the responsibilities and restrictions of family life.

At the beginning of this century, Cicely Hamilton (1909) referred to marriage as a sort of trade for women, since it was an economic necessity for many 'genteel' women of that period. Women's position in the labour market has improved since the 1900s, but marital status is still an important influence on women's lives. Nowadays the financial aspects of married life tend to be glossed over: love and romance are supposed to reign supreme.[6]

Most of the young white women I spoke to felt trapped by this ideology of romantic love. Meeting 'Mr Right' was supposed to be a spontaneous event, and yet girls' magazines were full of hints and strategies for attracting, getting and keeping him (McRobbie, 1978a). The marriage market was also a kind of sexual marketplace, in which maintaining a good reputation was essential — and a constant worry (see McRobbie, 1978b; and Chapter 5).

Although marriage and motherhood seemed relevant to the fairly distant future, most young women were involved in what was often a precursor to marriage and/or motherhood: managing pressures to get a boyfriend. Having a boyfriend was seen as a mark of adulthood, and a move away from the child-like status of the schoolgirl. It was also seen as proof of 'normal' (i.e. heterosexual) femininity. Social and financial pressures to marry developed from social and financial pressures to find a boyfriend, as part of the complicated process of 'getting a man'. These pressures were most acute in young women's leisure time, and they formed an increasingly important part of young women's lives as they grew older.

5
Leisure: deffing out and having a laugh

The meaning of 'leisure' cannot be taken at face value, since it reflects numerous assumptions about 'free' time, and what constitutes 'real' work. In capitalist societies, leisure is time outside of waged work which should allow people to recover from their labour in order to return, presumably refreshed, for the next day's work. This is literally 're-creation' time.[1] This relationship between leisure and waged work means that only those with full-time jobs are seen to really deserve their leisure time. It also means that housewives, school students and unemployed people amongst others are assumed to have nothing but leisure, since they are not supposed to be doing any *real* (i.e. waged) work.

Women's unpaid housework and childcare has no real place in the leisure/work relationship, and some studies in the sociology of leisure have even referred to housewives as having 'nothing but free time'. Stan Parker's (1971) influential study of contemporary leisure took men in full-time employment as the central category against which everyone else was judged (cf. Roberts, 1970, 1978; Parker, 1976). Women's leisure and domestic work were seen as something of a problem, since they did not conform to this male 'norm'.[2]

Research on youth sub-cultures has looked at young people's leisure activities, but this has concentrated on the experiences of white working class 'lads' (see Hall and Jefferson, 1975, for review). Feminist critiques of this work have shifted the focus towards young women's leisure and this led to a debate on young women's relatively marginal position on the edges of male-dominated youth cultures (see McRobbie and Garber, 1975; Powell and Clarke, 1975; and McRobbie, 1980). Dick Hebdige's analysis of the race-specific nature of most youth subcultures work, like the feminist critiques, said little about the double invisibility of young black women in these studies (Hebdige, 1979).

Leisure played an important part in the lives of the young women I interviewed. It was the area in which pressures to get a boyfriend were most intense. Getting a boyfriend was seen as proof of young women's 'normal' heterosexuality and more 'grown-up' femininity. Heterosexuality was not experienced as a freely chosen sexual preference: it was seen as 'natural' and inevitable. Alternatives to heterosexuality (e.g. bisexuality, celibacy, lesbianism) were seen as deviant, abnormal and pathological. For most young women they were dismissed as 'just a passing phase' in the supposedly natural process of maturing towards heterosexuality (Hemmings, 1982).

Heterosexuality is supposed to be *the* normal and natural sexuality for all women and men: a fundamentally biological phenomenon. Historical studies have shown that patterns of sexual behaviour vary considerably in different societies and in different periods (e.g. Foucault, 1978; Faderman, 1981). Heterosexuality is therefore very much a *social* phenomenon, which some feminists have referred to as the social institution of compulsory heterosexuality (see Rich, 1980; Rubin, 1975). In this sense, sexuality can never simply be a free choice or a natural behaviour, because of the numerous sanctions against supposedly deviant sexualities, and the extent of pressures to be heterosexual, preferably within marriage.

The institution of compulsory heterosexuality was certainly important to the young women I interviewed. Maintaining a good sexual reputation was crucial, and 'getting a bad name' as a slag, a slut, a whore or a pro was something to be avoided at all costs (McRobbie, 1978b; Cowie and Lees, 1981). Young white women sometimes used such insults as terms of racist abuse of their Asian and Afro-Caribbean peers, but it was the lads who had the most power to make or break a girl's sexual reputation:

Joy: He said he'd had it away with me. He never did — I wouldn't *look* at him never mind that. Everyone believed him of course. They always do. I was *furious*.

(Tildesley, white fourth former)

Labelling young women 'slags' drove a divisive wedge between 'good' and 'bad' girls: those who will and those who won't (Griffin, 1982b). This was a game that young women could never win; if you said 'yes' you were a slag, and if you said 'no' you were frigid or a lezzie (lesbian). The crucial dilemma was 'what to do if a boy asks you for sex':

Treena: But if a bloke asks you for sex, what do you do?
Brid: I'd tell him to go off and have a wank!
Stella: You dirty thing!
Kate: It's wrong, you ought to get married in a white dress.
Stella: But I don't think it is — if you like the bloke why not? Why wait till you're married?
Treena: She's talking — I bet she's done it!
Kate: You ought to sleep with a bloke if you loved him and he asked you to.
Stella: But you just said that you have to get married in white!!

(St Martin's, white fourth formers)

Relationships with boyfriends were supposed to be based on 'true love', but there was no easy way of fitting male demands for sex into this romantic fantasy. Pressures to get a boyfriend had a considerable influence on young women's leisure, especially on friendships between young white women.

Deffing out: the breakdown of female friendships

Much of these young women's leisure time was spent in the home, and centred on female friendship groups.[3] Young women would meet after school in each other's houses, usually in their bedrooms for privacy. They might play records, experiment with clothes or make-up, have a surreptitious smoke, and talk about teachers, boys, school and sex.

These friendship groups were close, and arguments could be emotionally traumatic. Many 'best' friendships lasted over several years.

CG: Who do you spend most of your time with outside school?
Cathy: I'm best friends with her [pointing to Jeanette]. We go around everywhere.

CG: D'you argue?

Cathy: Oh yeh — that makes it even better. I think if you didn't argue it'd be a strain (laugh). It can be awful though.

(Lodgehill, white fifth former)

Elaine: I see June mostly, we're best friends. She's like part of the family now, 'cos my parents know hers. I see her after school, I've known her since primary school.

(St Catherine's, white fifth former)

Berni: Her, she's my best friend. I love her [hugging Sue] . I can talk to her, tell her all my secrets (laugh).

(St Martin's, white fifth former)

These best friendships were typified by young women going everywhere together, walking along arm-in-arm, wearing *exactly* the same clothes, shoes, hairstyles, even jewelry. Apart from such best friendships, the exact make-up of female friendship groups was continually changing, as young women argued and shifted their allegiances elsewhere. One white fifth former at St Martin's school showed me a crumpled note which had been passed around all her friends:

'Dear Jenny, I'm writing this to tell you that I didn't mean what I said and that I still want to be friends. We can all three go around together, Shelly, Jenny and Marie. I said I wouldn't deff you out and I never will, OK. So let me know what you think and we can be friends always.

Jenny: [to me] She's gonna get it, that Marie. Me and Shelly are friends but not with her. I've told her to her face.

These female friendship groups were very different from the larger, looser 'gangs of lads' which have been regarded as the basis of youth cultures (see Hall and Jefferson, 1975; Corrigan, 1979; cf. Davies, 1979). If a young woman started to go out with a fairly regular boyfriend, she gradually lost touch with her girlfriends, often at the young man's insistence. This 'deffing out' process was even more prevalent after young women had left school, because they could no longer rely on the daily contact with girlfriends at school.

There was no equivalent breakdown of male friendships if a young man began to 'go steady' with a girlfriend. 'The lads' continued to see their friends in local pubs and at football matches (cf. Willis, 1977). Some young women had to tag along with a group of young men when they saw their boyfriends, as the latter incorporated 'going steady' into their usual leisure activities.

Sandra: Mandy's been out with a few boys, and whenever she does, she never bothers ringing me. Or she goes out with them and doesn't tell me, and I'm stuck in all the time. Whenever I go out with Mandy she's with her fella, and she leaves me with all his friends. They're all going on about this girl and that, so I try to get up another conversation. It's no fun standing around listening to them go on about sex and girls. We always said at the beginning that we wouldn't deff each other out if we went out with fellas, but she always does in the end. I could kill her sometimes, it gets on my nerves. If I do meet someone, it doesn't last, or I don't like them much (laugh).

(St Martin's, white fifth former)

This 'deffing out' process was most marked amongst young white women, since their Asian and Afro-Caribbean peers did not experience pressures to get a boyfriend in the same way, and they could draw on stronger cultural traditions of female friendship and support. Most young women had a fairly low opinion of their male peers at school, and their most valued friendships were with other young women.

CG: Do you go around with any of the boys here after school?
Janice: Have you *seen* them? Ugh.
Jilly: We mix with them in school though. They're a laugh.
Von: But you can't talk to them, they're like kids.

(Tildesley, white fifth formers)

Older lads, and especially those with jobs, could provide access to more exciting and expensive leisure activities, and close friendships sometimes developed from these relationships. Once a young woman was 'going steady', her leisure activities would increasingly centre on the male/female couple (see Griffin *et al.*, 1980).

Having a laugh; young women's leisure activities

So what did most young women do in their leisure time outside of school? The most common activity was 'dossing'; hanging around in a group of 'all girls together'.

CG: What do you think you enjoy the most that you do?
Jane: I like going out with my friends, buying clothes. I've nowhere to wear them mind you, but just buying clothes I think about going out. Just having a good time, having a laugh.

(Tildesley, white fifth former)

'Having a laugh' on their own terms was not always easy for these young women: the biggest problem was having nowhere to go and no money. They lived between two and five miles from the city centre in council and private housing estates which had been built during Birmingham's slum clearance programme in the early 1960s. The cost of travelling limited most young working class women to their local areas, although the most exciting places to go were in the city centre. Those from more affluent middle class families could rely on a lift from their parents, and they had more pocket money to spend.

In 1979 and 1980 return bus fares to the city centre varied between 30 and 80 pence, depending on where the young women lived. A visit to a city centre cinema cost around £1.50 (£2.00 by 1982); skating was about £1.00 (£1.50 by 1982); entrance to clubs and discos varied from £1.00 to £1.50 (up to £2.50 by 1982). These prices were beyond the reach of most working class students, apart from the occasional treat. Visits 'up town' usually took place on Saturdays, when groups of young women (and men) would spend the day hanging around, window shopping, stealing from shops, watching other young people, and 'winding up' the police.

Sonia: A group of us cleared a whole counter of make-up once in [a large department store] up town. Nicked the lot (laugh)!

(Lodgehill, white fifth former)

Those with no source of extra money from part-time jobs had to rely on their parents for money. This soon went on sweets, comics, magazines and cigarettes. Some young women went without school meals and spent the money on cigarettes or records. Smoking was an important means of resisting their child-like status as schoolgirls, along with getting drunk on cider or lager. When the prices of alcohol and cigarettes increased and 'nicking' was too risky, sniffing glue took over as a cheaper substitute.[4]

Most young women relied on their parents for buying clothes, and this was often a source of resentment and conflict with their mothers.

Von:	Our mam takes me to get clothes.
CG:	And do you get on OK?
Von:	Yeh — so long as you have what she says (laugh).
Janice:	If you go with your mum and you want something really *weird*, you know, it's no good.

(Tildesley, white fifth former)

Some young women spent money on make-up, although this was not a widespread practice. Most borrowed their older sister's make-up for special occasions, or for 'mucking about' and dressing up. They bought and swapped comics and girls' magazines, for reading at home, on the bus, and in lessons, both alone and in groups of other young women. These varied from the *Beano*, *Bunty* and comics for a younger age group, through to the more expensive *Vogue* and *Cosmopolitan*, with *Jackie*, *Blue Jeans*, *My Guy*, and *Photo Love* among the favourites.[5]

The most common local leisure facilities were pubs, although school students had to pass as 18-year-olds in order to drink there. Knowing that this was illegal, and wary of what might happen if they got very drunk, most young women who went to pubs avoided alcoholic drinks. Other local amenities included swimming pools, ten-pin bowling, youth clubs and (unlicensed) discos, sports halls and parks, depending on the area. Bingo halls were another widely used local leisure facility, and most of their customers were older women. Those amenities which were intended for young people usually required some form of entrance fee, and they tended to be dominated by young men, even if they had not been designed to appeal mainly to 'the lads'. These places had little to offer young women, especially given the various restrictions on their leisure time (see Hanmer, 1964; Carpenter, 1980).

CG: Do your parents let you go out like in the evenings or weekends? Are they strict or don't they mind?

Sonia: No we're not allowed to go out — got to do the housework
an' that.

Carol: They don't let you out (all laugh). Princess in the tower me.
There's nowhere to go really 'cos what we go to they don't
want us to go there because there's trouble, too much
trouble.

Mandy: 'Cos there's too much boys and too much drink.

Carol: That's true.

Mandy: 'Cos everywhere you go there's all alcohol and the discos
you go to now even the pictures have got bars in them (all
laugh).

(St Martin's; Carol and Sonia are Afro-
Caribbean, and Mandy is a white fifth former)

'Trouble' in this context had a range of meanings, the most common
of which was young men's violent behaviour. Several researchers have
described the aggressive bravado of white working class lads in positive
terms as a form of cultural resistance (e.g. Robbins and Cohen, 1978).
This behaviour also had oppressive consequences for young women
and black people when it took sexist and racist forms (Willis, 1977).

Two young women discussed the difficulties involved in going to
the local youth club:

Sandra: It's a drag, we can only go down every so often. . . . We have
to babysit an' that.

Cheryl: Yeh and when you *do* go it's all boys fighting. You can't get
a game of pool or table tennis. You have to watch. The
discos are OK, except there's always trouble.

(St Martin's, white fifth formers)

Although the combination of 'too much boys and too much drink'
restricted many young women's leisure activities, it would be a mistake
to see them as passive wallflowers. A single-sex disco at a girls' school
might be fairly safe for young women, but it would not necessarily
be a quiet or uneventful affair:

CG: Does this school have discos?

Tracey: Oh terrible!

Kim: We've had two.

Tracey: It's a bit difficult at this school 'cos the girls go to fight.
It's hard to get a disco in this school.

(St Catherine's, white fifth former)

An experienced part-time worker at the youth club which was close to Moorcroft and Tildesley schools saw considerable differences between the aggression of young women and men:

Liz: The worst fight we've had here was two girls, funny isn't it?
'Cos the boys are certainly a rough lot. We had to have the
police down to stop the girls. It's as if when the boys fight they
are playing at it — trying things out. When the girls fight they
really mean it.

'Trouble' also referred to the risk of sexual harassment and assault. Most young women had experienced some form of harassment, from 'flashing' to rape and sexual assault. In the area around Moorcroft and Tildesley schools, girls had regularly been followed by a man who would change into women's clothes in the streets in broad daylight, and carry on following them. Another man had waited outside the school gates and followed girls home. There had recently been two (unsolved) rapes in the area, involving girlfriends of the young women I interviewed.

El: Like that man that dresses up in women's clothes round here.
You shouted at him. Well I wouldn't as long as he didn't *do*
anything.

Sally: But he might. I'd shout at him. He *did* do something to me —
he nearly killed me with fright.

Cathy: I mean *all* of us have been followed home from school in daylight or flashed at by the same man.

El: Well that bloke got out of a car and ran after me — I was only
14. Luckily I was near my gran's so I ran in there.

Cathy: They're terrible, they just get away with it, how can they have
the nerve? Why do they need to do it?

El: You can't go on your own anywhere. I saw that bloke the
other day. Only I can't tell my mum. She wouldn't let me out
and my dad'd belt me.

Sally: A man did that to me and Pat in the park. We always walked
through together. He came up to us and got his wotsit out. I
just ran like mad. I was scared — terrified. She stood there and
said: 'Is that all you've got?'

Cathy: That's what you should do — they expect you to run away.

(Tildesley, white fifth formers)

Young women seldom reported these incidents because they feared
that if they did, they would not be believed, or else that *they* would
be blamed. These fears were not without foundation, as one local
teacher proved when he mentioned the same incidents to me:

Mr Yates: Some of the girls have been saying they've been attacked
coming from school.

CG: Yes some of them did mention that to me.

Mr Yates: Yes, well you don't believe them do you when they say
that?

CG: But if they're worried about it. . . .

Mr Yates: Yes but some of them wouldn't know what it means.
They're just having you on. These attacks are just nothing.
They're not serious you know (laugh).

(Tildesley, fifth form teacher)

All teachers and parents might not necessarily react in the same
way, but the expectation that they would kept young women silent
about their experiences. Their parents, and especially mothers, were
aware of the possibility of sexual assault, and placed restrictions on
their daughters' leisure activities as a result. Some young women even
felt that women who had been attacked must have 'asked for it', in
line with dominant ideas about most female victims of rape and mur-
der (cf. Birmingham RCC, 1980).[6]

Cathy: I think that girls who go out in slit skirts, and minis like,
they deserve it. They're asking for it.

CG: Would you go out in a mini?

Cathy: Oh yeh sometimes.

CG: If you were attacked, would you think it was your fault?

Cathy: Oh no course not.

(Lodgehill, white fifth former)

Young women resented the restrictions placed on their leisure activities whilst acknowledging that their parents' worries were well-founded. They were particularly annoyed because these restrictions seldom applied to their male peers, who were often the cause of any 'trouble'.

Elaine: Well I don't go out all that much, but once they [parents] know who I'm with and how I'm getting home, if I'm staying anywhere, who I'm staying with (yes) they're all right. There's one particular girl I know, once I mention her name everything is OK, you know (yeh) because we've been going around together for eleven years, we're best friends. They've never bothered as much about my brother though, it's not fair.

(St Catherine's, white fifth former)

Young women with no local girlfriends faced particular problems:

CG: Do you know many people round where you live?
Sandra: No, I used to but they all moved away to places, and I don't go out now at all, only local discos of a night-time — I stay in babysitting, I can't go out alone.

(St Martin's, white fifth former)

Young black women (and men) faced an additional restriction on their leisure activities: racist harassment. The prevalence of racist attacks on black people, and of the harsh police treatment of black youth, made most Asian and Afro-Caribbean parents understandably anxious about their children's safety (see CRE, 1979; Gilroy's article and 'Notes and Documents' in *Race and Class*, 1981; and Parmar and Mirza, 1981). Young women were the most affected by these restrictions:

CG: And what about after school? Going out or. . .?
Nasim: Well we can only go out early on. My parents wouldn't let me out later. It's too dangerous round where I live, especially after dark. But all the clubs and things are too late, they start at 7.30 p.m. I wouldn't go anyway.

(Moorcroft, Asian fifth former)

Young black women had developed their own ways of dealing with and challenging the everyday racism of their white peers. Young white women's racism took different forms from that of their male peers, and it was an important part of their leisure activities. Young white women often focused their more general anxieties about male sexuality and violence on to black men.

Janice: Well I don't mind coloureds — apart from Pakis [i.e. Asians].
I would go out with a black [she means Afro-Caribbean]. It'd be more than my life's worth. I'd become an outcast. I'd lose all my friends, my family'd go mad, my dad would kill me. There's too much to lose.

(Tildesley, white fifth former)

This fear sometimes extended to young black women's supposed aggression:

Sally: There was gonna be a crowd of black girls come down here [park] to beat us up. They don't like us.

(Tildesley, white fifth former)

Young black women would certainly have been justified in 'not liking' their white peers. Some young white women saw verbal abuse and even physical attacks on local black people as an integral part of their leisure activities: and a potential source of entertainment. 'Going nicking from the Paki shop' was particularly common. When occasional rumours of 'gangs of black kids coming to get us' circulated, this was seen as reprehensible behaviour, and a good excuse for a fight. It was not seen as a justifiable defence strategy on the part of local black youth who refused to suffer racist abuse (and worse) from their white peers. The almost hysterical local and national press coverage of 'muggings' during this period only reinforced the views of young whites (see Hall *et al.*, 1972 for an analysis of the racist implications of the term 'mugging').

Not all young white women shared these racist views. Loz was white, and her family on her stepfather's side were from Pakistan, including her half-brother Ali.

CG: What about going out or. . .?

Loz: You're joking! Near where I live it's all kerb crawlers. It's lethal. I still go out, but if any bloke came up to me when I was walking round there I'd go *mad*. I was going to the bus-stop with my brother Ali and. . . Well to me it's not the women round there that cause trouble it's the men in their cars stopping you all the time. Anyway this man came up to me and said 'how much love?' Then he saw Ali and he turned really nasty, saying 'Paki lover' and all this. He would have really beat us up. I was terrified. We ran off quick.

White racism drove a wedge between young whites and blacks, but young working class people in general had some sense of unity as a group in opposition to the police and teachers. Those whose families had a history of immigration to Britain or England also had some basis of common experience:

El: I want APL written on each shoe and tattooed on each arm. And red shoelaces in my Docs — that's APL, yellow is NF, white is BM.[7]

CG: You don't really though, I mean. . . .

El: Oh well OK, all right I mean my best mate's a black bloke. Why do you like 'em? I suppose some are OK.

Andy: APL is what's shit.

Marie: Yeh it's terrible, say Anti Police League instead.

Mick: Well that's crap 'cos I'm better than all them. They're useless.

Deb: What you mean 'cos you're white?

Mick: Yeh, they can't be British they ain't white.

Andy: Well that's rubbish. It's bad to say things like that.

Marie: Yeh I mean I'm Italian I know the trouble you get here as immigrants. You should too, you're Irish.

> (ex-Tildesley fifth formers; Deb is white from a mixed race family, Marie is white from an Italian Catholic family, Mick and El are white, from Irish Catholic families, and Andy is 'mixed race' from an Anglo-Asian family.)

Young women spent much of their leisure time maintaining female friendships groups, which were threatened by pressures to get a boy-friend and the prospect of leaving school. Most students kept to separate-sex friendship groups after school as well as during school hours. What is meant to be female or male, and the relationship between the sexes, was experienced through these 'separate spheres'.

6

Separate spheres: gender divisions in school

Gender refers to the socially ascribed characteristics and behaviours associated with being female and male, to dominant ideas about what women and men *should* be like, and to definitions of femininity and masculinity. Our understanding of gender and gender differences concerns more than collections of personality characteristics or 'sex-role stereotypes': it also relates to gender-based divisions of labour.[1] This covers differences between what women and men actually do, and assumptions about what women and men *should* do.

The education system is one of the most important social institutions through which these gender divisions are transmitted and reinforced (Deem, 1978). This chapter looks at young women's experiences of gender divisions in school; at differences between mixed and single sex schooling; between 'female' and 'male' school subjects; and at their expectations about 'women's' and 'men's' work.[2] Behind these experiences lay young women's relatively separate female friendship groups and their low opinions of their immediate male peers.

Gender divisions are maintained in part by the establishment of separate female and male spheres. This is usually justified by the argument that women and men are suited to different work because of biological differences in their physical and psychological make-up. The separate spheres argument that women and men are 'naturally' different (and that women are naturally inferior) has played an important role in the political arena: it was used to oppose women's demands for the vote (Harrison, 1976). In many societies, women have used their relative separation from men to develop female cultures

72

and support networks (e.g. El Saadawi, 1980), and this chapter considers how specific groups of young women responded to the relative separation between female and male spheres in school.

Mixed and single sex schools

The most obvious reflection of gender divisions for most students lay in their experiences of mixed or single sex schooling. In Britain, the more privileged daughters of the bourgeoisie and the aristocracy were the first to benefit from feminists' demands for girls' education (Delamont, 1980; Marks, 1976). Their schooling followed the pattern of their male peers, and was based in single sex establishments.

This association between academic privilege and single sex schooling continues to this day. It has led many radical educationalists to equate coeducation with more progressive and egalitarian systems such as comprehensive state schooling (see Education Group, 1981). Recent evidence suggests that coeducation tends to benefit boys more than single sex schooling, whilst for girls the relationship is reversed (see Lavigneur, 1980; Shaw, 1976, 1980).

Young women viewed the question of mixed versus single sex schooling in this context, so that going to a girls' school was associated with academic privilege. All of the more academic sixth formers were in girls' schools, so for these students, going to a mixed school would mean working with their immediate male peers, who were mainly white, middle class, and highly academic. The young women did not relish this prospect:

CG: D'you have much contact with the boys' school, 'cos it's very near?

Julia: More now in the sixth form. But I think it's odd here 'cos the boys aren't sort of normal boys (laughs). It's the only way of putting it, they've got such big egos, you can't talk to them like . . . arrogant . . . they're always being told how clever they are. Going to the same school as them? I'd hate it.

(Woodborough, sixth former)

Those students who had been to mixed comprehensive or grammar schools could make direct comparisons:

Maddy: I've been to a mixed grammar, and there's more competition between the girls. A lot of the time you're trying to impress the lads, especially if you're under age, no not academically, but showing off and that. I think girls do better academically anyway. It's just a general thing, your attitude to work changes, the way you think. When I came here I found the difference in the sort of work, the attitude to work. It doesn't make you not want to work like at a mixed school.

(St Catherine's, sixth former)

Less academic working class fifth formers at the same school weighed the advantages of an all-female institution against the possibility of 'missing out':

CG: D'you think you would have liked to have gone to a coed school?

Elaine: I don't really know. I think you miss out a bit, if you go to an all girls' school, 'cos like if not for for working where I did [Saturday job], I wouldn't have been able to get on with boys who work there. If you go to an all girls' school, it's just girls to get on with. You can't sit down and talk to a boy as if he's just a friend. You'd get all tensed up and everything . . . I don't know, I enjoy being at the girls' school. It's much more close. Girls are closer (hmm) and we never have any of that . . . bitchiness, you know, certain people that don't get on with other certain people.

(St Catherine's, white fifth former)

'Missing out' in this context referred to the everyday contact with male students in mixed schools. This was assumed to smooth the supposedly 'natural' process of maturation towards heterosexuality (e.g. Dale, 1974), and to alleviate girls' anxieties about boys, male violence and sexuality. Some of the working class students at one girls' school preferred to avoid such contact with male students and the associated pressures to get a boyfriend:

CG: Would you have preferred to have gone to a mixed school?

Girls: No, it'd be worse.

CG: Why worse do you think?

Sue: Dunno, it must be. You'd find girls going out with boys (laugh). And you couldn't concentrate (laugh).

Mary: We don't anyway (laugh).

Sue: No, but boys are violent — all — well most are (laugh).

(Moorcroft, white fifth formers)

Single sex schooling for girls is highly valued in some cultures, and especially for Catholic, Muslim and Sikh girls. Students from these groups were less likely to express any regret at having 'missed out' on coeducation, since girls' schools were an unsurprising and acceptable part of their lives.

All-male establishments, from bars and football changing rooms to elite London clubs, are viewed as quite normal, whilst all-female spaces tend to be described as 'unnatural', even 'unhealthy' (Imray and Middleton, 1982). Young women at the girls' schools objected to 'being called names' by local lads:

CG: Do you prefer being at a girls' school, or. . .?

Sue: You get called names, but you get used to that.

CG: What, from your friends (all laugh)

Sue: No, from the boys, being an all girls' school they call you lesbians.

CG: Why d'you think that is?

Sue: 'Cos it's all girls.

Loz: But they're the first ones to the gate in the afternoon (laugh).

(Moorcroft, white fifth formers)

Working class students at mixed schools associated single sex education with the more academic 'snob' schools, and attending such a 'posh' girls' school was not an attractive prospect. These young women were ambivalent about their experience of mixed schooling. The attention-seeking behaviour of their male peers might make lessons more exciting, but it could also be annoying and disruptive (cf. Stanworth, 1981).

CG: What about being at school with boys, d'you notice any difference between boys and girls . . .?

Sue: No they're all horrible.

Liz: They try to make theirselves noticed don't they?

(Tildesley, white fifth formers)

CG: What about being at school with boys?
Penny: It's exciting with the boys.
Marjory: They're *not* exciting though. They're boring in here mate (laugh). It's horrible. They're all horrible.
Penny: Not all, the ones I like. . . .
Marjory: They're nice but I wouldn't go out with any of 'em.
Peach: They always play up.

(Lodgehill, Afro-Caribbean fifth formers)

The behaviour of most male students was taken as evidence of their immaturity and stupidity. Young women did mix with their male peers in school, but they tended to avoid 'the lads' whenever possible, and especially for 'serious talks' (see Chapter 5).

CG: What about being at school with boys?
Sharon: They just run around and get in your way, and they always hit yer.
Marion: Boys are violent. When we want some peace we go and sit in the toilets.

(Tildesley, white fifth formers)

Penny: Boys mess around more than girls do.
Jacinta: Only if they feel like beating the drums.
Vanessa: That's only 'cos they don't know the work.
Penny: All that moaning. If they don't feel like working.

(Lodgehill, Afro-Caribbean fifth formers)

Ann: It doesn't bother us. We (laugh) just stay away from them most of the time. Don't really mix, but we do talk to them. Girls seem to stick to their own group, but boys aren't really fussy.

(Tildesley, white fifth former)

Asian, Afro-Caribbean and 'mixed race' students experienced frequent racist abuse — even attacks — from white students and teachers.

Some young black women found their most positive source of support and understanding from other young women of their own culture:

CG: Do you have particular friends at school?
Satjinder: Yeh. There's a few of us Asian ones we usually stick
            together. The others call us names.

(Lodgehill, Asian fifth former)

Those non-academic fifth form girls who had 'had enough' of school supported the lads when their disruptive behaviour stemmed from a similar boredom and rejection of school. It was when male students' behaviour took particularly violent or arrogant forms ('beating the drums'), that young women dismissed it as immature and stupid. The low esteem in which most young women held their immediate male peers was seen to be mutual.

CG: D'you think there is any difference between the way that
         girls and boys behave or not?
Elaine: I don't really know. I think the things girls think important
         boys just think, oh that's rubbish.
CG: What do you think that girls think is important then?
Elaine: Well clothes and records and pop stars, whereas boys think
         sports, and it's mainly football. But all the girls in our class
         are football fanatics!

(St Catherine's, white fifth former)

Gender-specific subjects in school

The relative separation between female and male friendship groups was linked to distinctions between 'female' and 'male' school subjects, and to expectations about 'women's' and 'men's' work in the home and the labour market. In the less academic schools, 'girls' subjects' were domestic science, cookery, needlework, childcare, typing and commerce. 'Boys' subjects' included woodwork, metalwork and technical drawing (TD). When the Sex Discrimination Act became law in 1975, schools were officially obliged to give all students the chance to take all of these subjects. Female and male students were supposed to have equal access to all subjects, but woodwork and cookery classes did not suddenly become evenly mixed on gender lines in 1975. Unsympathetic teachers could then blame female students for not taking up these 'equal opportunities', and for their subordinated positions in the job market.

Ms Barnes: Each sex can go into all subjects, but it's the boys who go into girls' subjects like catering or commerce, and there are no girls in woodwork or TD. They don't all rush into the opposite sex options, so they haven't been discriminated against.

(Tildesley school)

The ideology of equal opportunities, as expressed in Britain's Equal Pay and Sex Discrimination legislation, assumes that women and men can both be discriminated against because of their sex to a broadly equivalent extent (Snell, 1979). There was nothing equivalent about the treatment of boys taking cookery or typing, and that of girls taking metalwork or TD. If any group benefited from moves to promote equal opportunities, it was most likely to be the boys:

CG: Do girls tend to take different subjects from boys?
Ms Barnes: We've always had boys who want to do catering and go on to be chefs. Some girls in the fourth year did put in to do woodwork but it's not for jobs. Those are girls with no ability, they're layabouts. They'll go because of all the boys in the class, for a laugh. The girls who do TD are very good, and exceptions really, or they're groups who like boys.

(Tildesley school, deputy head)

Ms Pearson: Well most still stick to the same girls' and boys' subjects here. But last year we had a few boys doing cookery and we put on an extra class after school for them. They were really keen, they wanted to be chefs.

(Lodgehill school, headmistress)

Male students who took 'girls' subjects' were assumed to be learning a skill for future use in the labour market. They were taken more seriously than their female peers in the same classes, to whom such skills were supposed to come naturally for use in their future roles as wives and mothers (see Dyhouse, 1977). Female students who took 'boys' subjects' were either presumed to be interested solely in flirting with the boys, or discounted as unique exceptions.

Those who were fifth formers in 1979 were the last year under the old system, before most schools offered female and male students the chance to at least try non-traditional subjects. Many of these young women resented the fact that they had 'missed out' in this way. Those who were doing 'male' subjects had needed considerable determination to convince teachers and parents of their serious intentions (see Chapter 11).[3]

Paranjit: It's getting better for girls now. Well I wanted to do TD and I fought for it. The lower school can now each do both. I wanted it for an engineering job. I enjoy it now though.

(St Martin's, Asian fifth former)

Young women in girls' schools were the least likely to be taking 'boys' subjects'. Asking them whether they would have liked to try such subjects was a relatively meaningless question:

CG: Have you ever fancied doing things like metalwork or TD?
Elaine: But I don't know, 'cos I mean you know what they say, what you've never known, you never miss (laugh). I've never known it, so I didn't really miss it.

(St Catherine's, white fifth former)

Women's work and men's work

There were clear links between gender-specific school subjects and traditionally female and male jobs. Young women's experiences of gender divisions in school shaped their expectations about their own future job prospects as well as those of their male peers (see Griffin, 1983).

Sharon: There's one boy doing typing. I dunno why, I mean a boy can't be a secretary (laugh).

Marion: They can now, can't they? You can have male secretaries.

Sharon: Well not secretary, they can be male office.

Marion: They wouldn't want to sit there typing all day, and there's more jobs for boys anyway.

(Tildesley, white fifth formers)

CG: D'you not fancy the sort of jobs that boys do?

Jane: No I'd be no good at them things. Maybe if I was good at woodwork, I might try and do something but I've never imagined myself working there or doing anything like that. I mean like what my dad does I wouldn't like that, 'cos it's doing the same thing every day. He doesn't like it himself, it's just that he's got to do it.[4]

(St Martin's, white fifth former)

Many of the sixth formers I interviewed expected to go into traditionally female jobs as teachers or nurses, but a significant proportion hoped to take 'male' subjects like medicine, economics or physics at university. Most fifth formers expected to try for 'women's jobs' in offices, shops and factories — or to go on the dole (see Chapter 7). At first I was surprised that so many young women seemed to be 'choosing' traditionally female occupations. In fact about one third of the students I interviewed had been interested in a 'male' course or job at some stage. Discouragement, overt opposition and lack of support from teachers, careers advisers, relatives and friends had pushed most of them back towards more acceptable 'choices' (cf. Blackstone and Weinreich-Haste, 1980).

Despite such discouragement, I assumed that 'men's jobs' would present an attractive prospect for most young working class women, because they offered the chance to earn a reasonable wage and to learn a recognised skill. These students did feel pressured into traditionally female jobs, and they resented this, but getting a 'man's job' was not necessarily seen as the path to equality and liberation. Most young women had realistic and pragmatic reasons for preferring 'women's jobs'.

CG: Have you ever thought about doing jobs like engineering or mechanics?

Monica: I've thought about electronics, that would be only to fix my own TV though (laugh).

Lorna: Some of the boys' jobs are too messy, you know, spoil your hands.

Monica: Yeh, you see them with their crummy fingernails and it looks revolting.

(Moorcroft, Afro-Caribbean fifth formers)

'Men's jobs' were associated with brothers' or fathers' experiences of hard manual work in dirty and noisy conditions, doing long hours of overtime in order to earn 'a living wage'. Going into such a job would mean being the token woman in a predominantly male workplace, and this could be lonely and miserable for young women. 'Women's jobs' might be poorly paid, low status and boring, but they did include the support and 'laughs' of working with other women.

Given the importance of pressures to get a boyfriend, having some men around in a predominantly female workplace was seen as potentially exciting. If the focus of young women's attention shifted towards getting a boyfriend, the company of other women came to seem less interesting. This exacerbated the breakdown of female friendship groups as young women began to 'go steady'.

CG: So would you mind working with blokes at all?

Sheila: I wouldn't mind (laugh).

Lorraine: Not just girls though, I couldn't. I've had enough of sitting by girls at school (all laugh).

Mary: She's boy-mad ain't yer!

Lorraine: I'd only want to work with men if they were nice looking. It'd be more interesting than working with women (laugh).

(Moorcroft, white fifth formers)

If all the young women had been totally caught up in the process of getting a boyfriend, then one might have expected them to rush into jobs where they would be surrounded by men. Even those who had 'had enough of sitting by girls' at single sex schools preferred working in a 'women's job' to being a token female presence in the male world of engineering or motor mechanics. Working as 'one of the lads' with oily overalls and calloused hands hardly provided a suitably romantic atmosphere for getting a boyfriend, and there would be few other young women with whom to gossip and 'have a laugh'. Such gender divisions and pressures to 'get a man' were only some of the factors which shaped young women's expectations about their future job prospects.

7

Looking forward: young women's expectations about full-time employment

Most studies of what has been termed the 'transition from school to work' have used linear models to understand students' experiences (e.g. Carter, 1962; see Brannen, 1975 for a review of this research). Many working class school leavers move from casual part-time jobs into full-time employment, and rely on informal job-finding networks, so the 'school to work transition' is not always a sudden move involving official agencies like the Careers Service or Job Centres (see Finn, 1981). Most studies have either ignored young women altogether (e.g. Carter, 1966), or tried in vain to fit their experiences into analytical frameworks which were designed to explain young men's position (e.g. Maizels, 1970). This chapter looks at young women's hopes and anxieties about entering the full-time labour market, but it begins with an analysis of their involvement in part-time 'Saturday jobs'.

Part-time jobs and the child labour market

Overall, about 40 per cent of the students I interviewed had had some form of part-time employment, and this included 50 per cent of the young working class women (see Table C). These figures are comparable with the national study quoted by McLennan (1980), and with Dan Finn's research in Coventry and Rugby (Finn, 1981).[1]

Dan Finn found that young women and men had similar levels of overall involvement in part-time jobs, although when he spoke to them, 72 per cent of 'non-academic' girls and 47 per cent of their male peers actually had casual jobs. These young men tended to have multiple jobs (up to three at once), to move around more often, and to work mainly in manual jobs in garages and factories. Young women were usually employed in local shops or hairdressers, often in addition to home-based jobs such as babysitting or childminding (Finn, 1981).

The young women I interviewed had similar patterns of casual employment, but there were considerable differences between the experiences of young middle and working class women, and between white and black students. Only 13 per cent of the young black women had part-time jobs, compared to 50 per cent of their white working class peers. This was not out of choice, since most Asian and Afro-Caribbean students had tried to find casual work without success, in some cases for well over a year. Working for relatives or family friends was their only alternative.

The mainly white middle class sixth formers had fewer difficulties finding part-time jobs than their working class and black peers. They worked mainly in city centre department stores, cafés, shoe shops and boutiques: 'You can't go up town of a Saturday now, it's full of St Catherine's girls!' Some part-time jobs reflected the students' own cultural backgrounds, such as selling skis in an upmarket sports shop; working as an unqualified laboratory technician in a local hospital (where dad worked as a consultant); giving piano lessons; and making the teas for their father's cricket teams.[2]

Those sixth formers without part-time jobs were often unable to get a job because of schoolwork, which was their main commitment out of school hours. Most of those in casual jobs were horrified at the prospect of doing such work on a full-time basis, as their black and working class peers were compelled to do. Some sixth formers used their own distaste for these jobs as evidence of other young women's stupidity or lack of ambition:

CG: And what do you think of the job you're doing?

Fiona: I work in a newsagent's, but I could never do it full-time, it's too boring. It's different for these girls who do it full-time, they're used to it. I shouldn't say this I suppose, but they couldn't do anything else really could they? They just want to get married and have loads of kids.

(Woodborough, white sixth formers)

Marie: I've worked in this certain chain store (all laugh). I was there for a whole week not just Saturdays, and I've *never* been so bored in my whole life, you can see the seconds dragging by. It wasn't sales, it was waitressing. I had dogs coming to the table and drinking out the cups — off the plates (all laugh). You can't say anything to them because it's customers like. The conversation is real trivial with the full-time girls too.

Donna: We've been conditioned to think that though.

Marie: But they pick up £29.00 for that boredom, I couldn't do that all the time.

(St Catherine's, white sixth formers)

Contrary to Marie and Fiona's assumptions, most working class students dreaded the possibility of continuing their part-time jobs on a full-time basis. They were no more likely to be satisfied with their work than were their middle class peers. Young working class women simply did not have the same access to well-paid, high status careers, so the distinction between the part-time and full-time labour markets was not so clear cut. Some of these young women worked alongside older married women in local shops as 'Saturday girls' and part-timers respectively. Elaine worked with her mother in a local greengrocer's shop:

CG: And how did you get the job?

Elaine: My mum works there. She stopped for a bit but she's back now on 17½ hours a week. There's quite a few, you know, middle-aged women casual workers. There's hardly any full-timers there — one boy started this morning.

CG: So he [manager] gives women with children time off in the school holidays and takes you on?

Elaine: Yes, and it's not costing him too much at all 'cos he can pay at a lower rate 'cos they're girls and young. We get 69p an hour now, but it was 57p when I started. Full-timers it's £1.05p an hour over 18 though. It s hard work, it really tires you out, takes a lot out of you, you don't get paid all that well. It s just that it mounts up after a while and . . . it's covenient. It's just pocket money.

(St Catherine's, white fifth former)

The part-time employment of women and young people as cheap casual labour certainly benefited employers (see Bruegel, 1979). There was a great deal of uncertainty about appropriate rates of pay, and considerable variation between different jobs. Young women's pay ranged from nothing for babysitting, housework or working in a family business; 50p an hour for babysitting; 50-70p an hour in local shops; 80p an hour in some supermarkets and department stores; through to £3 for five days' childminding during half-term.[3] Sixth form students were mainly concentrated in the better-paid jobs.

This casual labour market also acted as an informal trial period for some employers, who could take on young people as part-timers before deciding whether to offer them a full-time job.[4] Cathy had a regular Saturday job at a local chemist's throughout her final year at school (Lodgehill). Despite teachers' encouragement to stay on, she decided to leave and get a full-time job, since she had such a low opinion of the school. Three months before leaving school, she was still undecided as to whether to continue full-time at the chemist's, to search for an office job, or to take a full-time reception work course at college. The chemist's offered training in dispensing, but such was the glamorous image of office work that Cathy eventually started as an office junior on worse pay and doing more menial work than at the chemist's.

For most young women, the work involved in part-time jobs was boring, menial, poorly paid and *hard*. Despite these disadvantages, casual jobs were a source of much-needed cash, and they did have some good points:

Carol: I've got a part-time job cleaning up town.
CG: How is it?
Carol: I like it — the atmosphere and the people there.

(Tildesley, Afro-Caribbean fifth former)

Elaine: All the girls get on pretty well and he's a good boss. We have a laugh, we enjoy it. That's what I'm going to miss. The fun and everything.

(St Catherine's, white fifth former)

Young working class women were not the brainless dupes that their middle class peers took them to be: they did object to the poor pay and working conditions in casual jobs. Arguments with employers often developed, with young women eventually leaving or getting the sack. Jilly had hoped to use a part-time job in a local hairdressing salon as a stepping stone to a full-time apprenticeship. Unfortunately the manager was 'a right slave-driver' who would not even let her wash hair.

CG: So you think you got a . . .?

Jilly: A rough bargain with that one. He was terrible he was, 'cos he thought he was high and mighty you see 'cos he'd got two shops and he was quite well established. Oh I couldn't stand him, 'cos everybody else they just sort of creeped round him, but I can't do that. So I left.

(Tildesley, white fifth former)

Some of the more academic fifth and sixth formers had been prevented from getting part-time jobs by their parents, who demanded that they spent any spare time doing schoolwork. The situation was more likely to be reversed for their less academic peers, with some parents explicitly pressurising them to find casual work.

CG: And do you work on Saturdays for money or for getting a job when you leave or . . .?

Janice: Me, I just work 'cos if I didn't our mum would call me all the idle things under the sun. She goes mad: 'Why don't you get a job? So I got a job and she's much better. She sees no reason when there's jobs to go and fetch why you don't go and get one. *She* says it's to prepare you to go to work [full-time] , but it doesn't prepare me.

Von: Our mum just about lets me work of a Saturday.

Janice: What, she don't like you going?

Von: Not while I'm at school, she don't like me working while I'm at school. She wants me to get my exams.

(Tildesley, white fifth formers)

Young women's experiences of casual employment affected their expectations about full-time jobs and their view of school:

CG: And you think it's different at work to school?

Lorraine: Oh yeh. Well like in a job you're getting paid to work
and you've got to work. At school you muck around a
lot. I know it will be hard work if I get a [full-time] job
'cos of this waitressing job. Doing that I found it very hard
at first. I'm used to it now but when I first started I used
to get terribly tired, standing up all day.

(Tildesley, white fifth former)

Careers advisers, teachers and social scientists have seldom recognised the importance of this 'child labour market'.[5] The latter have
also tended to underestimate the role of informal job-finding networks
and the influence of young women's families on their move to full-
time employment.

Getting a job: family influences

The families of young working class women played an important
role in their job-finding through informal contacts in local workplaces.
Employers were wary of taking on school leavers, even as relatively
cheap labour, but they were more likely to do so if there was some
adult (preferably a relative) who would vouch for and discipline the
young person if necessary. It was difficult to estimate the extent of
this informal job-finding network, but Easter school leavers and those
in factory jobs were the most likely to have found jobs through family
contacts (see Part II).

Some young women's families had their own businesses, however
small, and helping out on a part-time basis (paid or unpaid) whilst they
were still at school sometimes continued as full-time employment after
they had left. A number of young Asian women were expecting to
work in relatives' firms (cf. Wilson, 1978).

Charno: My relatives have found me a job — textile packing. It was
a job I've done on Saturdays and afternoons which I'll carry
on full-time. So I'll be with all my friends.

(Lodgehill, Asian fifth former)

Ms Preedy: There is race and sex discrimination from employers. It
happens all the time, and there's not much that these

laws can do. They've all had to change the wording of
ads, and so on, but they still say to us that they want
just girls or either girls or boys, or that they don't want
black youngsters. I really don't know what to do about
it.

(White careers officer)

Those students who recognised the importance of informal job-
finding networks tended to dismiss most careers advice as irrelevant.
Filling in job application forms and learning how to smile at the interviewer was seen as a waste of time (see Chapter 2). Outside the area
of the official curriculum, some teachers did mention the role of
informal job-finding networks. They saw this as relevant to a minority
of school leavers who were seen as 'lower ability', 'troublemakers', and
as incapable of finding jobs of their own accord. Two teachers mentioned informal job-finding networks in connection with another
potential job for young women: prostitution. This situation was not
seen as a cause for concern, but was accepted by the headmaster with
a genial laugh, as an indication of these young women's 'natural'
destinies.

Ms Barnes: Most girls' mothers' get them jobs — the sensible parents
who can watch them. Mind you, lots of them stay on
'cos they can't find jobs now. Some of our kids don't
get jobs but they manage all right. Some girls will find
work all right — they go on the streets — some of them
are already — while they're still at school.

Mrs Hughes: Their mothers are prostitutes too. It's the oldest pro-
fession and the girls get their training there (laugh).

(Tildesley, headmaster and deputy
headmistress)

Not all prospective school leavers could rely on informal job-finding networks, and they had to use more official channels:

CG: D'you know what you'll do when you leave?

Berni: I'm just leaving school (laugh). Just leave that's enough. I'm
not sure really. Look all round, I'll just start tramping round,
hope there'll be a job (laugh).

Shelly: I'm looking in the paper too me — and the Job Centre.

(St Martin's, white fifth former)

Most sixth formers felt that their parents (and their teachers) expected them to go on to college or university after their 'A' levels. Some of these students' parents had not been through higher education themselves and they simply wanted their daughters 'to make the best of their education'. Some parents preferred more vocational courses to strictly academic subjects.

June: I don't think my parents would have let me go to university
          if I hadn't been training to do something. They wouldn't like
          me to do a classics degree.
Fiona: Yes, they're quite keen on you going to university to fit you
          for something at the end of it, they're *not* keen on what my
          my mother calls the 'airy-fairy subjects' (all laugh).

(Woodborough)

Although young women's ambitions often coincided with those of their parents, conflicts did sometimes arise. Students would then try to 'talk them round', or would defy their parents on purpose.

Yvonne: They want me to go to university otherwise it'd be a waste
           of an education, *they* say. And their pride at having a
           daughter go to university.
June: Yeh, they wanna be able to show off to their friends (all
           (laugh).
Yvonne: And I'm going to do an ecology course, they can't bear it
           (laugh). Just to annoy them.

(Woodborough)

Some parents had quite specific ambitions for their academic daughters, which were sometimes closer to their own concerns than to their daughters' aspirations. One young women interrupted a group discussion in Woodborough sixth form common room to tell me about her experience:

Helen: My father has vague ambitions that I might do something
          scientific, because nobody in the family is the least bit scien-

tific, and I'm doing chemistry, maths and physics 'A' level.
Then I turned round and said I wanted to do economics, he
wasn't very pleasant. I mean nobody said anything particularly discouraging but nobody was very encouraging either.

CG: You mean that's not scientific enough? He wanted . . . .

Helen: Oh no, that isn't scientific *at all* (laugh).

Despite the restrictions which still exist for women in medicine,
several parents wanted their daughters to become doctors.

CG: Do your parents want you to do anything in particular or
not?

Julia: Well my parents wanted me to do medicine, and they didn't
want me to do engineering, 'cos they didn't think it was a suitable career for a girl. But I've talked them round now just
about. I think they're more pleased now 'cos I've got myself a
sponsorship . . . I think they thought that somebody must
think that she's worthwhile anyway (laugh). Even if *we* don't.
But they weren't happy about the idea of a girl going into a
man's world really.

All of these sixth formers took their parents' interest and encouragement almost for granted. Parents' ambitions for their daughters' academic and professional success did not always mix with the latters'
expected future position in family life, although there were exceptions:

Babs: My mum's pretty keen on my doing teaching 'cos that's a nice
steady job and it fits in with domesticity and all that (laugh).
The thing is that's what I wanted to do really . . . anyway
(sigh).

(Woodborough)

The prospect for less academic fifth formers were very different
from those of their white middle class peers. They could stay on in
schools which were ill-equipped to accommodate sixth forms; go on
to full-time college courses with a slim chance of getting an LEA
(Local Education Authority) grant; or go into the labour market.
The latter course might mean unemployment, joining a YOP scheme,
or a full-time job in an office, shop or factory, with poor pay and
worse prospects.

Most fifth formers said that their parents 'don't really mind what I do', but gradually a picture of subtle persuasion and encouragement emerged.

Mary: You're lucky to get somewhere, qualifications or career. I don't think any parents really want you to just do nothing. They'd like you to get good qualifications, but sometimes some parents say 'it's your life'. Mine, she just wants what's best for me as long as I get a job.

(Moorcroft, white fifth former)

One area of potential conflict lay in the decision to stay on at school or to leave. For some young women, their parents' views were uncomfortably close to those of the teachers, and they preferred the competition of the job market to the boredom of staying on at school:

Berni: My mum wants me to stay on.

CG: Does she?

Berni: Yeh — I'd be so bored, God! I don't see the point. I'd rather work anyway. You just do exactly the same work [in the sixth form] as you do in the fifth year.

Shelly: Yeh, 'cos we have the sixth year in our lessons.

Jenny: They're all trying to get yer to stay on till you're 18.

Sonia: They don't teach you nothing anyway.

Jenny: It's better to get out, get a job and earn money.

Berni: Mmm, go out and enjoy yourself. You only live once.

Sonia: Not according to my mom.

CG: What does your mum say?

Sonia: You've got to learn everything when you're young. She wants me to stay on but I'm not staying on.

(St Martin's; Shelly, Berni and Jenny are white, and Sonia is an Afro-Caribbean fifth former)

Most young women did not differentiate between the attitudes of their mothers and their fathers. When sixth formers experienced particular (and not always welcome) pressure from parents, it often came from their fathers. Fifth formers were more likely to talk about their mothers' views, which partly reflected their closer relationships with their mothers (see Chapter 13).

Sandra had continual arguments with her mother because she wanted to do a hairdressing course at college, and her mother had other ideas:[6]

CG: Did they want you to go to college then?
Sandra: No me mum didn't want me to go, no.
CG: Would she rather you'd get a job?
Sandra: I don't know. She's a bit funny. She keeps on to me to go
          with my sister in an office, and for that you need 'O' levels.
          I keep telling her, but she won't listen. And I don't want to
          get into an office anyway. But she won't listen.

(St Martin's, white fifth former)

When I talked to these students about their parents' attitudes, I had no means of comparing their responses with their parents' own views, because I only met some of the young women's families when I visited them at home after the students had left school. However, students' expectations about full-time employment were shaped by their parents' experiences of waged work (see Chapter 6). Elaine found out about the oppressive nature of waged work for many working class men through watching her father. She had also seen his power in the home, to make decisions about her mother's employment.

Elaine's father was on twelve-hour shifts at a local motor manufacturing company. He was offered a similar job in another section in the summer of 1979, working fewer hours for the same pay. He wanted to move, but the foreman would not let him go, because he did not want to lose a good worker. Elaine's father was then trapped in an exhausting work routine, compelled to work long hours in order to earn 'a living wage', but he refused to allow her mother to get a part-time job.

CG: And has your mum had a job before working with you in
          the greengrocer's?
Elaine: Yeh, she used to work in a hospital, er, bed making and
          that. . . . Well she'd worked practically all her life when she
          gave up work, and being in the house all the time depressed
          her. And then she started bringing outwork for my uncle,
          but she found that a bit monotonous. Then she started

work in a hospital, but that involved weekends. She had to give up the hospital job though, it was all right for a while, when I managed dinner and things like that, but then my brother started missing her a lot (yeh). He got funny and mopey and all moody . . . so she gave it up (yeh). I don't think my dad likes her to be working. He thinks she should be at home. But then you have to look at it from her point of view, in the house all day.

CG: When did she give up working altogether? Was that long ago?

Elaine: A year ago. She lasted about six months without a job, and then she couldn't do it any more. She was getting on our nerves as well, because when we came in, she was in a mood and being in the house all the time got on her nerves. We all got together and persuaded him to let her go back to work.

(Moorcroft, white fifth former)

Several white working class fifth formers mentioned similar family arguments when fathers tried to prevent their mothers from getting a job, and their mothers' depression at being stuck in the home all day. Whilst mothers often made connections between their own position and their daughters' lives, the latter seldom saw any direct links with their mothers' experiences. After all, mothers were older, married, with a family to look after, and this seemed far removed from the position of young single women who were still living at home.

Most fifth formers described their parents' views in terms of what the latter would *not* want their daughters to do. This mainly involved factory work, prostitution, joining the Police or Armed Forces or going on the dole:

CG: Is there anything they'd want you to do — or not?

Cheryl: Prostitute (all laugh).

CG: What do your parents think of you wanting to try for the Police? Or do they want you to?

Clare: My dad does but my mum doesn't. She wasn't too happy about the idea. Hard life, she's frightened I'll get beat up (laugh).

(St Martin's, white fifth formers)

Pippa: My dad wouldn't let me work in a factory, it's too dangerous.

	My mum worked in one and she had the end of a finger off.
Babs:	He says I can make up my own mind as long as I choose a good job and not a dead end job.
Jan:	They don't want me to go into a factory or anything like that.

(Lodgehill, white fifth formers)

A good job for a girl: young women's expectations

Young women's hopes and fears about their future employment were partly influenced by ideas about 'a good job for a girl' from parents, teachers and careers advisers. These messages about suitable female employment varied for different groups of young women, but behind them lay definite social and financial pressures to get a job.

In 1979, most sixth formers could adopt a fairly casual attitude towards unemployment, because they did not expect it to play a significant part in their future careers. Some young women adopted this casual attitude to irritate their parents, and as a rejection of academic pressures at school.

Anne: Yeh, I said to my parents that I might go on the dole, and they went mad – horrified. I don't particularly mind – I don't care.

(St Catherine's, white sixth former)

Fifth form students took the prospect of unemployment far more seriously, viewing it with anxiety or a certain resignation. Although many of these young women were worried that they might not be able to get a job immediately after leaving school, unemployment did not present the almost unavoidable prospect that it was to become some three years later (see Chapter 12).

CG: I'm doing this project talking to girls in schools and following some after they've left to get jobs.
Jenny: If they *can* get jobs you mean!

(St Martin's, white fifth former)

The unemployment rate for young black women in 1979 was

higher than for any other group (Malcolm, 1980), and black students realised that their employment prospects were not good:

CG: And what about you, when you leave school?
Penny: I'm gonna be a Giro technician, me [go on the dole].

(Lodgehill, Afro-Caribbean fifth former)

These young women were not prepared to take 'shit jobs' simply for the sake of being employed. Surviving without waged work or unemployment benefit had been an unpleasant part of the British colonial legacy for black students' families in parts of Asia, Africa and the Caribbean (see Foner, 1978; Race and Politics Group, 1982).

Joining the Police or the Armed Forces was definitely not seen as suitable employment for young women, and I was surprised at the number of fifth formers who saw these as desirable jobs.

Ms Haden: A lot of girls say that they want to go into the Army or the Police. We soon get them out of that.

(Moorcroft, careers mistress)

All of the students who wanted to join the Police or the Forces were white and working class. Their Asian and Afro-Caribbean peers vehemently rejected such jobs, since these institutions were seen as part of the state system which was harassing them, their families and their friends:

CG: I've talked to some girls who like, they're going into the Army and that.
Peach: Oh no, I don't think I'd wanna do that — ever.
Marjory: No, I don't want to do nothing like that, just do a normal job, right.
Penny: I wouldn't like nothing to do with Police or law. Them Babylonians [Police] are just no good man, they press down on yer all the time.

(Lodgehill, Afro-Caribbean fifth formers)

The Police and Armed Forces presented an attractive prospect to young white working class men because they seemed to offer a secure job, good money, the chance to learn a trade, and to express a particular kind of patriotic aggression:

CG: So what do you think you might get?
Brian: Police.
Rest: [all black students] Oh *no*, ugh.
CG: What made you want that job?
Brian: The authority and the danger . . . . Power.

> (Lodgehill; Brian is white, and the
> rest of the group are Asian and Afro-
> Caribbean fifth formers)

Mick: I'm gonna join the Army me — or the coppers. There's no
         jobs round here anyway.
CG: But you hate the coppers round here.
Mick: Yeh, but I wouldn't be in the police round here. They send the
         dregs here to this [local] station. I wanna go to Brixton to
         beat up blacks or to Ireland to kill paddies.
CG: But you've just said you're half Irish when you were on about
         voting Labour not Tory?
Mick: Yeh, but I'm British, it's not the same — none of *them* are
         British.

> (Tildesley, white fifth former)

Young white women did not want to join up in order to exercise power in such overtly aggressive and racist ways, although a few did look forward to 'being bossy'. They wanted to avoid the dole and the uncertainties of the labour market; to have a good social life and an interesting job 'working with people'; and the chance to leave home without getting married.

CG: Have you any idea what you'll do when you leave school?
Loz: Going in the Army. Not yet though, they want me when
         I'm 16 and 5 months.
CG: What made you think of that?
Loz: It's a good life, you get out a lot, get away from people and
         you meet different people then, different friends. It's to get
         away really. Specially from home — mind you I've already
         left home. I live at my sister's now. I just like wearing a uniform.

Cathy: Yeh, never wear the school uniform though (laugh).

(Tildesley, white fifth formers)

The age limits and entry requirements for joining up combined with the disapproval of parents and teachers meant that few of these young women would actually end up in the police or the forces. The minimum age for applying to join the Army is 17 years and 3 months; 17 for Naval ratings; 16 for Police cadets; and 18½ for the Police Service proper.[7] Some sections of the Army require Grade 3 CSE's or Maths and English 'O' levels, but all applicants must at least pass the relevant entrance exams. The Police require applicants to pass a recruitment exam, and at least three Grade 1 CSE's or 'O' level passes. The most important aspect of young women's ambitions to join up was their reasons of wanting to leave home; to travel and be independent; and to avoid unemployment and the exploitation of the local job market.

Prospective school leavers were subject to considerable pressures to be 'realistic' and get suitable jobs (see Chapters 2 and 6), but they did not accept such pressures with acquiescence or passivity. Young women had their own ideas about 'what makes a good job'.

Satyinder: I want to stay on or go on to sixth form college and do pathology. I'm ambitious really — but they [teachers] say it's not realistic. I wanted to do TD, and to get an engineering job. They didn't like that either. I'd like an interesting job with variety and chances of promotion.

(Lodgehill, Asian fifth former)

One of the most important qualities of a good job was 'variety' and 'interesting work'.

Berni: I'd like to have a different job every week me (laugh).

(St Martin's, white fifth former)

This was partly a reaction to fifth formers' experiences of boredom and monotony during their final months at school and in their part-time jobs. Several studies of the school to work transition have attributed young people's dissatisfaction with poorly paid menial jobs to adolescent irresponsibility or youthful energy (see Cockram and Beloff, 1978 for review). Young women's desire for variety and interesting work was not a particular characteristic of their age: they simply preferred not to work in boring, unskilled and low status jobs (cf. Rauta and Hunt, 1975).

Pay and working conditions were also important, although few of these fifth formers stood much chance of earning enough money to leave home and live as independent women. Young working class women did not see the size of their future wage packet as an index of their competence or their femininity in the same way that the wage packet was central to the masculine identity of their male peers (see Willis, 1977 and 1979). Feminine identity was more closely related to getting a boyfriend, marriage and motherhood (cf. McRobbie, 1978b; Pollert, 1981). Young women were used to working, or seeing their mothers and other women working for nothing in the home, and in this context any wage at all was a welcome prospect. Good wages were important, but they were often weighed against other factors such as variety and a good social atmosphere.

CG: What makes a good job?
Sandra: Whether you like it. Whether it's interesting. The money isn't . . . if you get a low wage, you're not going to like that much, but if it's not a very good job with high pay, I wouldn't like that. 'Cos then you're not enjoying it. I'd rather enjoy a good job, not get so much, but then get promotion later on, mainly.

(St Martin's, white fifth former)

CG: What's important about a good job then?
Shelly: Money, you do need that.
Berni: Yeh you need to earn more money when you go to work to pay your keep and clothes and food.
Shelly: I think you'll have to be more responsible when you work too. They expect you to be adult and you'll have to act it — not muck around all the time.
Berni: I'll still be mad though (laugh).

(St Martin's, white fifth formers)

Most students valued the social aspects of waged work, and especially the importance of 'getting on with the people you work with'.[8] Working with other young people was seen as the most important requirement for a good social atmosphere. The prospect of meeting a new group of people at work was viewed with a mixture of eager anticipation and wary apprehension.

CG: What do you think is the most important thing about . . . what makes a good job?

Elaine: You get on with people and enjoy the work you have to do. If you really enjoy it, you put your whole heart into it. If you don't enjoy it, then you just wanna get it over as quickly as possible (hmm). I think you meet new friends, a new atmosphere, you know, new surroundings.

(St Catherine's, white fifth former)

CG: So what do you think is the most important thing about a good job?

Jane: To make friends, that's most important or it'll drag on. I think it's important to get to know everybody else that's there.

(St Martin's, white fifth former)

The distinction between office and factory work

One of the most important ways of defining a good job for a (working class) girl was via the distinction between office and factory work. The latter was rejected as boring, insecure and unpleasant by parents, teachers and young women: 'not a nice job for a girl'.

CG: And is there any sort of job you wouldn't like to do?

Cheryl: Oh factory work. Just sitting at a machine a long time, doing the same thing.

Clare: You've got to have good working conditions to enjoy it and good friends. Now a bad job would be in a factory, that's too dirty (laugh). Office work is cleaner, I don't want an old office though, I want a nice modern one, a proper one.

(St Martin's, white fifth formers)

June: Me mum works in a factory and she says it's not . . . it's sort
of work for money. So you sort of keep going. She said it's
not a good job at all. In a factory you just work for money,
not like a proper career, she says.

(Moorcroft, white fifth former)

Office jobs had a more glamorous image as clean, secure work
which gave young women the chance 'to dress nice', even though they
might not pay so well as some factory jobs.[9]

CG: So why do you want to work in an office?
Von: Oh just to do typing.
Janice: And dress nice, yeh 'cos it's clean.
Von: I don't wanna work in a factory.
Janice: I'm not fussy I'll do anything.
Jilly: It's good money but I wouldn't work there [factory].

(Tildesley, white fifth formers)

Not everyone shared this positive view of office work. Young
women whose mothers or sisters were in office jobs were more critical
of their glamorous image, as were teachers at the more academic
schools like Moorcroft and St Catherine's:

Ms Haden: A lot want the more glamorous jobs, like hairdressing
and secretarial work — so *they* think. But I don't think
hairdressing *is* glamorous.

(Moorcroft)

Not all young working class women had such a positive view of
office jobs. They rejected the work as boring, and derided those who
hoped to go into office work as 'snobs'.

Viv: Those lot that want to do office jobs, they're snobs. Think
they're it.
Loz: Yeh, look down on us lot.

(Tildesley, white fifth formers)

Penny: It'd be boring man, in an office, I couldn't stand it, me.

Jacinta: Sitting down all day. Being nice to people. Huh.

> (Lodgehill, Afro-Caribbean sixth formers)

Office jobs were also associated with typing and commerce lessons in school, which some students found boring.

CG: What about office work, have you thought about that?
Cath: Oh *no*, I wouldn't like that.
Marjory: Not a secretary, it's boring enough sitting down in typing [lessons] never mind in an office.

> (Lodgehill, Marjory is Afro-Caribbean,
> Cath is a white fifth former)

Young women's views of office and factory work did not necessarily coincide with their eventual destinations in the job market (see Chapter 1). The distinction between office and factory work was very pervasive, and it was partly an expression of divisions between various groups of young women in school. Those who were seen as 'troublemakers' or 'low ability' felt consigned to a future as 'factory fodder' by parents and teachers.

CG: So do your parents want you to do anything in particular or . . .?
Sue: No, not really, well anything as long as you get money, 'cos I ain't got any brains for a proper job like a secretary or something like that. That's what they all say.

> (Lodgehill, white fifth former)

Part of the attraction of office work for some students was that it represented an idealised form of femininity. A job in an office (or a city centre boutique or hairdressing salon) conjured up a picture of clean modern rooms, full of 'nice' smartly dressed and made-up young women; a polite white and middle class image of femininity (Winship, 1980). Office jobs rarely conformed to these expectations in practice (see Chapter 9), but these prospective school leavers were concerned with *anticipated* experiences of particular jobs.

Those aspects of office work which attracted some young women as potential means of 'getting on' put other students off. Some young

Asian and Afro-Caribbean women and several of their white working class sisters objected to the 'snobby' attitude of those who saw office work as clean and glamorous. They had no time for 'nice' feminine behaviour such as talking in a 'posh' voice, or adopting a servile and flirtatious manner. These young women expected to feel more at ease in the 'friendlier' atmosphere of factory work.

Penny: I *wanna* work in a factory (all laugh).
CG: What sort of factory work do you mean, or don't you know?
Penny: I don't know really. I don't think I'd like office work you know, sitting in an office all day doing the same thing all the while. You make more friends in factories anyway, they're friendlier.
Vanessa: I make friends with my family when I come home.
Penny: Aah, but can't make friends with your family all the while, you've got to make friends and that ain't ya?
Vanessa: If you're doing the work I want to do [legal assistant] there's gonna be somebody there you'll be friendly with, but I wouldn't be a secretary or typist and that. Too boring.
Jacinta: I'd hate that. It would be boring in an office. The same routine over and over again.

(Lodgehill, Afro-Caribbean fifth formers)

Vanessa was hoping to be a legal assistant, which was strictly an office job. Whilst she defended her decision to her friends, she shared their dislike for the glamorous image of office work, and their disdain for those 'snobby' students (mainly young white women) who hoped to become secretaries and typists.

Office work seemed to offer young working class women the chance to 'get on', and out of their expected position in the lower status, poorly paid sectors of the job market. Potential escape routes included promotion from the typing pool to a job in sales or as a personal secretary; and meeting eligible men in higher status staff jobs, or in reasonably well-paid skilled production jobs. Few of these young women were likely to earn enough to live independently, and their futures would depend on whether and whom they married. Meeting 'a nice bloke who won't bash you around' with a secure well-paid job was an important social and financial consideration. Young women were not obsessed with 'getting a man' at the expense of their own future employment prospects, but such pressures were part of the potential attractions of office work (cf. Griffin *et al.*, 1980).

Young working class women talked about employment in general, and office and factory work in particular, in fairly broad, sweeping terms. When it came to their own prospects of finding work, these general assumptions were less important than what type of jobs were available, strategies for finding employment, and comparing experiences with their peers. As they approached the end of their compulsory schooling, these more immediate and specific issues began to occupy their thoughts. Despite their differing preferences, most students had similar hopes and fears about entering the job market. They wanted interesting work, reasonable pay and working conditions, 'a good group of mates' and a tolerable boss. Chances of promotion or training were important for those who had a specific job in mind, otherwise students realised that few jobs would be likely to offer training or promotion. Their immediate concern was to leave school and to find a job: a passport into the full-time labour market.

PART II

PART I

8

Entering the full-time job market

The second part of the book documents the experiences of a small group of young women as they moved from school into their first two years in the labour market. I followed twenty-five young white working class women from various Birmingham fifth forms into a range of jobs and through periods of unemployment. Their academic qualifications ranged from none to four 'O' levels, and they had all found jobs between one week and one year after leaving school (see Table D).

The decision to leave school or to stay on was not always quick or straightforward. Ten of these young women found jobs before or soon after leaving school, and eight found work during the summer. The remaining seven were still looking for jobs in September 1979, and some were tempted to return to school, but they all decided to continue trying to find a job.[1]

Jane: I couldn't have gone back to school, it was too boring. If I hadn't got this job, I'd just have gone on looking until I got something, *anything*, even if it wasn't office work.

Nine young women found office jobs, seven moved into traditionally female factory jobs, and four worked in the 'male' world of engineering. Their experiences are covered in Chapters 9, 10 and 11 respectively. A further five school leavers found jobs in shops, boutiques and hairdressing salons, but I was unable to visit them at work.[2] It was clear from talking to young women in school that two aspects of full-time employment were particularly important: the difference between 'female' and 'male' jobs, and the distinction between office and factory work. Although a significant proportion of female school leavers do go into shop work and hairdressing,[3] I decided to concentrate on young women's experiences of 'women's jobs' in offices and factories, and in the 'male' world of engineering (Tables E to J put these young women's position in national and local context).

The following five chapters are based on a series of informal interviews with these young women, with their families and friends, and on visits to ten different workplaces. I spent about two weeks in each company, watching the young women at work, and talking to their employers, supervisors and workmates. These workplace case studies relied less on taped interviews, unlike my visits to schools, and more on observation and informal discussions. The noise level in most firms was too high for tape recording in any case.[4] It was especially important to keep comprehensive and accurate field-notes, so I paid numerous visits to the Ladies toilets to scribble notes, writing these up in full at the end of each day.

This research did not involve true participant observation (PO), since I did not work alongside the young women (cf. Willis, 1977, 1980). To do this I would have been working without pay, which I preferred not to do in a situation of rising youth unemployment. It would also have been highly disruptive for me to take on general office duties or typing with minimal knowledge of the firm, or to learn sewing machining or assembly work. The 'fly on the wall' technique allowed me to observe the pattern of the full working day and the social structure of different workplaces without undue disruption. Employees were curious and uneasy at first, but once they knew that I was 'finding out what X's job involves for a study', most people relaxed and told me that they had soon forgotten about my presence altogether (see Griffin, in press).

Interviews with young women at their homes and in city centre coffee bars after they had left school were more of a two-way process than the schools' interviews. At school, young women had asked how I had got the research job, and how I had felt about leaving school. After leaving school, they tended to ask more about their ex-school-friends, using me as a means of keeping in touch. I never treated these questions as irrelevant or unwanted intrusions. My role was not to act as a passive recorder of people's experiences who would then disappear to 'analyse the data' (cf. Oakley, 1981; McRobbie, 1982; Hobson in Hall *et al.*, 1980). Young women used me as a source of information on their girlfriends; on how to join a union; and as a link with the local careers centre, as well as 'someone to moan to' when they were depressed.

The young women felt more relaxed talking to me outside of school, and more able to look back on their experiences at school after they had left.

Kim: It was a terrible atmosphere that first time at school, us all sitting there thinking 'Is she a teacher?' 'Cos you assume that anyone who comes in is a domineering sort of person, it's just not relaxed. We were taught to respect people, speak properly to them, but you can't respect and be relaxed (laugh).

They missed the close and enclosed community of the school; their own group of girlfriends, gossiping about teachers, 'having a laugh' and 'nicking off'. It became increasingly difficult to keep in touch with ex-schoolfriends as they moved into different jobs, college courses or unemployment. Friendship groups seemed strangely different without the shared daily routine of school life, although young women were less concerned about losing touch with their male peers.

CG: Do you still see your friends from school?
Shelly: Not so much, no. It's strange, 'cos we used to be such a good group of mates. We've all gone our separate ways since we've left to different jobs.

CG: Do you see much of the boys from school?
Jeanette: Oh God, those idiots, no (laugh).
Cathy: As boys go, if they were the last men on earth I'd turn queer (laugh). No, some were all right, we used to have a laugh, play teachers up. But we didn't speak a word to them, none of us had anything in common. Some of the more intelligent ones we could talk to for a *few* minutes without them saying something stupid.

Despite some regrets, most young women were relieved to have finally left school, and especially the tedium of revision lessons and the anxiety of exam nerves.

CG: Do you miss school?
Jane: I miss my friends and the laughs, but that last year was terrible,
it *really* dragged. It's just going over and over your exam
papers and what you'd already done.

Kim: I miss the chats and the dinner hours, the security, because
everything is put there for you. But I felt really pressured at
school, all for exams. They don't make you want to work,
they *tell* you. I didn't like being forced to, which is bad I
suppose. Before the exams, I was physically and mentally
shattered, by the end I got so tensed I thought I'd crack up
(laugh). Dunno how I kept sane, I was like a robot.

The less academic students had not been so affected by exam
tensions, but they had felt rejected by the school.

Monica: I never passed no exams, but I'm glad to have stopped
those revision lessons. They never bothered with those
that wasn't doing many exams really.

Wendy: I'm glad I've left. It was a good school, but it was snobby.
I'm Irish, and I got trouble for that, plus I didn't live in a
posh area like most of them.

Young women were particularly relieved to have left the strict
system of control and supervision in school, which treated students
as irresponsible children even in the fifth form.

CG: Do you feel any different now you've left school?
Pippa: People treat you as if you're grown up, where at school
you were treated like an infant. It was terrible, they wouldn't
let you wear anything other than uniform. I thought they
made our school like a prison, they were ever so strict.

Cathy: I hadn't got any faith in that school. I mean there was some
of us who were interested, we could have got 'O' levels if
we'd been pushed. But we weren't given enough responsibility, weren't taken seriously, or treated as, er, teenagers.
They wouldn't have prefects or school council, nothing.

As they looked back on their time at school, young women compared this with their experiences as full-time employees. Those in office jobs:

CG: Do you feel any different now you've left school?

Berni: At work you can please yourself, you can go out and get a coffee, have a break when you want, well I can. At school it's all 'please miss I wanna go'. I miss the laughs.

Elaine: The main difference for me is the people, working with older people, old women. At school you're working with your friends, keeping the teacher at bay (laugh). On the bus you're treated as older in your own clothes, than in school uniform, though I don't feel no different in myself.

In factory work:

Shelly: I'm feeling more independent now, earning money, buying my own clothes.

Liz: Yeh, I feel older. The woman who teaches you what to do at work tells us when we go wrong, but a teacher would tell you off and you get the blame for everything. They shout at you and show you up in the class. Well some, not all teachers do.

These different experiences in the world of full-time employment meant that young women had less in common with their girlfriends who had stayed on at school or gone on to college. Those in engineering apprenticeships found that their 'man's job' formed an additional barrier between themselves and their old schoolfriends (see Chapter 11).

Jill: I see some of my friends, but they don't want to know you, 'cos they're at college and you're doing engineering. Oh God, shock (laugh).

Kate: Yeh, and if they've stopped at school it's even more difficult. They're still friends, but you can't have a conversation. It sounds really terrible, as if they're really immature. We try to keep in touch, but it'd be no good, we've nothing in common.

Jill: Yeh, and all the ones in [women's] jobs are with other girls
          our age, so there's no change of environment, but we have to
          get on with 60-year-old men (laugh).

The difference between life at school and in a full-time job came
as something of a shock to most young women, even those like Elaine
who already had a part-time casual job. There was some resentment
that schools had done so little to prepare students for their first full-
time jobs.

CG: What was it like, starting work compared to being at school?
Jenny: You're stepping into something that's completely new from
          school, you're on your own now. There's no one behind you,
          you've got to go out and do it yourself. Everything is dif-
          ferent, it's all change now. It's so different to school you
          wouldn't believe it. But no one tells you that.

Elaine: At school, the very name *school* makes you feel about 14,
          but at work it's more adult. I can still remember my first
          day at work, and I never want to go through anything like
          that again. I was so nervous it was unbelievable. They don't
          prepare you at all, you don't know what you're facing.

The following chapters look at the various changes in young women's
lives after they left school and entered the full-time job market. Apart
from case studies of offices, factories and engineering training schemes,
this also covers young women's involvement in Youth Opportunities
schemes and their experiences of unemployment. Young women's jobs
did not always match up to their expectations, but life in the full-time
labour market was certainly very different to being at school.

9

Office work: a good job for a girl?

Office jobs are the first full-time employment for a significant proportion of young working class women (see Tables E and F; and Careers Service Survey, 1982). Office work is a predominantly female occupation, with women concentrated in the lower status, poorly paid clerical and secretarial jobs (McNally, 1979). In 1979 and 1980, 70 per cent of office staff and 99 per cent of typists and secretaries were women, and yet they made up only 14 per cent of office managers (Counter Information Services, 1981a; Downing, 1981).

The office has not always been a primary site of women's employment: it was dominated by male clerks until the late nineteenth century. The prospects of the mainly white and middle class clerks declined with the introduction of new mechanical equipment and of compulsory elementary education in the late 1870s. This brought a flood of working class commercial workers who could operate the new typewriters and calculating machines, and who were used as a cheaper and more productive labour force. It was only *after* this initial decline that women began to enter office work: women were not strictly replacing men (Downing, 1981).

'Office work' is frequently used as a unitary term, but it covers a wide range of jobs and skills, which can vary depending on the size, structure and function of an organisation. Young women's office jobs involved typing, making tea, running errands, telephone and reception work, photocopying, filing and coding invoices through to using computer terminals. I visited six young women at work in various different office jobs, and this chapter is based on their experiences.

The office junior

Ansteys, Townsend Graphics and Midlands Stationers

Most of the young working class women who moved into office work were taken on as office juniors or 'Person Fridays'.[1] These jobs were often menial and poorly paid (see Table D), and young women soon found out that office work did not always match up to its glamorous image.

Berni started as an office junior at C.M. Ansteys on £34 a week in July 1979, just as Jeanette began work at Townsend Graphics on £39 a week. Clare joined Midlands Stationers in January 1980 on £39 a week after a disastrous experience as a data processor for the city council. I visited all of these young women at work in the spring of 1980.

C.M. Ansteys was a wholesale suppliers of general electrical goods. It was a small family business which occupied cramped and dingy premises close to Birmingham city centre. Ansteys had about thirty employees in 1980, half of whom worked in the ground floor stockroom, with the rest in the offices on the floor above. The firm was run on fairly traditional lines, despite the recent addition of a microcomputer which monitored each day's trading.

There were clear divisions of labour at Ansteys with older middle class white men in the most prestigious and powerful positions. The firm's owner, Mr Anstey, had retired, and the business was run by a managing director, a sales manager, and Mr Crossland, the office manager. The office workers were all female, and the stockroom was staffed by men. All of the employees were white apart from two young Asian men who worked in the stockroom.

Within the area of women's office work, there was also a distinction between full-timers and part-timers. The former were mainly young and single like Berni, older single women, or young married women without children. The part-timers were all older married women who had returned to paid work after bringing up their children. They were employed as a cheap and flexible labour force to do the most tedious office jobs (cf. Bruegel, 1979).

Mr Crossland: I take on the school leavers full-time, then the part-timers are older married ladies who do the accounts. They sort out their own hours to suit school holidays. They don't want responsibility or promotion, they

just come in for something to do and the pin money.
So we give them the work that the full-timers wouldn't
do (laugh), the really boring work, and they'll do it.

This view was not shared by the women themselves, who had no
alternative but to take boring, badly paid part-time jobs.

June: It's not too bad here because they let you have time off when
you need it. The work is *so* boring, but I need the money
with the kids to feed, and there's nothing else part-time really.

Berni had few illusions about office work, since she had not been
attracted by its glamorous image (see Chapter 1). She had little time
for workmates who were obsessed with 'looking posh'. Buying suitably
smart clothes on her paltry wages was extremely difficult: Berni preferred to spend her money on 'punky clothes' for going out at weekends.

CG: So what do you think of this job?
Berni: The money I like, but it just goes (laugh) on clothes. Oh
God, all these girls at work come in so posh, and I go just
like a tramp. They're always saying 'oh God, I saw that on
you before'. You've got to have something different *every*
day.

Berni's job involved general office duties like filing, coding invoices,
and later recording orders on the computer. Apart from her sporadic
use of the computer, Berni was bored by the monotony of her job
and the whole office atmosphere.

Berni: I quite liked the job at first. I still do, well the computer bits
anyway. They're gonna let me learn more about it. So I'll
stay I expect, plus I think it's harder to get another job now.
But this place is *so* boring, and the job is boring too, every day
the same. It's such a dusty old place. I mean there's some
women who've been working in this office for twenty years!

Despite her misgivings, Berni was still at Ansteys in 1982. She had
learnt more about computer operation, but she still found her job
boring and missed the company of other young people: 'a good group

of mates to have a bit of a laugh with, brighten the place up'. The increase in youth unemployment rates between 1980 and 1982 made her reluctant to risk leaving Ansteys to look for another job (see Chapter 12).

Jeanette's job at Townsend Graphics was slightly different, because she sometimes helped out with production. The distinction between office and production work was less clear-cut, although there were still various divisions of labour similar to those at C.M. Ansteys. Townsend Graphics was a small printing and photocopying company which had once been part of the university. It had been forced to become a private company during a reduction in university spending in the mid-1970s. It dealt mainly with reprographic work for the university, along with various external orders.

Townsend Graphics occupied two large adjoining rooms close to the university, which were full of noisy printing, collating and copying machines. Jim Bayliss, the overall manager, had an office in a nearby building, since he was also responsible for a stationery suppliers. Jim was a middle class white man in his early thirties: all the other employees were working class. This included Tom Nicholls, a white man in his fifties, who was directly responsible to Jim Bayliss as the production manager of Townsend Graphics.

The company had about twenty-five employees, most of whom worked on specific machines. Jeanette worked in a partitioned-off section, answering the phone, coding invoices, writing job sheets, working on reception, and helping out with collating, binding and photocopying during busy periods. The work organisation was informal and flexible, with few apparent distinctions within the mainly young workforce along race or gender lines. Closer inspection revealed that the firm's pride and joy, a two-colour printing machine, was the sole responsibility of two skilled white men. The less complex machines were operated by younger, Asian, Afro-Caribbean, and/or female employees, and office work was always done by the three young white women: Jeanette, Shirley and Liz.

During busy periods, cooperative and flexible working was essential, although both Jeanette and Jim Bayliss had noticed gender differences in this respect.

Jim Bayliss: We have equality here, the women and men do the same things. Mind you, women work together better than men. If there's a big collating job which needs

four people, the men all say 'no' and disappear, so all
the women do it together.

Jeanette: Women are better than men at work. They work harder
and do it quicker. Women get down to it — men disappear.
It is true though, this place is *really* run by women.

Despite the apparently egalitarian working practices at Townsend
Graphics, older white men had the better-paid skilled jobs. Repetitive
office duties were a strictly female province, and these were also the
lowest-paid jobs.

Like Berni, Jeanette had not been impressed by the glamorous image
of office work. She took the job at Townsend Graphics as a temporary
stop-gap until she could join the Army 'for the sporting facilities' at
17½. Jeanette liked the job because it was varied and interesting, with
a lively informal atmosphere and a fairly young workforce. She usually
wore casual clothes and jeans rather than 'posh office togs', because
her job included working with machines. Jeanette was working on the
boundary between 'a nice clean office job' and 'dirty factory work',
and she felt more at ease with the latter.

Jeanette: It's more like a factory than an office here. It's loud, you
get dirty if you work on some of the machines, it's not
posh at all. But you get these people from the university
who are *so* snotty. They think they're it. Just 'cos their
offices are all carpet, and you should see the Ladies' bog
at the Registry, it's *so* smart. I know, 'cos I have to go
in and feed job sheets into the computer. They all have
to wear posh clothes, and they look down on you. If you
go in there they look at you as if to say 'who's she?' My
sister works in staffing and she doesn't do anything (laugh).
She just sits about all day looking pretty. My mate who
worked there said you go in the loos and they're all in there
putting on make-up to go for lunch for twenty minutes!

Like Jeanette, Clare had gone into office work as a temporary
measure until she could join the Police Force at 18, and again like
Jeanette, she was still in a full-time job in 1982 at the age of 19. Clare's
second office job was at Midlands Stationers, who supplied engineering
firms in the West Midlands with stationery and office supplies. The

company was based in a spacious, fairly modern (early 1960s) building in Birmingham city centre: a marked contrast to C.M. Anstey's
cramped premises and the noisy production rooms at Townsend
Graphics.

Midlands Stationers employed about sixty people in 1980. There
were around fifteen secretarial, clerical and administrative staff, five
managers, twelve sales representatives, and about thirty storeroom
staff and drivers. Once again, older middle class white men occupied
the senior administrative and managerial positions; all of the secretarial staff were white women apart from one young Asian woman.
The drivers were all white working class men, as were most of the
stockroom staff, apart from three young Afro-Caribbean men. The
sales staff were all in their twenties and thirties, all white men with
the exception of two young white women.

The company was organised on formal lines, with a fairly rigid
hierarchical structure. Clare was directly responsible to Mr Morris,
a middle class man in his fifties who was the local area sales manager.
The office area was a large open-plan room: only the top managers
had their own offices. Clare's desk was literally overlooked by Mr
Morris, as she sat coding invoices, taking his phone calls and filing
orders. Mr Morris was out on sales business several days a week, so
Clare was often working on her own, left with a list of jobs to do
in his absence.

There seemed to be no obvious division between female and male
staff in the open-plan office, apart from the all-female typing section.
In fact, the only time that women and men worked alongside each
other doing similar jobs was in the accounts section. Here the men
were some twenty or thirty years younger than their female colleagues,
and on the lower rungs of a promotional ladder to which women's
access was limited. Ms Haines, a married woman in her forties who
worked in the accounts department, felt that women were restricted
to lower status jobs.

CG: So will you try for promotion here then?
Ms Haines: Oh no (laugh). It's a fairly good job, but women just
            don't get on, they stick in one place for years.

Clare was happy with her job, especially in comparison with her
problems at the Data Processing Centre. After a few months she began
to learn how to deal with orders for an expensive line in specialised

stationery, and her work became more monotonous and routine. Unlike Berni and Jeanette, Clare was more attracted by the glamorous image of the 'office girl', and welcomed the chance to 'dress up and look smart'. This was partly because Clare's workplace was more conducive to 'looking smart' than Ansteys or Townsend Graphics, and partly because Clare had never objected as strongly as Berni and Jeanette to the 'snobs' and 'pets' at school who hoped to get office jobs.

Clare's appearance changed radically after she left school and started her first job. She wore full face make-up, smart skirts and blouses with high heels, rather than school uniform or casual jeans and jumpers. Her hair was cut short, straightened and dyed blonde to affect a complete transformation. She looked so different when I visited her at home for the first time that I hardly recognised her.

The other side of this smart glamorous image of the 'office girl' was reflected in the everyday office culture. Flirtatious banter and innuendo characterised relationships between female and male employees in all the firms, but it was particularly marked at Midlands Stationers when the sales*men* (sic) dropped into the office for their regular weekly visit. They told a continuous stream of 'dirty' (i.e. sexual) jokes, flirting with and 'touching up' most of the women. Older married women like Ms Haines would turn this 'harmless banter' around to embarrass the younger men, but Clare, as the 'baby of the office' simply had to grin and bear it. Her immediate boss Mr Morris continually mixed references to her stupidity with sexual innuendoes and jokes. Clare was in no position to reply in kind, since this would be taken as evidence of unfeminine vulgarity or promiscuity. Despite these drawbacks, Clare stayed in the job since it seemed to offer some prospect of promotion.[2]

A chance to get on? Banking and telephone sales

Working in a bank is seen as one of the most secure and prestigious jobs for a young working class woman, offering the chance of training and promotion. Elaine and Kim worked in different branches of one of the 'big four' banks, and whilst their training and promotion prospects were better than those of most office juniors, the picture was not quite so rosy as they had been led to expect.

Elaine was based in a fairly small city centre branch with only ten employees, and Kim worked in a far larger and busier branch near the university on the outskirts of the city.[3] Elaine's workplace had clear divisions between women's and men's jobs. The branch manager had his own private office, and the assistant manager worked in a semi-enclosed space. Up to four people (three women and one young man) worked at the tills as cashiers during busy periods. Four men covered specialist areas such as loans or securities in an open plan area behind the tills, each working at individual desks.

In marked contrast to this quiet, spacious area, four women worked in the cramped and noisy conditions of what the manager, Mr Shaw, called 'the production room'. Here the records of each day's trans-actions were processed and recorded by electronic and mechanical calculators, on paper and at the new computer terminal. This repeti-tive and painstaking work was carried out by Elaine, Nicky, Gill the typist, and their supervisor Gail.

All of the employees were white and middle class, with the excep-tion of the younger working class women in the production room. The branch operated according to a strict hierarchy, with the older middle class men in the most powerful senior positions. The manager, Mr Shaw, saw banking as an 'ideal job for a girl', and boasted of the job security it could offer them.

Mr Shaw: It's ideal for a girl, good clean conditions, nice people. The job itself is repetitive at first, but there is job security once you get in, as long as you don't do something awful (laugh). And girls can get on now, there are women even in management, if they've got it.

Mr Shaw was approaching retirement age (65), but Mr Harrison the assistant manager was some ten years younger, and he saw women's improved position in banking as a potential problem.

CG: Is it normal policy for all girls to do day release?

Mr Harrison: It is now, because of this sex equality. In my day there was no day release at all, it was all night classes in your own time. Then they started day release, the sex equal-ity act came in, so the girls joined in as well. Unless they want to make a career of it (laugh) it's a bit of a fiddle to be honest. They get the time off, but very few progress further than the first stage. The men of course

CG:

are likely to plod on because you get nowhere if you don't. In fact, it's gone to a far higher standard than when I did it.

So you have to carry on with the courses to get anywhere?

Mr Harrison:

Yes, you *have* to. There are residential courses too, it's a hell of a struggle now, but they've all been opened to men and women. There is no sex discrimination, there are equal opportunities for all young girls. Equal pay for equal work too, which is good, so the opportunity is there if they want it, but most of them don't. Most of them end up as cashiers, and don't wish to go any further up. Very few do go up to managership, though I know of one woman assistant manager.

Elaine was determined to complete her training, and did two years' day release at college before moving on to Birmingham Polytechnic in 1982 to continue her courses. Bank employees needed to complete at least four years of day release and evening classes in order to gain qualifications with any significant value in promotion terms. Elaine was relatively unusual in this respect; most young women were like Kim, who gave up the day release classes after the first year. They were either unaware that the Institute of Bankers qualification took four years to complete, or they had taken one look at the exclusively male management hierarchy in their branch, and decided that 'getting on' beyond a cashier's job would be very difficult indeed.[4]

Office jobs offered young working class women the promise of promotion, holding out the chance to move from the typing pool or an office junior's job into a higher status post as a personal secretary or even into administration, sales or management. Hazel Downing (1981) has referred to this phenomenon as 'the illusion of upward mobility', because so few women ever reach the higher levels of the office hierarchy.[5] Most young women realised that their promotion prospects were limited, even Tracey, who was being trained for the top secretarial jobs:

Tracey:

I mean, however far we go, we'll never be the bosses will we? We'll always be the secretary to the boss (laugh).

Tracey's supervisor agreed with her, complaining that women's secretarial skills were not recognised, and at the muddled distinctions between different office jobs.

Ms Stewart: Secretarial work *is* skilled, and it's not recognised. So there's no distinction between office juniors and women just out of training who all call themselves secretaries.

The illusion of upward mobility in women's office work rested on this ambiguous job hierarchy, and on the lack of a uniform and accredited training system. Most formalised training in office work skills such as typing and shorthand takes place in schools and colleges, funded by Local Education Authorities or the students themselves, and not by employers. This is a marked contrast to the on-the-job training schemes, apprenticeships and strict job demarcations found in many areas of skilled 'male' manual work (see Chapter 11).

The lack of promotion prospects was one of the reasons behind Cathy's decision to leave her office junior's job at Courtfields solicitors:

Cathy: Once I'd started there, I thought 'oh God, a 6-year-old could do this'.
CG: Didn't you think it would change at all?
Cathy: No, 'cos the next step up would be either in accounts, which I'm hopeless at figures, or as a typist cum secretary to one of the solicitors, and I didn't want to do any of them. That was the main reason I left, there was no future in it really. But I couldn't ever have got the job at Gaskells without it, 'cos it gave me the office experience.

Cathy was the only young woman in office work who managed to 'get on' to any significant extent. She started as an office junior at Gaskells, typing and answering the phone, before moving to better paid telephone sales work. Gaskells was the Midlands office of a national supplier of expensive office equipment and partitioning. Eight people worked at this office in a smart and modern block on the outskirts of Birmingham city centre.

All of Cathy's co-workers were white and middle class, and in their twenties and thirties. Dick Cooper was in charge as the area manager with his own office, Jim and Mike the two surveyors shared an office, and Ann worked on reception. Cathy worked with Julie and Sue, the two telesales workers, in 'the women's room'. Sue was in charge of telephone sales, which was a predominantly female occupation. Gaskells operated an unofficial (and illegal) sales policy which did not allow saleswomen out 'on the road'. This was supposedly because (male) clients 'wouldn't like it', according to head office in London.

Sue Godard was an extremely efficient saleswoman who had struggled to maintain some degree of autonomy from the firm's head office. She resisted their attempts to introduce a logging system of sales contacts, and to transfer requests for technical information to salesmen.

Sue: This logging contacts business I wouldn't have anything to do with. First thing you know head office would be asking us to get more and more contacts each month, it'd be impossible. And they don't want us to deal with technical calls, well that's daft because we know as much as the men. London want us all to act like silly little telesales girls.

Sue and Julie could never be described as 'silly little telesales girls', and their room bore little resemblance to the stereotyped image of nice young ladies at work. A torrent of swear words alternated with jokes and witty comments, most of which were directed at male colleagues and sales contacts. This barrage of sarcasm and insults was interspersed with quiet, serious and businesslike phone conversations with these same colleagues and prospective clients.

Sue, Julie and Cathy could continue with this distinctly unfeminine behaviour because they worked away from direct male supervision. Cathy had noticed a male double standard regarding women and men swearing.[6]

Cathy: Honest, the air is blue. I swear more since I've worked there. Mind you men don't like you swearing, but *they* can, oh yes. I mean they trip up and say 'oh bloody hell', and you do it, and they turn round real sharp and say '*what* was that?' All snooty.

Sue had no time for the expensive accessories required to 'look smart' in the office, much to Julie's consternation:

Sue: God my hair needs a wash.
Julie: What shampoo do you use?

Sue: Washing up liquid.

Julie: What! You don't use normal mascara or make-up either. Do you use anything that normal people do? You're terrible. What do you use for soap then?

Sue: [quickly] Shit covered in sugar, what do you think?

Julie: [shocked intake of breath] OK. I wondered what the smell was (laugh).

Cathy enjoyed the atmosphere at Gaskells, and she was excited by her promotion. She started in February 1980 on £40 a week, and began to train in telesales work six months later at Sue's suggestion. By April 1981, Cathy was a full-time telesales worker, earning around £60 a week including commission. This was far more than any of her peers who had gone into traditionally 'female' jobs. Cathy had benefited from working with other women who encouraged her to train in telephone sales, having noticed her abilities relatively quickly. Male supervisors rarely expected young women to have any long-term potential beyond menial office jobs. Like Mr Harrison at the bank, Tom Nicholls of Townsend Graphics blamed women for not 'getting on':

CG: Do many people leave or move on?

Tom Nicholls: Not many leave because they don't like working here. Men leave to get more money and go into printing works. One woman left to get a better job 'cos she was getting married. I dunno what women do, become ladies of leisure I suppose, just housewives. They could get on, but they just don't seem to want to.

The lack of in-service training and promotion prospects in office work was found in most 'women's jobs' (Benett and Carter, 1983). The Universal Metals secretarial school was an exception to this trend, since it provided full-time training in various aspects of secretarial work on the employer's premises.

Service with a smile: Universal Metals secretarial school

The UM secretarial course was interesting for a number of reasons. It was a standardised in-service secretarial training course; a female equivalent to UM's craft apprenticeship in engineering (see Chapter 11); and it included training in the non-technical side of women's office jobs. The relevant technical skills were typing and shorthand, and the non-technical aspect covered appearance, deportment, and 'social skills'. Tracey and her fellow trainees were learning to become polite, smart personal secretaries to UM's top management.[7] A particular form of 'nice' femininity was required for such jobs as part of the secretary's 'service with a smile' (cf. Downing, 1981; Griffin, 1982b).

The secretarial school was based at the Birmingham headquarters of UM, a large multinational corporation with interests in wrought and refined metals (especially copper and titanium), general engineering, plastics, heating systems and building projects. UM's pre-tax profits for 1979 were £34.5 million, with overall Group sales of £612 million. About 10,000 people worked at the Birmingham site, out of 26,500 across Britain, and 32,700 more around the world (UM's annual report to the shareholders, 1979). The main site was dominated by the rigid hierarchical structure and the formal management style which belied UM's origins in the Victorian metal manufacturing trades.

The secretarial school was housed in dingy rooms above the extremely plush director's offices. Tracey and nine other young women started the eight-month course in September 1979 on a training allowance of £22.50 a week. The course was supervised and mostly taught by Ms Stewart in the school's main classroom. Apart from the technical lessons in shorthand and typing which made up most of the course, there were also lectures and practical sessions on personal hygiene, grooming, dress-sense, make-up, elocution, social skills and contraception. Tracey discussed these classes with two of the other trainees:

Tracey: We went for this make-up demonstration which UM paid for, 'cos it's grooming and everything (laugh). Two of the girls were made up as guinea pigs like, it was a laugh, but really expensive. I mean this little pot of cream for cleansing was about nine quid. I tried all these perfumes, about thirty quid a bottle they were, so I'd better not wash for a bit (laugh).

Katie: Yeh, and do you remember that contraception one? (laugh). This woman was throwing johnnies [sheaths] all round the room.

Janie: The company don't want us to get pregnant and leave. See now they've trained us they can't afford it, so they're teaching us how not to get pregnant.

Katie: Say no, that's the best way (all laugh).

Tracey: We have to take turns at being Ms Stewart's secretary, answering her 'phone and that. It's OK, but sometimes I just forget and say 'hello, who's calling the Golden Shot?' [in Birmingham accent] , like at home (laugh). That's what we have our oral communication lessons for, to learn how to speak proper (laugh).

The secretarial school was an exclusively female domain. No young men had ever applied for the course, which was designed with young women in mind, to develop the particular form of 'nice' feminine appearance and behaviour required of the secretary. About a hundred young women applied for the ten trainee places each year, so the competition was fierce. Ms Stewart selected and interviewed the most likely applicants, looking for a combination of academic and commercial qualifications and 'the right personality'.

Experience of typing or shorthand was not an essential part of the course's requirements. Three of Tracey's peers were middle class 18- and 19-year-olds, with three 'A' levels each, and the remaining six were 'academic' working class school leavers with between four and six 'O' levels. Only two of these young women had ever done shorthand, and two more could just touch-type. In most cases Ms Stewart was starting the secretarial training from scratch, hoping to have the trainee typing one hundred words a minute by the end of the course.[8]

Having 'the right personality' to learn the non-technical aspects of secretarial work was an important criterion for selection. Learning to give that 'service with a smile' demanded a particular form of white and middle class femininity.[9] Young white working class women could pass as middle class by 'talking posh and acting snooty' as Katie put it. As the daughter of a working class Spanish family, Tracey would pass as 'slightly suntanned' or 'exotic looking', but it was far more difficult for young black women to fit in with this image of the 'nice office girl'.

No young Asian or Afro-Caribbean women had ever been accepted on to the UM course, although Ms Stewart did admit that 'quite a few' Asian school leavers had applied.

CG: How do you decide who to accept then?

Ms Stewart: Well cutting out the first lot is easy — they just haven't the qualifications. We ask for four 'O' levels and a certain degree of ability in English. Well with the Asian girls, it's the language that lets them down.

Since Birmingham Careers Service statistics indicated that the majority of black school leavers had been born and brought up in Britain, Ms Stewart's concern about Asian applicants' supposed 'language problems' appeared somewhat suspect. She went on to justify her views with what she subsequently realised was a double standard:

Ms Stewart: I get annoyed really, because if people expect to come to this country and use our facilities, they should be prepared to change and adapt to western culture. Mind you, if I went to Singapore, say, I wouldn't want to give up my ways and eat grasshopper or whatever (laugh). I'd find people like myself and stick to my British ways.

A greater proportion of white female school leavers in 1979 went into 'clerical and related occupations' in Birmingham compared to their Asian and Afro-Caribbean sisters (Careers Service statistics). Racist assumptions about the most appropriate jobs for young black women were extremely pervasive. I interviewed Ms Jameson, a middle class white woman concerned with further education provision in Birmingham, who had a young Afro-Caribbean woman working as her secretary. Ms Jameson had employed Yvonne because of her efficiency and secretarial skills in a spirit of positive discrimination. She was horrified to discover that most of her white visitors assumed that Yvonne was the office cleaner, simply because she was black (see Griffin, 1982b).

The non-technical aspects of office work are concerned with women's appearance and manner, and with their servicing role, and they are not confined to women's office jobs. Waitresses, air stewardesses, hairdressers, prostitutes and some shop assistants are all required to develop particular styles of feminine 'service with a smile' as part of their jobs. This non-technical side of women's office work was important to many male managers, and it influenced their criteria for selecting female office staff.

The Alfred Marks Bureau carried out a survey of 650 male managers in 1975, which looked at the attributes of their ideal secretary.[10] Forty per cent preferred secretaries from a similar cultural background to their own (i.e. white and middle class); 62 per cent preferred to employ women aged between 20 and 25. Their selection criteria were race-, age-, class- *and* gender-specific, as well as disbarring those with any form of recognised disability.

The attributes of the ideal secretary included 'personality', good grooming, clear speech, and a sense of humour. The employers' list of dislikes was longer, including body odour, bad accents, bad speech, bad grooming, no personality, affected speech, heavy make-up, way-out clothes, and sticky hands. Their personal dislikes included strident laughter, spots, gossipers, self-assertion, rudeness, bad manners, no sense of humour, and women with more than three children. The overwhelming emphasis in these lists was on the appearance and manner of the ideal secretary, with little reference to technical skills.

An important part of young women's office work was what Hazel Downing has called their role 'as objects on which to pin his [male manager's] sexual fantasies', which provide 'a break from the routine of his work' (1981, p. 196). Ms Stewart recognised this when she advised the UM trainees of ways to 'get around the boss'.

Ms Stewart: [to Janie, slouched over her typewriter in class] : That's not the best position for 120 words a minute is it Janie?

Janie: My arms ache (rest of class laugh).

Ms Stewart: Well, you'll have to hitch your skirt up a bit higher to distract your boss's attention and get out of it (all laugh).

The trainees were already well aware of their status as potential objects of male gaze after their visits to different parts of the UM site.

Tracey: This one place we walk up this road on the site. They never do any work and they just stand there waiting for you, and there's us ten walking up and they're just in streams. Ten on that side, and ten on that side all along, and you have to walk through them. They go 'cor she's nice', or 'she ain't bad', and you feel so embarrassed. You feel the blood rushing to your face, and oh God, it's terrible.

The trainees did not accept this treatment passively unless they were heavily outnumbered. Otherwise they played men at their own game, 'eyeing them up', and commenting on their physical appearance. This could and did unsettle some of the men, but it was a limited threat because the young women were playing men's games on men's terms.

Tracey's experience at Universal Metals was not an isolated event: in 1977 a man had broken into the office block where Gaskells was based and hidden in the women's toilets before attacking a female employee with a knife. All the women's toilets had then been fitted with locks, but by 1979 no one bothered to use them. When I visited Gaskells the main problem was the porter, a middle-aged white man who loitered inside one of the women's toilets pretending to change the hand towels. Most women preferred to walk up two flights of stairs to the next nearest ladies toilets if he was hanging around.

Another potential danger area was the office party. Young women noted the advice of other female employees about which men tended to develop 'wandering hands' when drunk. Jeanette had overheard her boss boasting drunkenly to other men that he had sacked a young woman for refusing to 'come across' at the previous year's office party. Jim Bayliss may have been indulging in a bout of inebriated male exaggeration, but sexual harassment was a distressingly common experience for female employees. Objecting to a man's advances could lead to their dismissal or hinder their promotion prospects.

As Catherine MacKinnon pointed out in her study of sexual harassment in North America, 'the very qualities which men find attractive in the women they harass are the real qualifications for the jobs for which they hire them' (1979, p. 23). Sexual harassment is here defined as 'any repeated or unwanted sexual comments, looks, suggestions or physical contact that women find objectionable or offensive and causes them discomfort' (Working Women United Institute, also quoted in Backhouse and Cohen, 1978). Hazel Downing's study of female office staff confirmed the extent of sexual harassment in Britain (see Downing, 1981 and Read, 1982).

The importance of these non-technical aspects of women's office work has been demonstrated by recent attempts to introduce new technology into Britain's offices. For all the promised financial benefits, male managers have been notably reluctant to swap the personal services and presence of their secretaries for a microprocessor (see Downing, 1981).

New technology: the office of the future?

The introduction of the first office machinery, such as mechanical typewriters and calculators, had little impact on the traditional manual methods of information processing. More recent technology, such as electric typewriters and audio-typing equipment (tape recorders, earphones, etc.), have not transformed office work to any significant extent. Decades of minimal change in office technology came to an end with the developments in computing and data processing in the 1960s. Banks, finance and insurance companies that need to process quantities of numerical information were the first to introduce this technology, which allowed them to reduce their use of paper — and labour power.

The assistant manager at Elaine's workplace was wary about the future implications of these changes for banking practice:

CG:	And what about computers and new technology generally?
Mr Harrison:	Well, in a bank there are literally *millions* of pieces of paper every day for cheques, and you can get rid of all those and have just people to feed it into a computer. You're saving a *tremendous* amount of money; paper and staff — about 70 per cent of a bank's cost is the staff. The whole of the bank is run on *one* computer. It's amazing, you can get at a press of a button information that used to take weeks to work out. Accurately too (laugh).
CG:	So that will restructure banking?
Mr Harrison:	Oh yes, and a lot of jobs will be lost. I'll be glad when I retire actually (laugh), it'll be a whole new generation.

Data processing involves the manipulation of numbers, and this does not affect office work which is based on correspondence and written information. The word processor (WP), however, allows for the manipulation of words, sentences and paragraphs, and has the potential to transform the office and to deskill many women's office jobs.[11] A WP usually consists of a standard QWERTY keyboard, instruction keys on either side with facilities to programme a microchip computer, a printout, and a VDU to replace the paper in the typewriter.

Most of the young women who had any contact with new technology only worked on it for short periods, and they were usually as enthusiastic as Tracey on her first visit to the UM teleprinter room. Her enthusiasm was not shared by the women telex operators:

Tracey: Like the teleprinter room. I'd like to work there, we visited it, it was really interesting. They're introducing new telex machines, like typewriter carriages and keys. 'Cos *now* telex machines are different to typewriters, and all the teleprinter workers, the girls know those keys off by heart.

CG: So now they've got to learn it again?

Tracey: Yeh, and they can just employ ordinary typists to do the teleprinter work. So they're complaining about that 'cos they'll be out of a job, 'cos they're the only skilled people, and they don't want that.

Berni and Elaine were similarly impressed with the data processors they used for a few hours each week. Only Clare had worked full-time with new technology in her first job at the city council's Data Processing Centre. This was close to Clare's ideal 'nice clean office job' that she had described to me just before she left school. In practice, the job was far from ideal. Clare worked in a sort of VDU typing pool, typing in data with one hand, and flicking through accounts information with the other. She earned more than most of the other young women with office jobs (£42 gross a week), but she handed in her notice before the end of her six-month trial period.

Clare worked continuously at the VDU from 8.00 a.m. to 4.00 p.m., with a one-hour break for lunch and two quarter-hour tea breaks. Her productivity was monitored closely, since the keyboard contained a mechanism which counted every key press.[12] Clare had to reach a minimum of 6,000 key strokes per hour after two months, 8,000 after four months and 10,000 after six months. Each operator's average hourly rate for the day was displayed on a notice board in the office. After two months Clare was up to 6-7,000 strokes, but felt frustrated that she could not improve on that rate, and because trainees received so little encouragement from supervisors.

The mental and physical strain of the work eventually forced Clare to give up the job. She had backache from sitting in one place for long periods, with headaches and eyestrain from concentrating on the VDU screen (cf. Counter Information Services, 1979; and *Women's Voice*,

1979, on the hazards of new technology).

Clare: At first I was bad, I had to go to the doctors. 'cos I always got headaches and that. He says it's probably just strain leaving school, completely different change of life and everything. Said I'd get used to it after a while. Well I did a bit, but not altogether. You was just bored sitting at a machine all day, bosses watching over you, frightened to move, having a cigarette just in *their* breaks. It just wasn't normal, so I left. The pay was good, but money isn't everything is it? I know you need it, but I used to get up of a morning and I'd be crying thinking I had to go.

All of Clare's co-workers were young white working class women like herself, her supervisors were slightly older women, and the department manager was a white middle class man who had little contact with 'the girls'. All of these supervisors had once been full-time data processing operatives themselves, since the only escape route from the hated VDUs was via promotion to supervisor and later to section leader. The high labour turnover meant that most women left before becoming eligible for promotion, and few wished to join the ranks of the loathed supervisors.

Office automation was being hailed as the saviour of British industry in the late 1970s: by the early 1980s, it was clear that this was not the solution to the problems besetting British industry. Eighty per cent of offices employed only five or six people, so they were unlikely to invest in expensive new equipment. Drastic reductions in the manufacturing industries were leading to staffing cuts and increased workloads in the office. New technology has resulted in the loss of hundreds, even thousands of jobs, but as Hazel Downing has pointed out, no amount of increased productivity can replace women's role as status symbols, decorative sex objects, waitresses and even mistresses in the office.

New technology brought production line methods and the labour process of the factory floor into office work. Trade unions in many organisations have opposed office automation or been closely involved in its introduction to prevent staffing reductions (see Counter Information Services, 1979). Clare could have joined NALGO, the union for local government employees to complain about her work, but she was unsure how a union worked. Her limited understanding of the history and role of trade unions was shared by other female school leavers. Only three of the nine young women in office jobs were unionised. Elaine and Kim had joined BIFU, the union for banking, insurance and finance staff, and they saw pay negotiations as the most important part of the union's role.

Jeanette had been asked to join NALGO because of Townsend Graphics' previous close links with the university. She eventually joined CASA, the Clerical and Administrative Staff Association, because she felt that it would produce more in the way of financial and social benefits. Most of her co-workers were NALGO members, but Jeanette was 'against unions 'cos all they do is strike', and she preferred the outings to London shows offered by CASA.

Jeanette and Cathy were best friends, and when I visited them at Cathy's house one evening, Cathy described her problems at Courtfields.

CG: Is there a union at Courtfields?

Cathy: No, if you have any problems you go and see the personnel
             manager. What I find funny is that there isn't a standard
             scale of pay, all the secretaries are earning different money.
             I don't know *how* they work it out. Everyone seems to be
             on different scales of pay.

They did not connect Cathy's low wages with the lack of union organisation, nor Jeanette's far better pay and conditions with the activities of NALGO and CASA. This was hardly surprising, since the history of workers' organisation had not been included in their school curriculum, and given the degree of opposition to trade union activity in the popular press. Their main source of information about unions was from the experiences of relatives and friends, but union organisation was a predominantly male tradition which tended to place women on the edges of the action (Boston, 1980).

Cathy's situation at Courtfields was similar to that of most of her peers in office work, since she had no union or staff association to join. Many young women in factory jobs were in the same position, but they soon understood the potential value of union organisation from their experiences working at piecework rates in crowded or unhealthy conditions.

10

Factory work: producing the goods

Factory work in Birmingham follows the nineteenth century pattern of numerous small workshops and family firms concentrated mainly in the 'small metal trades'. There are more family-owned small businesses in Birmingham than in any other British city; a total of 3,540 in 1980, when 41 per cent of all Birmingham companies employed less than ten people, and 81 per cent employed less than fifty. Almost half the local workforce are employed in the light and medium manufacturing industries, which is a far higher proportion than the national average (C. Webb, 1980).

Birmingham industry has been heavily dependent on motor manufacturing since the 1960s, and many of the larger manufacturing companies such as Lucas's, GKN Sankey and Dunlops supplied components to the various British Leyland plants in the Midlands area. Most of the young women's parents and older relatives and friends were employed by these larger companies, whilst they worked mainly in smaller family firms. Larger companies were notoriously reluctant to take on school leavers with minimal experience of assembly line work disciplines (Ashton and Field, 1976; Roberts and Sharpe, 1982).

Birmingham's manufacturing industry is unusually concentrated in the 5,000 hectares of the inner city core area. In 1980, this contained some 5,000 factories, 80 per cent of the city's industrial buildings, and it accounted for 62 per cent of all manufacturing employment. Many small family firms are housed in the so-called 'jewelry quarter' in the Hockley district of the city. This area has traditionally been involved in the production of cheap metal goods, and most companies still occupy cramped multi-storey, multi-occupancy premises which date from well before 1914.[1]

About half the male 16-year-old school leavers in England and Wales entered manufacturing jobs in 1979, compared to a quarter of their female peers (see Table F). Just under half of these young men were working with metal and electrical equipment, while most of the young women worked with other materials, and they were far less likely to have apprenticeships. The situation in Birmingham was similar, with over 75 per cent of male school and college leavers in manufacturing jobs, compared to 16 per cent of their female peers. The majority of Asian and Afro-Caribbean students moved into routine unskilled jobs, with almost 80 per cent of young black women employed in this sector (see Tables G and J; Smith, 1976).[2]

Most young women were employed in traditionally female factory jobs, and these were mainly working class school leavers with few academic qualifications. They moved into a narrower range of jobs than their male peers, and comparatively few areas of skilled manufacturing employment in Birmingham were open to young women. Although factory work was a last resort for some school leavers, it was still preferable to 'waiting about on the dole' (see Chapter 12), and young women's actual jobs were not always as bad as they had expected. I visited eight young women at work in four different companies, and this chapter is based on their experiences.

Skilled Factory Jobs

Sewing Machinists at Dalcourts and Lycetts
One of the few areas of skilled work which was available to female school leavers in Birmingham was in the declining local 'rag trade'. Birmingham has never been a major centre for clothing manufacture, unlike parts of Northern England (see Coyle, 1982), but it did have a small but flourishing 'rag trade' until the early 1970s. By 1979 this sector was struggling to survive, unable to meet department stores' demands for cheap mass-produced garments, or to compete with overseas manufacturers who exploited the cheap labour rates in parts of South-East Asia.

I visited two of Birmingham's longer-established clothing manufacturers, Dalcourts and Lycetts, two white-owned family firms which had adapted to the changing economic situation in different ways.

Liz and Jan worked at Dalcourts, and Jenny, Monica and Babs were employed at Lycetts. Young white women tended to look for jobs with companies like Dalcourts and Lycetts rather than Asian-owned firms. The former did employ Asian and Afro-Caribbean women, but they worked mainly in the least remunerative routine jobs (cf. Hoel, 1982).

Dalcourts was based in a spacious and fairly modern building near the jewelry quarter, and it had a good local reputation for offering reasonable pay and working conditions. The firm employed about 150 people, of whom one hundred mainly white working class women worked as sewing machinists on the four assembly lines, with a minority of about twenty Asian women doing the least skilled jobs like pressing, packing and basic seams. Ten middle-aged white women supervised production, and the twenty management and sales staff were mostly white middle class men. The fifteen designers and cutters worked in separate premises, and had little contact with the production workers. This group of white middle class women and men were in their twenties and thirties, like most of the sales staff and lower management. Mr Appleby, the production manager, who showed me round Dalcourts, was in his late twenties, with an aggressive and forthright management style.

Dalcourts had a large production area which was well-lit and venti-lated, and an excellent subsidised canteen. All of the production workers were female, and although their ages varied from 16 to 60, they were always referred to as 'the girls' (cf. Pollert, 1981). Dalcourts had responded to changes in the clothing industry by specialising in high quality upmarket garments such as ladies' tailored suits which retailed at £80 (in 1980), and by a radical reorganisation of their production processes.

Dalcourts' assembly lines stretched along the shopfloor, with con-veyor belts connecting the machines operated by a supervisor at a large control panel at one end. When a machinist required more material, or had completed a batch, she pressed the appropriate buttons next to her machine, and the supervisor would send along the relevant items. It was therefore possible to monitor each worker's output with considerable precision. Piecework rates for each job were set on the basis of time and motion studies, so that machinists had to reach a given speed in order to earn their basic rates. A young white woman who had started the year before Jan and Liz explained how this payment system worked:

Jo: You have to do sixty minutes an hour, each job is worth a set
        number of minutes which is set by the work study people.
        Sixty minutes an hour is called earning your money, you're
        supposed to do that anyway to get your basic. Then whatever
        you do over sixty minutes you get more than your basic, that's
        when you can really earn some money. But it's hard to do that
        sometimes. With some jobs, it's really difficult to do more than
        the basic, and it can take a while to get your speed up with a
        new job. It's got a lot harder to earn your money since I've been
        here [November 1978].

CG: Do you all try to go as fast as possible?

Jo: Yes (laugh), but not all the time. You know if you're getting
        good money, they'll have a go for it, and you have to have a
        go anyway. It does make a lot of difference what job you're
        on, you'll work harder if you know you're getting the money
        for it.

CG: And if you're not. . .?

Jo: You just do a day and then go home (laugh). It's right that is.

Fitting a skirt waistband was assessed at two minutes, so that
machinists had to produce thirty an hour to earn their basic, which
was around £45 a week. The most complex and skilled tailoring jobs
were not always more remunerative than less complicated jobs like
making skirts. Machinists had to work a lot harder to 'earn their money'
on the simplest seams, because they had to produce more to get the
basic rate.

There was no pool of experienced sewing machinists on whom
Dalcourts or Lycetts could draw, because the local clothing trade
was fairly small, so both firms had to train most of their own labour
force. Conversely, skilled machinists were dependent on a limited
number of companies for employment, unless they joined the hidden
economy by making clothes for friends and relatives.

Dalcourts and Lycetts both used government sponsored YOPS Work
Experience schemes as part of their recruitment and training policies. Jan
and Liz started at Dalcourts in January 1980 on the YOPS rate of
£23.50 a week for six months. They moved straight into the small training school above the main production area for at least six weeks to learn
basic seams and operations before moving down on to the assembly lines.
The YOP scheme acted as a trial period during which Mr Appleby could
decide whether to keep the trainees on as permanent employees.[3]

Although some trainees had been recruited to Dalcourts through Job Centres and the careers service, Jan and Liz had heard of the vacancies through relatives and family friends who worked there. Mr Appleby valued such informal recruitment methods as a means of 'keeping it in the family', because trainees were then under the dual control of supervisors and older female relatives or family friends. This system operated mainly within the local white working class community, and subtly excluded Asian and Afro-Caribbean applicants.

Liz had been interested in a sewing job since a careers interview in late 1978, and from her sister-in-law's positive reports of the good working conditions at Dalcourts. Factory work was not Jan's first choice, and she had heard about Dalcourts through a friend of her mother's. Jan was far less happy with her job than Liz when I visited them at work in November 1980.

Jan: I didn't want to go into a factory when I left school.
CG: Why was that do you think?
Jan: 'Cos I don't like it now (laugh), and I didn't want to then. It's the work, you feel as though you're shut indoors all the time, it's a weight. I don't like it (laugh).
CG: Would you like to have a job outside then?
Jan: Yeh, in the shops, before I got this I did a bit of casual work in kiosks in the city centre. I had fifteen other interviews before I got this and I was a bit desperate for a proper job, I'm still looking for other jobs though, I'm not staying here unless I have to.

Jan was still working at Dalcourts a year later. The contracting youth labour market had discouraged her from leaving to look for another job, and she gradually felt more at ease in the production room. Jan and Liz were both taken on as permanent employees after the YOP scheme ended. By the end of 1981, they were taking home around £40 a week. As trainees they had learnt the simplest operations like darts and side seams, before more skilled jobs like fitting waistbands and zips. Once they had built up their speed, trainees moved on to the assembly lines, and on to piecework rates. Liz remembered this as a fairly traumatic experience:

Liz: It was terrible at first. I thought I'd never pick my speed up. It was horrible, I hated it when I first came down. It was a worry

really, 'cos everyone else was getting on all right, and I thought
I'd never do it, but you do get into it. It just takes a bit of time
– practice.

The introduction of assembly line production at Dalcourts had
been designed to increase efficiency and to minimise employees'
disruption of the work. All 'unnecessary' talking or movement from
the machines was forbidden without the supervisor's permission. As
Mr Appleby informed me with a gratified smile: 'the girls don't need
to move at all.' The degree of concentration demanded by the work,
the layout of the assembly lines, and the music blaring out over the
clatter of the machines combined to make communication between the
machinists extremely difficult.

Dalcourts had changed their production processes and altered
working hours without consulting their employees. Management
realised that these changes were far from popular, but were able to
act as they did because of the ban on union organisation. Trainees
as well as more experienced employees were critical of management's
actions, but they were also well aware of the fate of those workers
who had tried to organise resistance in the past.

CG: So what about unions? Is there one?
Jo: Oh no, they wouldn't have a union. You have to look after
yourself here. If you've got a complaint you tell your supervisor, but she's for the management all the while, so you're on
your own. If you feel that strong and you want to complain,
you've got to go up yourself on your own, and you know it's
you yourself. No matter how bad it is, you won't want to go
up. Some of the girls tried to get a union up not long ago, but
they wouldn't have it (laugh). And the girls got into trouble
as well for trying to start it.

The situation at Lycetts on the opposite side of the jewelry quarter
was somewhat different. The firm's owner had retired, and the company was managed by his son-in-law, Mr Stockton, who was in his late
forties. The company had originated as a manufacturer of children's
clothes supplying small local shops. As the latter were forced out of
business in the early 1970s by the rise of larger department stores and
supermarkets, Lycetts shifted to mail order selling in order to survive.
By the end of the 1970s, they were mainly supplying bulk orders to

department stores around Western Europe in an extremely competitive sector of the market.

Lycetts employed around sixty machinists in several different teams. About twenty white women worked mainly on the more lucrative skilled jobs, with as many Asian and Afro-Caribbean women working on the lower-paid, lower status operations. There were five women supervisors, a management and sales force of about ten people, and a further ten designers and cutters. Unlike Dalcourts, Lycetts occupied far older, more cramped and dilapidated premises, and they organised their training and production along more traditional lines. Despite these differences, both companies operated similar divisions of labour along age, class, race and gender lines. Older middle class white men (e.g. Mr Stockton) occupied the more prestigious and powerful management posts, whilst younger, black and working class women were concentrated in the less lucrative, least skilled jobs.

At Lycetts, teams of about six machinists worked around their own long tables. The two junior teams did the simpler jobs, and the most experienced top team were given the more skilled jobs. The latter were all white women, and they could decide amongst themselves who should work on each seam or operation. Lycetts took on about six school leavers each year, either individually or as a group, to replace staff who had left. They joined one of the junior teams at once, learning basic operations from the team supervisor, and gradually building up their speed.

Mr Stockton: We have two good junior teams now, but we really have to press them very hard indeed. We've had to change our methods of working recently, and I don't think we're all that popular.

Until late 1979, most teams had produced complete garments as a group, with each machinist doing different operations. Mr Stockton then introduced a new split work scheme in an attempt to increase production. Everyone in each team worked on the same operation, then passed batches of half-completed garments on to the next team along, with the exception of the top team, who continued as before. This new scheme was unpopular with the machinists, who found it more boring and repetitive, and harder to earn their money.

Machinists were paid on a piecework basis which was similar to the system at Dalcourts, but the rates for each job were not calculated with such precision. It was impossible to monitor each machinist's output in the same way, since the production rate of each group depended on the slowest worker. This was a major problem for Mr Stockton, because speed and flexibility of output were essential in the clothing industry, where production was geared to regular annual seasons.

Babs and Monica started at Lycetts in September 1979 as YOPS trainees, and neither had family contacts in the trade. Despite the short-term financial advantages of such schemes, Mr Stockton and Ms Granby, Lycetts' chief supervisor, were unhappy with them as a basis for training and recruitment.

Ms Granby: We've had some real problems with the Work Experience girls. We can't do much with them here — the training on these machines is quite long. It's a skilled job is sewing, so you can't just sit them down at a machine and fit them in. It can take two or three years to get a full training. They come here and expect to do office work, they won't look at the sewing. They don't come because they *want* to do sewing, or because their mum did. We're not taking on so many now anyway.

Managers and supervisors preferred informal family-based recruitment methods to the more official channels which were usually used by YOP trainees. Babs heard about the job through an advert in the local paper, and Monica had been recruited through the careers centre. They discussed their disappointing experiences of full-time employment with Nadine, a young Afro-Caribbean woman on the same junior team, when I visited them at work in December 1980:

GC: When you were at school, did you think you'd be in a job like this?

Nadine: No (sigh).

CG: Had you any idea what you did want to do?

Babs: Something but not *this.*

Monica: Yeh, I never thought it'd be like this. When I left school I thought, well it's this or probably on the dole waiting, so I thought I'd better take this. It's better than sitting there on the dole taking the money, bored stiff.

Nadine: I wanted to be a designer, I should've gone to college, I got a place but I took this when it came up (raised eyebrows). The careers officer said 'don't get a sewing job if you want to be a designer'. She was right too (laugh).

Mr Stockton complained about trainees' ambitions to be designers.[4] He visited local schools every year in an attempt to recruit machinists, but with little success. He viewed sewing as a valuable skill which would be particularly useful for young women's future domestic role. Their ambitions to be designers or office workers appeared unrealistic and incomprehensible to him.

Mr Stockton: I mean some of our girls have been with us for fifty years with the factory. If a girl gets married at 20 or 25 she's been sewing for five or six years. She can earn a lot of money at home making jeans and her children's clothes. She's got a real skill, and she can come back into it.

Young women's skills were seen as the company's property because the firm had subsidised their training. Management were far from happy if employees attempted to exercise control over their working lives.

Ms Granby: We had one girl who was here for five years, really experienced, then she left and said she wanted a rest. She was unemployed for two years, it was a waste of our training.

Mr Stockton: (head in hands) I'll tell you my main problem. We've tried and we really do need them to work because we have to get these orders out. They just don't care. We tried making it worth their while to work harder but they don't want the money. These girls (sigh). Perhaps it's my age, getting older. I'm sure young-sters didn't used to be like this.

His despair at trainees' apparent intractability stemmed from a profound mismatch between his expectations and their experiences. According to Mr Stockton, trainees could quite quickly be earning £40 a week. Speaking some six months after they had moved on to piecework rates when the YOP scheme ended, the young women told a very different story.

CG: How's the pay?

Monica: Well put it this way, we do a five-day week, 8.30 a.m.-
5.30 p.m., and we work all the time. We end up getting
about 50p an hour, and that's no good is it? We get ten
minutes off in the morning but not in the afternoon, and
half an hour for lunch.

Nadine: The pay's bad man, you might take home £21 at the end
of the week. It's hopeless, and it's not fair. The job she's
doing now [pointing at Babs], she can earn half as much
again as us. It's boring, all you do is churn it out, produce
the goods.

For Mr Stockton, the perfect machinist was hard-working, docile
and adaptable, but few young women matched up to his ideal.

Mr Stockton: That's Diane over there [pointing out a young white
woman], now she's marvellous. She started last year,
and she wants to earn money, she wants to work, and
she'll turn her hand to anything. I wish they were all
like her.

The atmosphere at Lycetts was very different to the strict supervision at Dalcourts. Talking was permitted in the teams provided that
it did not interfere with production. Mr Stockton and Ms Granby
complained that young women's talking frequently brought production
in the junior teams to a complete standstill. They focused their criti-
cism on young Afro-Caribbean women, drawing on a series of racist
stereotypes (cf. Lawrence, 1981).

Ms Granby: They've all had an easy time of it at school, these girls.
They just don't want to work. Especially the West
Indian girls, they don't care, they just want to talk.
They don't want to earn money. I don't even think
they give their pay packets to their parents. The little
Asian girls are the best.

Mr Stockton: Yes, the Asian girls are the best especially once they
get to 17 or 18 or so and they go over to India and meet
the mother-in-law. Then they have to prove themselves,
and they're judged on the amount they bring in, and they
can earn £70 a week. They really work.

Young Asian women were assumed to be quiet and hard-working, as compared to their supposedly lazy and disruptive Afro-Caribbean sisters (cf. Chapter 1). At Lycetts white and black employees worked alongside each other in the same junior teams, and they were all equally involved in talking and disrupting production. Afro-Caribbean trainees were not all lazy and talkative, any more than all young Asian women were 'good little workers' or involved in arranged marriages (cf. Brah and Golding, 1983),[5] but employers used these assumptions as a means of dividing Asian trainees from their Afro-Caribbean peers.

'Race' was a central element in white managers' treatment of black workers, whereas it was simply not an issue in relation to white employees, or white people in general (cf. Guillamin, 1972, quoted in Tajfel, 1978). This was not only relevant to managers and supervisors: white employees shared such assumptions, but they did not have the bosses' power to hire and fire.

These personalised assumptions had political resonances outside of the workplace, since black people were blamed for the declining rag trade and the crisis in British industry (cf. Hall, 1978; Hall *et al.*, 1978; Billig and Cochrane, 1983).

Mr Stockton: There used to be more places round here like us, there's only Dalcourts left now. There are all these smaller firms run by our Commonwealth friends, and they do work hard. They employ girls for a fraction of what we do.

Ms Granby: Well I've had no trouble with anybody except the black girls. They've got to realise that they're adults and they don't get paid for doing nothing, they've got to work. We can't afford to pay them . . . this is what's been happening to the country. We've been paying people who haven't been working. I think we're getting down to brass tacks now, firms aren't prepared to pay out to people who aren't prepared to earn it. It's as simple as that.[6]

As with Dalcourts, there had never been a recognised union at Lycetts, although the trainees would have welcomed one. When they complained about the unpleasant working conditions, and the management's ability to introduce new working practices without consulting them, they also remembered the fate of those who had tried to start a union in the past:

Nadine: It's dirty this job is, all the dust and fluff that goes up your nose (laugh).

Monica: Makes you cough too.

Babs: Yeh, you blow your nose and all the stuff comes out in it. I've got backache and eyestrain at the end of the day.

Monica: Yeh, it's with sitting still all day, stuck in one place.

Babs: It's terrible, you long for the breaks, you sit at lunchtime and look at the clock. Your heart sinks when you think oh God, you've only got one second left.

Monica: Yeh, and you're shattered at the end of the day. At first I could hardly move after a day here. Agony. And you can't complain 'cos there's no union.

CG: Is there no union here then?

Monica: Oh, they'd never allow any of that here. It's a family firm, well it's supposed to be. There was one once but they stopped it.

Nadine: Yeh, you'd get the sack for starting one, that's what they did last time.

Monica: I wouldn't know how to start one (laugh), but we do need one.

Paramjit: I'd start one me.

Monica: My dad's all for it, he thinks we should start one.

The experience of being young employees working for small non-unionised family firms was a common link between young women in skilled jobs such as sewing and those in semi- and unskilled factory jobs. The former could progress to more lucrative skilled jobs, but the latter had no such chances.

Semi- and unskilled factory jobs

Assembly work at Corbetts and Trenthams

Most unqualified school leavers moved into semi- and unskilled factory jobs as assembly workers in Birmingham's light engineering industry. Shelly and Ann-Marie found jobs at Corbetts, a small family firm in the jewelry quarter which had been part of Birmingham's 'small metal trades' for almost one hundred years. Sue was employed at Trenthams, another small business which manufactured specialist measuring equipment, as a circuit assembly worker.[7]

Corbetts occupied two floors of a Victorian factory in a street full of similar premises. The somewhat dingy and cramped main workshop was on the ground floor, and this doubled as a storeroom when the adjacent stockroom overflowed. The firm's owner had long since retired, so Corbetts was managed by his nephew, Mr Landham, a white middle class man in his forties. The twenty-five employees included twelve female assembly workers, two older women supervisors (Doris and Mary), a secretary (Mrs Landham), two salesmen, and two men in charge of stock and distribution. New products were designed by Mr Graham, a Corbetts employee of almost thirty years' standing, who was assisted by Nazira and Jill.

Apart from the Landhams and Nazira, a young Asian woman, all of Corbetts' employees were white and working class. Mrs Landham was the only office worker, and she did all the firm's secretarial and clerical work, as well as some book-keeping and accounts. She was fortunate enough to be paid for this work, since it was a common practice in many family firms for 'the boss's wife' to do the office work for nothing, or to receive minimal wages from the firm's petty cash.[8]

The Landhams worked in the two small offices on the first floor, opposite to Mr Graham's workshop area. Shelly and Ann-Marie worked downstairs in the larger workshop-cum-storeroom. They were part of the team of twelve young women who did the least skilled, monotonous assembly jobs. Mr Landham felt that this fiddly repetitive work was particularly suitable for young women:

CG: Do you take on boys from school?

Mr Landham: Yes, we've had boys as well, not so many though. The type of work is more suited to girls, the assembly work. That's why I mentioned to the careers office that it would be more suitable for girls. Though only one girl came to us from there. The lads have usually *not* been straight from school. They've had a job previously, or some sort of work experience. They usually go into the stockroom or something. Lads don't take to assembly work really.

Like Trenthams, Corbetts did recruit some school leavers and young workers from local careers offices and Job Centres, and like Dalcourts and Lycetts, they preferred to use less formal family contacts. This was relatively easy in the jewelry quarter, which was full of similar small firms with fairly high labour turnover rates. Shelly and Ann-Marie had both heard of the vacancies at Corbetts through Shelly's sister who worked nearby.

Mr Landham: Now Ann-Marie is fairly quiet and Shelly is totally different, full of life, but they've both settled in now. We had a few troubles with Shelly at first, she was a bit talkative doing her work, but she's settled down now. Now with Ann-Marie it's different because her parents have taken such an interest, come along to the interview and everything. That is helpful. *We* think it's an ideal start for them from school because it's a very friendly atmosphere.

In fact, Shelly's parents had been equally involved in her entry to the labour market. Shelly left school at Easter with no qualifications, desperate 'to get out and get a job'. Her mother worked part-time as a cook in a city centre restaurant, and had arranged for Shelly to work there full-time from early May 1979. Shelly had missed her exams at school to take up the job, which then turned out to be washing up from 12.00 a.m. to 6.00 p.m. every Saturday for £6. She looked for office jobs throughout the summer without success, and by the end of 1979, her sister had heard of the vacancies at Corbetts. Shelly informed her ex-school friend Ann-Marie who was also unemployed at that time. Ann-Marie's parents then accompanied her to the job interview, and made such a favourable impression on Mr Landham.

Like so many of their female peers at school, Shelly and Ann-Marie would have preferred office jobs to working in a factory:

CG: When you were at school, did you think about what sort of job you'd be doing once you left?

Ann-Marie: Well, no, I never really thought about it (laugh). I was looking forward to getting a typing job in an office, I wanted to leave school, I knew that. But then I didn't mind what I got as long as I got a job (laugh).

Shelly: I always thought I'd be in an office, I used to *dream* about
           an office job.
CG: Why do you think that was?
Shelly: I dunno (laugh). I used to do typing at school and I liked it,
           and I used to think I would never work in a factory ever, it
           seemed horrible, factory work. But I quite like it now, though
           I thought I'd be in a posh office or something. Now I wouldn't
           want to do it, it'd be boring, all that writing.

'The girls' worked in three groups, soldering, filing, assembling and
packing the products. Their work was supervised and checked by
Doris and Mary, who also trained new employees. Flexible production
patterns meant that their work was relatively varied, but it remained
at a fairly low skill level.

CG: The work you're doing now, are you always doing the same
           job?
Shelly: No, you do something different every day. It's all the same,
           I mean, I've done it all before, but you do different parts.
           I'm doing some filing now, when I've finished that I might
           do some knocking off, that's putting notes on badges, or even
           painting, 'cos we're decorating the factory (laugh).
CG: So you're not doing the same thing all the time then?
Shelly: No, that's what I like about it, 'cos some places you do the
           same thing all day and every day, I don't think I could do
           that. You'd be like a robot, wouldn't you?

Trainees began on £33 per week, and according to Mr Landham
they could be earning £40 fairly quickly once they had built up their
speed. In October 1980, after ten months at Corbetts, Shelly was
taking home £28 a week, of which £7 went to her mother for keep. As
at Lycetts, there was a discrepancy between employers' expectations
and employees' actual experiences.

Training at Corbetts was of the traditional 'sitting by Nellie' type,
with an official three month's trial period for new recruits. Mr Landham had considered using the government-sponsored YOP schemes,
but decided to continue operating with an adaptable and multi-skilled
workforce as the best means of minimising the costs of high labour
turnover rates.

CG: Do you have a trial period then?

Mr Landham: We do give them three months' trial officially, but in practice it's fairly vague. You have a few who leave in the first week, or you know they're not suited to the work. Others might stay for six months. Nothing you can do really. We did think of having a go at this MSC scheme, but it all seems a bit of a palaver to me. What we do now is to train people up so they can take over if someone leaves.

Mr Landham expected a fairly high labour turnover as young people either settled in or left during their first months at work. He attributed this 'settling down' process to the young employee's supposedly 'natural' (i.e. biologically determined) transition to responsible adulthood (cf. Ariés, 1962). These changes were more likely to stem from the new atmosphere and disciplines of full-time waged work.

Mr Landham: In the first six months, as girls come straight from school to work, we notice *tremendous* changes in their attitudes and their ways. They either accept it and settle down or after six months you can usually tell what they'll do, they'll wander around and not really know what they're doing. If they're still here then, they stick it out. We've had the same sort of problem with the lads, though most have had jobs before.

Mr Landham presented his recruitment of unqualified school leavers as a sort of social service, since he viewed many working class youths as 'a bit backward', from 'deprived' or problem families.

Mr Landham: Now we have one girl here, she's been with us eight months and she's had a hard life. We keep her on, feel a bit sorry for her really. She's not very well off, she's a bit backward, trouble with her family, her brothers are always in trouble with the law. She's had to look after the family. It'd be a great pity if she had to lose her job to look after them now. She's a little bit slow, but she's basically a good girl.

For Mr Landham, the informal atmosphere of the small family

firm was particularly suitable for school leavers, as well as being more efficient.

Mr Landham: Some of the senior people have been here for twenty years, we're all in the same team. And we are accustomed to helping school leavers through. We're *all* on first name terms, and they can come and talk to any of us. We've had girls come from other places who've said they've had trouble, unfriendly places. We find we get as much, if not more, work with this sort of atmosphere than the big companies.

There were three groups of four young women working together at Corbetts, but Shelly felt that they did not constitute 'a group', and would have preferred to work in a bigger company where she could 'have a laugh'.

CG: Are there quite a few girls coming and going here, or is it the same lot all the time?
Shelly: There's a few girls here, but not really a group. There used to be more doing enamelling, but they've stopped that. They don't do it no more.
CG: So do you think it's better being small like this than a bigger firm?
Shelly: I'd prefer a very big one, me.
CG: Why do you think that is?
Shelly: More people there, you can have more of a laugh, make more friends.

According to Mr Landham, trade unions were unnecessary in friendly family businesses like Corbetts, because workers' interests were well protected by benevolent management. Union organisation would dissolve the illusion of the happy little family firm by shining an unwelcome light on the power relationship between employer and employee.

Shelly was aware of the potential benefits of union organisation through the experience of (mainly male) relatives and family friends. Like many other young women, she was unsure of the exact function of trade unions.

CG: What about a union, is there one here?
Shelly: Oh no, it's a family firm, they don't agree with it?
CG: Would you join one if there was one? Do you think they
          should have one?
Shelly: Oh yeh, I'd join. I dunno quite what they are, but they're
          good to have, I do know that from my dad and my brother
          and that.

Unlike Shelly, Ann-Marie was noticeably unsympathetic to trade
unions, partly as a result of working at her uncle's newsagent's on
an occasional basis during the summer of 1979. She had been paid
£5 for working an eight-hour day.

CG: Would you join a union here if there was one?
Ann-Marie: No I don't think so, there's no point really is there?
            (laugh). When I worked in the paper shop they never
            had one. I dunno what good they do, all they do is
            cause strikes. You're forced into these unions, aren't
            you? I don't agree with it. I think they're terrible. I
            mean you're told what to do, once you're in a union
            you can only work on certain things in a shop. When
            you're on strike you *have* to go out, that's what my
            uncle says anyway.

Trenthams' employees were not unionised either, although the
working conditions and the production processes were somewhat
different to those at Corbetts. Trenthams was involved in a relatively
young industry, and they were constantly updating their products to
keep pace with new technological developments. The company was
based in a spacious modern building in a new industrial estate on the
edges of Birmingham city centre. The business was only ten years old,
and it was owned and managed by Mr Trentham, with a total of seven
employees.

Mr Trentham was a young man in his early thirties, the child of
a white working class family who had 'got on at school', gone to
university, and then set up in business on his own: an 'earole made
good' (cf. Willis, 1977). The company's employees included Sheila,
the secretary and general office worker, Rick, who was in charge of
production, a salesman, and four production workers. This last group
included Jim, Sue and Pat, the two young women from the EITB

scheme, and one other young woman. All of Trentham's workforce were white and working class, although a young Afro-Caribbean man replaced Jim in the summer of 1982.

The organisation was informal, and working processes were fairly flexible. Although Mr Trentham had overall control, he discussed most of his decisions with Rick and Sheila, and he did all of the design work and product development himself. Trenthams dealt mainly with science departments of universities and colleges, hospitals and specialist companies, and most of their work involved 'one-offs' or fairly low quantity orders.

Sue and Pat had joined the company through the job placement system that Ms Webb had developed for the EITB scheme (see Chapter 11). Sue started in November 1980, some six months after Pat, and I visited her at Trenthams in December of that year. Mr Trentham preferred to use informal recruitment methods for young employees rather than more official channels. He could not draw on the established family-based job-finding networks that Corbetts relied on in the jewelry quarter. The EITB scheme was an ideal combination of the two methods.

CG: Have you used the EITB before?
Mr Trentham: Yes, we have, it's better than the careers centres
                 because they've done some work before, know what
                 to expect. Mind you, that doesn't always mean they
                 stay once they're here. Some leave after a week, but
                 most stay longer. A couple left after about six months,
                 one after a year. I used to bother about it, but you
                 just can't tell who'll stay and who'll leave.

The company had two small offices, a large production area which doubled as the stockroom, and a small research and development room. Mr Trentham divided his time between his office and his 'inventing room', Sheila was in the other office, the salesman was usually out on the road, and everyone else worked in the production area. The men were at one end of the workshop assembling and testing the products, whilst 'the girls' worked at the other, assembling and soldering electronic circuit boards. Despite the apparently flexible working processes, young women did the more monotonous and least skilled production jobs, or worked in the office. Once again, men occupied the better paid and more powerful positions.

All of Trenthams' employees were paid on an hourly basis, and Mr Trentham had set Sue's wages (£42 a week) at the official minimum for her age group. Low wages were so common amongst young workers that Sue earned more than most of her peers in office, shop and factory jobs (see Table D). Although her co-workers were fairly young, they were few in number, and Sue found the atmosphere at Trenthams fairly boring.

CG: So how's the work here?

Sue: Boring. It was OK at first — all different, but now it's getting really boring. Nothin' ever happens. I can't be bothered really, there's no point. I couldn't bear to be here in two years' time. There's only us and Jim, no other young people, no crowd. We're the only girls too, apart from Julie in the office. It's just boring, all the same.

Like most employers, Mr Trentham had a limited understanding of his young female workers. Pat and Sue had joined the company with basic soldering and circuit assembly skills, and they received no further training apart from when Rick showed them how to assemble a new circuit board.

CG: How have the EITB trainees got on?

Mr Trentham: Well, I dunno, really. They've not much confidence, quiet, they stick together. I've had this lad [Jim], now he'd been on the dole a year since leaving school, that made him quiet and nervous. But he's not like them.

CG: Is he doing the same work as them?

Mr Trentham: Well no, he's doing wiring and putting the circuit boards into the chassis, as well as one day a week at college.

CG: Do you think the girls seem so depressed because they do. . .?

Mr Trentham: (interrupts): Well it isn't (pause) . . . actually to be honest, it *is* pretty boring, what they do. It'd bore me, but we do pay them more than what most girls would get. I just can't understand them really, why they're so depressed.

Sue and Pat found their work monotonous, with little chance of 'getting on' and no offers of day release. Jim had come to Trenthams with similar qualifications, but he was doing more skilled work, he had been offered day release, and he was learning about electronics at work. Whilst Mr Trentham was superficially sympathetic to the young women's position, he was unable to understand why they seemed 'so quiet and depressed'. He had never thought of offering them day release or encouraging them to develop their skills as he had with Jim. Young women were expected to leave in a few years to 'start a family', so it was hardly surprising that Sue and her peers felt bored and undervalued at work.

'The girls' felt decidedly uneasy working opposite a wall covered in pictures of naked women, which had been put up by Rick. They were far too embarrassed to complain to Mr Trentham, since Rick was their immediate boss, and pornography was supposed to be harmless and 'natural' (see Dworkin, 1981; and Griffin, 1981).

The young women also had to put up with constant jokes, sexual innuendoes and 'put-downs' from Jim (cf. Chapter 9).

Mr Trentham: Jim has had to be told to stop getting at the girls. He gets very arrogant. They can hold their own but it often ends in tears.

Like Mr Landham at Corbetts, Mr Trentham expected to have a relatively high labour turnover amongst his younger employees. This posed more of a problem for Mr Trentham because the assembly of electronic circuits required more skill than making buttons and badges, and because he had no access to the pool of relatively cheap and unskilled labour in the jewelry quarter.

Employers in all these four companies assumed that young working class women would be motivated mainly by money, and they were surprised when young women's behaviour did not fit with their expectations. Young women were not interested in poorly paid boring jobs with minimal training and limited prospects. They valued the social atmosphere at work, and 'having a good group to work with' in an informal friendly factory could make a boring job almost bearable. Those young women who went into 'men's' engineering jobs had better pay, training and prospects, but they never felt completely at ease on the predominantly male shopfloor.

11

Engineering: young women in a man's world

Engineering has been the main area of working class male employment in the West Midlands for decades. It is a long-established industry with rigid skill hierarchies, a comprehensive apprenticeship system, and strong union organisation. Female engineering trainees were moving into an almost exclusively male occupation. In Britain only one in 500 engineers is a woman, compared to one in fifty in North America and one in three in Russia (*Industrial and Commercial Training Journal*, December 1979).

Debates about women's position in non-traditional jobs have been dominated by the ideology of equal opportunities, particularly since the sex discrimination legislation was passed in 1975. In these terms, both women and men can be discriminated against on the grounds of sex, since there is no concept of differential power. Lone 'token' women (and men) in non-traditional occupations can then be presented as evidence that particular jobs are equally open to women and men.[1]

The craft apprenticeship at Universal Metals was a classic example of tokenism, since they had taken on one young woman out of thirty male trainees each year since 1976. The EITB schemes for female technicians and operatives were examples of 'positive discrimination', since they were designed to encourage young women to train as engineers. This chapter compares these two approaches to breaking down gender-based divisions in the job market.

Craft training at Universal Metals

UM's four-year engineering apprenticeship was based at their on-site craft training centre (CTC). The course began with a year 'off the job' training in the CTC, covering basic skills in electrical engineering, machining, fabrication, welding and bench work. During the second year, apprentices specialised in machining or maintenance via a module system, and worked on small set-pieces. The final two years were spent working on site to build up experience. All the apprentices did day release at a local college throughout the course, working towards a TEC Certificate.[2]

The scheme was taught by a team of white, middle-aged male instructors, with Mr Wright as the overall supervisor. Entrance requirements included a headteacher's assessment, and anticipated grades of at least CSE grade 3s in English, maths, physics and either metalwork, woodwork or technical drawing (TD). About 800 school leavers applied to join the course in 1979: only sixty were tested and interviewed. Mr Wright was a practical working class engineer of the old school,[3] and he regretted this reliance on academic qualifications.

Mr Wright: Society is piece of paper mad, even the simplest of jobs, we're looking for exam results now. We've gone *mad* on exams, and yet I get the impression that educational standards have dropped.

Mr Wright preferred to use an informal assessment system which tended to favour schools with better academic reputations. Most of these schools were outside of the immediate locality, which was made up of mainly Asian and Afro-Caribbean communities, so Mr Wright's selection system made it more difficult for local black school leavers to get into the scheme. UM took on about thirty apprentices each year, most of whom were young white working-class men, with around five young Asian and Afro-Caribbean men in each group.

The scheme had never recruited any female apprentices until 1976, when the EITB piloted their girl technicians scheme at UM's CTC. Seven young women worked alongside UM's 'lads' for the first year's off-the-job training. The course did not run smoothly, since the young women were on block release from college, and the lads were on day release. This mismatch created different levels of knowledge and competence, which were exacerbated by a fundamental cultural division, as Mr Wright explained:

Mr Wright: Now the problem there with the seven was they tended to form a club, and they didn't integrate. Now one girl on her own is forced to integrate and the lads are forced to accept her. Two girls tend to stick together although they are still accepted, but if they get more than three or four and they have one table at tea-break to themselves, they tend to become their own little community, and they just don't integrate so well.

The EITB scheme eventually had to move to separate premises because of the continual conflicts. The young women had clearly gained sufficient collective confidence to develop an autonomous female culture. This undermined and threatened the lads' conversations about bikes, cars and football, and their boasts about drinking, fighting and sexual conquests. As Mr Wright pointed out, token women were more acceptable, since they posed less of a threat to the dominant male culture.

Mary had been one of the original seven EITB trainees. She failed her first-year exams through difficulties with the college work, left the EITB scheme and applied to UM as their first female apprentice. This change undermined Mary's already battered self-confidence, but she preferred the more practical emphasis of the UM course. Janice was taken on as the next year's token woman in 1978, and Loz started in September 1979. They had all been compelled to integrate into their particular year as 'one of the lads'.

Mary: I mean when I first started with the lads I was the first girl, and they looked at me like I was a two-headed zombie that had just walked in fresh from the grave.

Loz: You get like a tomboy working with boys. You agree with them to keep the peace. At school me and my friends used to get together and argue all week about something with them. Now you just shut up. You find yourself thinking differently too. They don't think of me as a girl anyway (laugh).

On the UM course the young women were doing exactly the same training as their male peers, and yet supervisors were still reluctant to allow them to do heavy, noisy or dirty jobs. Mr Wright was concerned to protect them from particularly 'heavy' male cultures, and he used swearing as a sort of index of the latter.[4]

Mr Wright: Whilst we can use a lad virtually anywhere, use the big hammer and knock seven bells out of him, there comes a time when you're still reluctant, whether rightly or wrongly, to put a girl in that situation. The fallacy that she's physically weaker, or the situation where the air is blue with language, and you draw back from putting a girl in there.

Most of the female apprentices went into desk jobs, as work study engineers, or in the planning and drawing offices. Mary was relatively unusual, because she had gone into the rolling mill, which Mr Wright described as 'a very blue area language-wise'. She was not doing heavy physical work, but was logging and planning the preventative maintenance repair work in that section of the site. Mr Wright attributed Mary's success to her unique personal qualities and her ability to survive the men's continual intimidation. All of the female apprentices were seen as exceptions proving the rule that engineering was not *really* women's work.

Mr Wright: The problem is not the girls, the problem is the male chauvinists' ideas. . . . There's got to be a certain breed of girl who will stand the rigours of a factory like this, 'cos it is pretty heavy and dirty. They have to be pretty special.

Mary herself dismissed the view that women could not do engineering because they were too weak to lift heavy weights as misguided rubbish.

Mary: Everybody thinks that because it's a man's job that you are throwing lumps of metal about, you've about two ton in weight, just pigging 'em around for an encore, and it's just not true. Now I can show you places where men are lifting half a ton, a ton, and I can do it, 'cos all you need to do is go on a slinging course. You've got radio-operated cranes or

crane drivers, nobody lifts anything in this day and age.
Well they do, but not all the time. It's rubbish anyway, some
men are small and weedy, and couldn't lift a feather, and some
girls are dead strong.

Mary was undoubtedly determined and hard-working, but she had
developed these qualities at school in order to survive. As a scholarship
girl, Mary had been one of the few working class students at a prestigious mixed independent school. She was seen as a freak because of
her interest in engineering and technical drawing.

CG: So how did you get on at school?
Mary: Well, at the school I went to it was little girls do this and
         little boys do that, and nothing in the middle. So when I told
         them that I wanted to do engineering, there was trouble. The
         careers officer froze in his chair, and three minutes later he
         recovered. He was flabbergasted, whereas if I'd been a boy it
         would have been quite all right.

Mary was highly ambitious, aiming 'to have one of those 4.2 litre
Jags parked on the forecourt'. She took her work seriously, and objected when other people, particularly men, tried to undermine her
achievements.

Mary: People *always* say 'when are you going to get married or have
         kids?' Some blokes say 'why did you take it up? If my wife
         did I'd throw her out.' God, it drives me *mad*.

Mary had paved the way for Janice and Loz, who also had a long-
standing interest in engineering. They had experienced a mixture of
support and discouragement from families, teachers and careers advisers.

Janice: The careers teachers were useless, they tried to put me
         off, but my parents don't mind so long as I've got the
         craft I want to do. The careers officer gave me the addres-
         ses to apply to, and most of the firms — big and small —
         wouldn't have anything to do with me, 'cos I'm a girl. UM
         was OK, 'cos they already had Mary here. At school they
         just thought I wanted to do TD so I could be with the boys
         (laugh).

Loz: I got on really well with my TD teacher at school, he was ever
so pleased when I got in here [UM]. My dad wanted me to go
into hairdressing, 'cos he has his own salon. But me older sister
did that, and I saw enough of that not to want it. My dad's
really pleased now though, 'cos he knows I've got a trade.
Me mum's over the moon, what I'm doing is so different.

Like most of the apprentices, Janice and Loz had hoped to become
draughtswomen after doing TD at school. The intensity of the competition for these jobs in the drawing office soon persuaded Janice
to focus her ambitions elsewhere.

Janice: Most of the lads want to be draughtsmen, so I'll have more
chance of a job in capstan turning. I'm quite interested in
it, although I'm having trouble with milling at the moment.

All the female apprentices enjoyed the challenge and the variety
of their work, as well as the satisfaction of producing something tangible and useful.

Loz: I brought home a tool box I'd made, and my sisters went mad!
They didn't believe I'd made it, they thought I'd bought it. It
wasn't even very good (laugh). They think I'll be making thousands of tool boxes in the end, I bet (laugh).

Mary: When I was 11, I read about engineering, and I liked the
satisfaction of, when you'd done something, it was *there* to
move, or to do what it was supposed to do, and you could
see it. And it *is* like that.

Some of their peers in office or factory jobs talked about having a
pride in their work, but their efforts were seldom noticed by anyone
else. The engineering trainees were learning recognised skills, each of
which had their own place in an established craft. They also had a low
opinion of office work and their peers in the secretarial school, which
was at the opposite end of the UM site.

Mary: I'd hate an office job, I did one once and it was terrible.
My mum forced me to, 'cos she wouldn't keep me if I went
on the dole. It's boring, and there's no absolute top freedom.

You're never gonna be your own boss. In the secretarial
school, the competition is all over dress, they're all in there
plucking their eyebrows, doing their hair, thinking 'she's
worn that twice this week'.

Whilst the female apprentices had no time for the glamorous
image of office work and other 'women's jobs', they did miss the
company of other young women.

Mary: I missed the EITB girls after they'd gone, 'cos we were like
a commune, and now I've no one to talk about clothes or a
new hairdo with.

Loz: You know you sometimes get an off day, and you feel a bit
tired? I'd like to have a woman to talk to then. There's Janice,
I see her in the toilets, but she's different to me, we don't
have big talks. You can't talk to the lads always and some of
the things they talk about — sex an' that — I just go away.

These young women were particularly affected by the gradual
breakdown of female friendship groups as their girlfriends began to
go steady and get married, because they had so little contact with
other young women at work.

Janice: My girlfriends from school have all got married, and that's
not for me. I don't see 'em no more. They think I'm a bit
weird 'cos I do this job.

Joining the UM scheme had been a traumatic experience for all
the trainees:

CG: So what was it like at first?
Mary: Oh it was terrible at first, even though I'd been before with
the EITB girls. Then when I came back to the rolling mill
it was so bad I thought I'd never come back. They treat you
like a freak. But I've got used to it now. Where I work they
swear a lot, so I put a swear box on my desk, and every
time I catch one of them swearing they have to put some
money in it (laugh). It works too.

Loz: At first I was very wary, and scared of being the only girl.
That came as a real shock I can tell you. For the first month
I felt that I just didn't fit in, I was so quiet. I asked Janice
and she said it had been the same for her. It got better and
I like it now. I feel much more confident when I know that I
can *do* something.

All of the apprentices worried about making mistakes and being
'shown up', since a practical competence in manual skills was highly
valued in the male culture of the shopfloor (see Willis, 1977, 1979).
The onus to prove oneself fell most heavily on female trainees and
on Mary in particular, who also had to contend with racist jibes about
the supposed stupidity of Irish people (cf. Ullah, 1983).

Mary: Anything I do wrong, people laugh, they tend to put it down
to the fact that I'm female and Irish. The Irish takes more of
the blame than being a girl does. I ignore it, but I hate to make
mistakes. I don't take those little romance books to bed, I
take Kempsters 'Materials for Engineering' (laugh), because
people will try to catch you out, being a girl.

Mary was nearing the end of her apprenticeship, but even after
almost four years she still faced harassment and opposition from
male engineers. This ranged from finding a dead mouse in her locker,
being given impossible 'joke' errands and jobs, to receiving abusive
telephone calls.

Mary: It's OK with the blokes who know me, but I have to be
careful with those that don't. Even now, I get the odd joke
played on me, and some of them can be really nasty.

The difficulties of working in such a heavily male-dominated area
were offset by the advantages of strong union organisation. The female
apprentices had better pay, prospects and working conditions than their
peers in non-unionised offices and factories, but they did not always
recognise these as the fruits of union activity.

Loz: I dunno anything about the union, none of us do, but we're all
in it. I think they think we're too young. I just pay my sub
and that's it. We had two union people — I dunno what they're

called — down to talk about it, but it just went in one ear
and out the other. I don't really know what they do.

Mr Wright had twenty years' experience of the industry, and was
involved in the sensitive negotiations between unions and management
over the apprentices' wage levels. He felt that many of the older women
workers objected to being kept on the edges of union activities by the
mainly white male leadership (see Coote and Kellner, 1980).

Mr Wright: Some of the women aren't too pleased with the union,
because they're in TASS, which is part of the AUEW,
which is still very chauvinistic. Like about the timing of
union meetings, they get very cross, because they can't
even get to them, and they've invested as much in union
dues as the rest of the factory.[5]

In 1980, the British engineering industry was in the throes of a
major crisis. Mr Wright expected this to result in fundamental changes
of attitude and practice, including a shift towards a more flexible
and multi-skilled labour force. He was attempting to introduce an
extra module into the apprenticeship course, in order to produce 'a
multi-skilled bloke'. Mr Wright hoped to overcome what he called
'the political barrier' of union opposition to these changes although
he realised that doing so would not necessarily be in the best interests
of the workforce, the industry, nor of union-management relations.

CG: So how do you see the future?
Mr Wright: Well, we've had five or six hundred people made redundant so far this year on site. If by applying your multi-
skills you deprive someone else of a job, then eventually
you're cutting your own throat. And the BL situation at
Longbridge will have national repercussions especially
if Edwardes wins the day. It'll change the attitude here,
widen the gap between unions and management.[6]

The future of Britain's engineering industry looked bleak to Mr
Wright in 1980, and subsequent events more than confirmed his pre-
dictions. It was in this period before the crisis deepened that the
EITB piloted their 'girls in engineering' initiative. Their initial attempts
at training mixed groups had proved unsuccessful, so the EITB moved
off the UM site to concentrate on women-only courses.

The Engineering Industry Training Board schemes

The EITB initiative aimed to encourage more female school leavers into the industry, and to break down employers' biases against women engineers. These were not the first nor the only women-only training schemes,[7] but they were the first to be funded and publicised on a national level by an industrial training board. They made use of provision in the Sex Discrimination Act which allows educational and training institutions to practice positive discrimination in fields where there has been a serious imbalance in the ratio of the sexes.

The EITB began by sponsoring fifty young women in Birmingham and Croydon on craft technician scholarship schemes in 1976. By 1979 their Premium Grant scheme was funding 150 young women around Britain, rising to 250 in 1980. Ms Lowe supervised the Birmingham schemes, and she recalled the origins of the initiative, and her surprise at the poor local response.

CG:	Were you involved from the beginning?
Ms Lowe:	Yes, it all came from a TSA document on training opportunities for women in 1975, or the lack of it (laugh). The MSC and TSD were looking for training for women, and we were asked to do something.[8] Plus there was a shortage of technicians and school leavers coming into engineering, and we weren't making the best use of the girls we had anyway. So it was a sort of double situation. We had the chief education officer on the board, but we had terrible difficulty getting into schools. He wrote to them all, saying we could come in and talk to girls about engineering, and we didn't get *any* invitations at all. We were a bit stunned at that (laugh).
CG:	Why do you think that was?
Ms Lowe:	Well, they didn't want to be encouraging girls with 'O' levels to leave school, and the ones who *would* be leaving, well engineering wouldn't be good enough for them. Banking and the commercial world was far more acceptable for their young ladies.

The EITB then circulated publicity brochures and posters, and arranged seminars for careers advisers, teachers and employers. Increasingly amazed by the lack of response, Ms Lowe had to get in touch with young women directly – and quickly. The EITB ran advertisements in the local press and radio, and the response was immediate: over a hundred young women replied in a matter of days. Here was conclusive proof that the course would be meeting a genuine demand.

The craft technician scheme was launched first, and the official requirements were four 'O' levels, including English, maths, preferably physics and a technical subject. Ms Lowe and Ms Norton, who worked in the central careers service administration, were both aware that female school leavers were less likely to have done these subjects than their male peers (see Kelly, 1978; Walden and Walkerdine, 1982; Hartnett, 1979).

Ms Norton: There are so many barriers to be broken down which start right from when the girls are given the dolls and the boys get the pliers. There's all that to battle against, and the girl might not have had a chance to do physics or technical subjects. We've had a lot of opposition from fathers. We've even used aptitude tests to *prove* to parents the girls' ability.

The two-year technician scheme covered the basic engineering processes (fitting, machining, electrical wiring, soldering, sheet metalwork and welding), combining block release at college with periods of work experience in local firms. Since a full apprenticeship took four years, the trainees had to find full-time jobs for a further two years after completing the course.

The trainees were an even mix of young middle and working class women, whose academic qualifications ranged from eight 'O' levels to just below the entrance requirements of four 'O' levels or their equivalents. A minority had drifted into the scheme after failing exams or a period of unemployment, but most trainees had been interested in engineering for some years. Ms Lowe attributed the scheme's success to the trainees' commitment and motivation, which set them apart from their male peers.

Ms Lowe: There just aren't the differences between girls and boys, it all comes down to individuals. Girls are better in many ways. Not so much academically, but because they are more determined to succeed, motivation, dedication. The boys just go through an apprenticeship, don't put so much effort into it. I think that's why girls have come out extremely well in the companies, because of the way they work. It's not a *training* difference though.

Apart from Ms Lowe, their college tutor Mr Prestwood was also in regular contact with the trainees. A white middle class man in his forties, Mr Prestwood agreed with the general aims of the scheme. He had less sympathy for the views of the trainees, some of whom were overtly feminist and all of whom were questioning their own abilities, as well as women's position in general.

Mr Prestwood:	[to me] : I wanted you to see some of these girls because they've got very fixed ideas which they'll modify over the next few years.
Young women:	[who had overheard him] : On what?
Mr Prestwood:	On what? About these superior men.
Kate:	We're just as good as you.
Mr Prestwood:	(patronising) You're better, my dear, you're better. My wife has always been on a pedestal in my life. Women are much better than men, they just have problems proving it.
Lorna:	We're trying to prove that a woman can do the same things as a man, not that we *are* men.
Mr Prestwood:	Yes, but you don't have to prove that you can do a man's job. There are lots of jobs in industry that are suitable for women to do.
All:	Aah! (indrawn breath).
Kate:	No, but I can do exactly the same job as you. You have no right whatsoever to say 'oh that's a woman's job, that's a man's job'. I think he's trying to get us annoyed (laugh).
Mr Prestwood:	It's just that I think women are unsuited to certain jobs. Like a coalminer, say.
Kate:	No, but there are women that *would* like to go down a mine. They do in America as well. It's because men are so high and mighty that they think that they should always be protecting women. I mean, what

	right have they to think they're above women?
Lorna:	Some men are incapable of working down a mine, but they don't say 'no weedy men allowed'.
Mr Prestwood:	Yeh but what you're trying to do, you're trying to alter the structure of our society, which has been built up over centuries, and you can't do it.
Kate:	But if it needs changing you can't keep it.

All the trainees were white, as were their college tutors, apart from one Asian man who taught electrical principles. His classes were unpopular with some of the students, and they had expressed their dissatisfaction in racist ways. Eventually another group of trainees challenged this racism, as Ms Lowe explained:

Ms Lowe:	Some of the girls have said he can't speak English, they can't understand him. In fact he speaks fairly good English, maybe he's a bit impatient. But now another group of girls have said it's not that he can't speak English, because he can, it's the other girls who are prejudiced. Actually that group weren't too keen on his subject because they prefer *anything* to electrical engineering (laugh).

In the trainees' work placements with local companies, the main difficulties had been with unsympathetic male co-workers and supervisors.

Ms Lowe:	The most important thing is that girls are put with sympathetic people and treated as individuals. Quite a few have said, 'I don't believe a girl can do it, but OK, I'll tell her how', and then she'd have to be twice as good just to compensate for being female.

Like Mr Wright at UM, Ms Lowe was concerned about the 'heavy' male cultures of the shopfloor. She was less worried that young women might be offended by the men swearing than by the use of such language as a form of harassment.[9]

Ms Lowe:	Bad language *is* one of our worries, although the girls aren't really worried about it. Some of them have been offended, in one case in the technical department, not the

shopfloor. They were really being obscene *to* her. She had
to leave in the end, it was a really nasty situation. The girls
have to accept that engineers *do* swear, they always have.

Ms Lowe tried to put two or three young women together in a
company, in order to give them some support. Moving from the predominantly female college course into heavily male-dominated workplaces could be a traumatic experience. The young women had gained
a sense of collective confidence and support from the other trainees,
and were not always content to blend in as 'one of the lads' (cf. Newton, 1983).

CG:	How are you treated as a girl doing engineering?
Brenda:	Some are extra nice to me, and that really gets me (laugh). It's 'oh look after the little girl'. That's the older men mainly.
Jill:	If you have to work with someone they never leave your side, but with boy apprentices they go off and leave them to it. It's like they think you shouldn't be there.
Brenda:	I keep telling all the men, 'look I'm not a girl, just treat me as a fella!' (laugh).
Jill:	I'm a person, I don't wanna be treated like a fella! The worst is when they think you're in jobs that should go to boys. That's mostly on the shop floor. They say you'll all get married and have kids, and that'll be a waste of the training.

The young women worked on both sides of the industry, and
they had to alter their dress and appearance to suit drawing offices,
work study departments, and the shopfloor.

Ms Lowe:	They realise that jeans and leather jackets aren't so accept-able when you go for a job. Jeans are fine on the shop-floor. But in a skirt, you're gonna get wolf whistles (laugh). Now in a drawing office, mostly you'll wear a skirt prob-ably.
Jill:	I can't wear my V-necked T-shirt, or there's trouble. And you can't bend down. I didn't think at first, but I soon knew better. They seem to think any girl who's with a

bunch of boys is gonna be after all the men.

Kathy: And in the offices you get these really dreadful men who are after anything in a skirt. It's best to avoid them — bad news.

Brenda: And we're more manly in our way of dressing. Not that we dress like men, but we don't bother what we're in.

Quite apart from their appearance, female trainees were often assumed to be 'after all the men' simply because they worked in a predominantly male occupation.

Kathy: Boyfriend's won't accept that you can have workmates of the opposite sex. They think something's gone on. But they talk to girls in the typing pool don't they? *I* don't say they're all his girlfriends.[10]

Trainees' work placements varied considerably, and not all of them were valuable as engineering experience.

Jill: I spent a day sticking labels on plastic bags (laugh).

Rachel: I spent a week sweeping sawdust off the floor! (laugh) So much for technicians.

Kathy: And *then* you get the other side of it, 'cos for two and a half weeks I was sitting at a desk writing out batching sheets, '1234' all these stupid numbers.

The apprentices agreed that they could usually pass relatively unnoticed in smaller firms, but in large companies they tended to 'stick out like sore thumbs', and experienced more overt harassment. They were horrified by the class-based cultural chasm between the offices and the shopfloor.

CG: You've worked in the office and the shopfloor then?

Jill: Yeh, and what *really* annoyed me was in the offices they all talk about the assembly workers as if they're the lowest of the low: the idlest of all. It's disgusting. You see the offices hate the shopfloor and the shopfloor hate the offices.

Lorna: Yeh, you gotta do both, gotta be careful (laugh).

Jill: You see what doesn't get told. You'd like to tell them (management) but they'd never believe you.

Kate: There's like a complete block on communication. It's like war really.

The EITB trainees were no more likely to move into those engineering jobs that were seen as particularly 'male' than the female apprentices at UM. This was not a fault of the schemes, but an indication of the inflexibility and chauvinism of the engineering industry. The main advantage of the technician scheme was the support and confidence that the trainees gained from being on a women-only course. The EITB junior operatives course was also for women only, but it was not intended to be comparable to a craft apprenticeship, nor to encourage young women into 'men's' engineering jobs. The course aimed to give female school leavers some basic engineering skills, experience in waged work disciplines, and the confidence gained from training with other young women.

Although most of the trainee operatives went into 'women's' engineering jobs (e.g. circuit assembly, hand press operation) they *did* learn what were seen as 'male' skills. I was not able to follow any young women directly from school into the UM apprenticeship or the EITB technicians' scheme, but I did follow Wendy and Sue from Moorcroft and Tildesley schools respectively into the junior operatives course.

The fifteen-week course covered basic skills in electrical wiring, assembly, electronics, drilling, machining, some theory, maths and social skills. Originally funded by the EITB, the course later became part of the MSC Youth Opportunities Programme, with a weekly training allowance of £23.50. It had no formal academic entry requirements beyond a minimal competence in English and maths. Ms Lowe explained the original reasoning behind the course:

Ms Lowe: A third of the engineering industry is made up of operators, semi-skilled people, mainly with a short time to learn the job, and there's a terrific turnover of these people. A lot of companies are reluctant to take school leavers on, and to give them a bit of skilled training. They'd far rather take on someone with experience. And we had this experimental scheme for boys and girls, but very few girls applied. So we set up this one purely for girls as an experiment really, I suppose it was a bit like an equal opportunities thing.

The scheme had started with male instructors, but this had proved unsatisfactory.

Ms Lowe: A lot of the male instructors had trouble working with
              girls after working with boys in both schemes. So we
              got in a woman to run the operatives scheme, and it's
              been very successful.

Ms Webb, a white working class woman in her forties, supervised the course assisted by Mr Walker and Bob, two white working class men in their fifties and thirties respectively. These three instructors covered most of the technical skills, with tutors from the local college coming in to take classes in English, maths, and life and social skills. The training course was housed in dilapidated premises, surrounded by a jumble of small companies. It had a small training area, a cramped office and two classrooms. This was very different to the spacious and well-equipped training centre at Universal Metals.

Ms Webb was extremely interested in 'women's role' from her own experience as 'a woman in a man's job'.

Ms Webb: My big thing is women and work: our role. I mean I'm
              not an ardent women's libber, but we are restricted and
              looked down on. Like here it's easy to end up doing the
              cleaning up and tea-making without thinking. You have to
              keep fighting it. And purely as the *woman* in this set up,
              and the fact that it's all *girls*, they immediately relate
              mainly to me. I'm the one that's most under pressure,
              and I really identify with your study.

The trainees were all working class young women, about one-third white, one-third Asian and one-third Afro-Caribbean. Around twenty trainees were on the course at any one time, since it operated on a rolling basis. Some trainees (like Wendy) had a long-standing interest in engineering; others (like Bridget) had been unable to find a job, or else they had been expelled from school with no qualifications (like Sue), and had applied to the EITB because the course 'looked interesting and different'.

Just as the technicians' scheme had been careful to develop the young women's confidence in tackling scientific and technical subjects, maths was the sensitive area for the trainee operatives. One careers officer admitted that she rarely mentioned the maths component of the course, because 'so many girls are scared of it, or they think they're hopeless at it' (see Wallsgrave, 1983).

The trainees' reservations disappeared once they began to work on mathematical exercises which were relevant to practical engineering skills in a supportive female environment. The instructors were intrigued by the young women's complex attitude to maths:

Ms Webb: Some of the girls don't know any maths, they can't add up. But you can't diddle them out of money. And they know their rights — like where's the nearest social security office.

Mr Walker: It's the schools, they say they all hate maths and can't tell a metre from a millimetre, but they love the maths lessons here. We can't keep them out!

Many of the trainees had left school branded as academic failures, with several of the young black women labelled as having 'remedial language ability'. Some of these Asian trainees were actually bi- and even tri-lingual in Urdu, Gujarati, Hindi and/or Bengali, as well as English.[11] Supervisors tended to identify 'problem trainees' with reference to their family lives and cultural backgrounds, and their concern was usually focused on young Asian and Afro-Caribbean women (see Chapter 4).

Ms Webb: The problem girls usually have both parents out of work, which is usually the coloured ones. It's more difficult now, there's more genuine unemployment. Before if the father was at home you could say. . . .

Mr Walker: Layabouts. But now these Asian girls *all* say their fathers haven't got a job.

Ms Webb: Or else their mothers have jobs, that's the other problem.

Ms Webb had developed her own job placement system through contacts with local companies (see Chapter 10) rather than leaving young women to rely on Job Centres and the uncertainties of the local job market at the end of the course. She had particular difficulties with the larger companies.

Mr Walker: Placing anyone under 18 can be difficult, especially in big companies.

Ms Webb: They have their own training centres, and when you
ask about taking on someone under 18 apart from
their own trainees, they just don't want to know.

Large companies usually attributed their lack of co-operation to
the strict legislation limiting young people's conditions of employment. Ms Webb and her colleagues were unimpressed by this argument.

Ms Webb: Everyone bends laws, not just in engineering. It's the
non-union places that don't bother and take on under-18s.
There's no unions to get at them to stick to the rules.
People go on about unions, but it's easy to forget how
much work they've done, safeguarding people.

Most of the trainees went into smaller non-unionised firms to
work in 'women's' engineering jobs. Several were employed as electrical and electronic circuit assembly workers, although this had been
the least popular part of the course. This was in direct contradiction
to employers' widely held assumption that women are particularly
suited to such close, fiddly and monotonous work.[12] Pat and Sue
became circuit assembly workers at Trenthams, so whilst their training had been closer to that of the EITB craft technicians, their employment experience had more in common with young women in traditionally female factory jobs (see Chapter 10).

The junior operatives course had not been designed to help young
women move into particularly 'male' engineering jobs, but Ms Webb
felt that women should have equal access to all jobs. Her own experience led her to conclude that men on the shopfloor were the most
overtly opposed to women engineers, whilst management objected
to young people in general.

Ms Webb: I used to work on an all-male management team. They
seem much better about a woman being there — once
you've proved you won't be the little woman. Coming
back here it's like being on the shopfloor again. Those
men are awful, oh engineers are the worst, there's no
place for a woman. You have to *keep* proving you're as
good as them — if not better. We don't have so much

trouble with the employers usually about girls — it's young people they don't want.

In 1979 and 1980 the junior operatives scheme had a long waiting list, partly because of its good job placement record (around 90 per cent) and the lack of academic entry requirements. As youth unemployment levels soared in the early 1980s, the scheme suffered because of its connection with the YOPS programme. Increasing numbers of young people were becoming disillusioned with 'government schemes', and were rejecting the courses outright. Although the junior operatives scheme was funded by the MSC, Ms Webb prided herself on providing something quite different (even superior) to most YOPS schemes. By 1982, she could only watch in despair as her waiting list dwindled along with job opportunities for Birmingham's school leavers.

12

On the edges of the labour market: unemployment and the Youth Opportunities Programme

When I first contacted young women in the months before the general election of May 1979, an unemployment rate of 15 per cent in the West Midlands by 1983 seemed unthinkable. In 1978, the national jobless total had *fallen* by 4 per cent, and in Birmingham by 2.3 per cent.[1] When 1979's school leavers entered the job market, only 5 per cent of Birmingham's workforce were officially unemployed. By October 1980 the figure was 9.8 per cent, rising to 14.8 per cent in August 1981 (342,134 people, of whom 50,000 were school leavers); and reaching 17 per cent (386,666) in September 1982. By early 1983 one in five of Birmingham's population was unemployed, as were almost half of the city's 16- to 18-year-olds.[2]

I was mainly interested in school leavers' experiences in waged work, but the sharp decline in the Birmingham job market from 1980 onwards meant that most of the young women I interviewed were unemployed for between two months and two years. By 1981 and 1982, the situation had deteriorated to such an extent that I could hardly avoid looking at young women's unemployment and the expanding role of the MSC through the Youth Opportunities Programme.

Most of 1979's school leavers avoided the worst effects of the 'recession'. Eleven of the young women found a job soon after leaving school, eight were unemployed for six months or less before starting their first full-time job, and the remaining six were out of work for over six months. Young women in office jobs were more likely to stay in employment than their peers in shop or factory work, since the latter jobs were the first to be hit by the effects of the recession (cf. Friend and Metcalf, 1981).

Young women with full-time jobs were generally sympathetic towards their unemployed peers. Those in factory work attributed their friends' unemployment to the state of the local labour market, and saw clear connections with their own position.

CG: Have any of you been on the dole?
Monica: My mates are mostly on the dole, they've given up. One of them has tried for jobs, but they all want experience and not school leavers. Then when they don't get a job, their parents say it's their fault, and it's not, and they just give up. What's the point? I'll do that when I leave here [Lycetts].

Giving up the soul-destroying and increasingly futile search for jobs was not seen as a mark of laziness or irresponsibility, but as a refusal to accept poorly paid and exploitative 'rubbish jobs'.

CG: Are many of your friends still looking for jobs?
Shelly: All our brother's mates is on the dole, and none of them ever look for a job. They say 'no, I don't want a job, they're all rubbish jobs'. It's the girls as well as the boys.
CG: Why do you think that is?
Shelly: I dunno, it's a struggle too much.

All of the young women felt that older people, and especially parents, had little understanding of contemporary youth unemployment and the state of the local job market.

CG: How do you think you would have felt if you'd been out of work for months after leaving school?
Berni: I dunno.
Mother: She'd probably have got used to it, and I'd have been on the door giving her money. There is lots of jobs for boys and girls, but some of them are very fussy. I mean they just won't take a job just to tide them over for the time till something better turns up.

Many employers shared this view of young people as irresponsible and 'fussy'. Two supervisors at Dalcourts welcomed rising youth unemployment as a potential means of undermining young workers' defiance:[3]

Ms Jenks: The thing they don't realise is there's a lot of people
             out of work and they can't just sit there.
Ms Granby: I almost think it'd be better if they'd been unemployed
             or done another job before coming here. It would give
             them a taste of real life. People at school have been
             lenient with them.

Six young women were unemployed for periods of six months or more during their first two and a half years in the labour market. Sue and Wendy were out of work for seven and ten months respectively before they joined the EITB junior operatives' scheme in July 1980. Ann was unemployed for eighteen months until she found a job in a greengrocer's shop in November 1980. She spent the time doing voluntary work in a local primary school. Pippa was made redundant from her sales assistant's job in a city centre clothes shop in November 1980. She had been working there for one year, and lost her job on the 'last in, first out' principle when the shop reduced their staff, ostensibly as a result of falling sales.

Mandy and Sandra left St Martin's school together hoping to go into hairdressing, but they were both unemployed for long periods, and were still on the dole in 1982. Their experiences demonstrate the potential influence of young women's domestic commitments, and the monotony of life on the margins of the labour market. Mandy and Sandra had hoped to start the same hairdressing course at college in September 1979, but childcare responsibilities prevented Sandra from taking up her place (see Chapter 3). Mandy left college at the end of the first term, unable to afford the travelling costs without a grant, and upset by the 'snooty', middle class students.[4]

Sandra and Mandy eventually found jobs in different hairdressing salons in March 1980, each starting on £22 a week (see Table D). Mandy soon moved to a better job on £24 a week which offered day release training and bigger tips. Both young women contracted dermatitis (see Chapter 3) and, combined with the long hours, low wages and inadequate on-the-job training, this led Sandra and Mandy to leave their jobs in June and August 1980 respectively.[5] They were both sacked following arguments with their managers, and they refused to return to hairdressing, looking for jobs in shops and factories with little success.

Sandra never found another job, and she gradually became more isolated and depressed. The period of enforced childcare after she left school, the breakdown of contacts with ex-schoolfriends as they began to go out with boys, and living some miles away from most of her friends all increased Sandra's isolation. Her only regular outings were to the dole office and the Job Centre.

Sandra felt unfairly pressurised to get a job by her mother: as with most of her peers, Sandra's relationship with her father was somewhat distant.

CG: What about your parents?
Sandra: Well my dad, I can't really talk to, it's my mum, she's always
         at me to get a job. She doesn't understand that there are
         none, and it drives me mad.

Like many young women from Irish Catholic families, Sandra felt more at ease with her relatives in the South of Ireland. She spent two months in the summer of 1980 with her Irish relatives searching in vain for a job. A year later Sandra left home to share a rented flat with two girlfriends, desperate to leave her parents, but she was soon forced to return due to lack of money.

Sandra attributed her position to the declining youth labour market, which has been caused by economic and political forces outside her control. As the months dragged on, Sandra felt increasingly rejected by society, with no recognised role or value, and more personally responsible for her failure to get a job.[6] Long-term unemployment had positioned her in a social and psychological limbo.

Mandy's experiences on the more exploitative margins of the labour market had transformed her attitude to unemployment. When she started college, Mandy was extremely critical of her unemployed peers:

CG: Have most of your friends found jobs?
Mandy: If they wanted to, yeh, but a lot of them just can't be
         bothered. They hang around at home, walk about the streets.
         The girls are the worst, they're hoping the job will come to
         them. They just want a cushy job, like at school they picked
         the things where they do the least work.

After leaving college and the low-paid drudgery of hairdressing jobs, Mandy found work packing silverware at £32 a week at a small firm in the jewelry quarter where her sister had worked. This lasted from February to October 1981, when Mandy was sacked for demanding the rise to which she was entitled (and which the manager had promised her) on reaching 18, and for threatening to call in a union. Her disdain for unemployed youth had turned to anger at the lack of jobs available for young women.

CG: Are there many jobs around?
Mandy: There are always building site jobs, dirty work. Actually
         (laugh) I did go for one, but this bloke was really cheeky.
         He said he wouldn't take women. I said 'well what about
         the Sex Discrimination Act?' So he got nasty and said
         'OK, you can have a job if you'll strip to the waist'. Well
         I never got it. There are always more jobs for men though.

Mandy never found another job, and she survived by doing hairdressing from home.[7] She watched as employers benefited from rising youth unemployment, and saw the situation moving out of even the government's control.

Mandy: What these small firms are doing is making money exploit-
         ing young people, taking them on for a month or so trial,
         and then finishing them. One asked for maths and English
         CSE or 'O' levels for packing! I dunno how the government
         think they're gonna get things back. The way things are
         going it'll be World War Three next. I get so mad about it.
         Mind you I don't think these jobs marches are a lot of use,
         no one notices, they don't get the publicity.

Mandy was equally infuriated by older people's patronising and misguided assumptions about what it was like to be young and unemployed in the early 1980s.

Mandy: I got a slip from the dole office for £3.75p to give my parents
         for keep. If I gave mum that she'd laugh in my face, it wouldn't
         feed me for two days. It annoys me when people don't rea-
         lise that you have no money, can't afford your bus fare like.
         Older people just don't understand what it's like now. And
         they expect girls to get married 'cos we've nothing else to do.

Unemployed young women were often expected to get married and/or pregnant in a search for 'some identity' (see Cohen, 1982; Davies, 1983). Mandy got engaged in February 1982, and married in August of that year. This was not a search for 'identity', nor even financial security. Mandy's fiancé was made redundant from BL's Longbridge plant two months after their marriage and she could not leave home because they had so little money. Marriage was seen as an inevitable fact of social life rather than a means of avoiding the worst miseries of unemployment (cf. Leonard, 1980; and Chapter 4).

Unemployed young women like Mandy and Sandra felt trapped in an impossible situation: the choice between the dole and 'rubbish jobs' was no choice at all. They were receiving around £16 a week 'dole money', and paying half of this to their mothers as 'keep', like most of their peers in waged work. Many school students had dreaded the prospect of 'waiting about on the dole' (see Chapters 7 and 10), and some unemployed school leavers were reluctant to claim state benefits. Such sensitivity to the stigma associated with being unemployed was soon overcome by young women's parents. They argued that 'the dole' was not a charity handout, but part of young women's rights as prospective employees and the children of employees (cf. Presdee, 1982).

YOP schemes were not always seen as a solution to unemployment. Sandra was offered a place on a Work Experience (WEEP) scheme as a sewing machinist, but she left when she found that she was the only white trainee on the scheme. Like most white people, Sandra only felt comfortable when whites were the 'ethnic majority'. Mandy rejected such schemes on economic grounds.

Mandy: I mean young people have got no choice now, you have to stay in work but the pay is terrible. These government schemes are the worst. They should pay a real wage. I mean working a forty-hour week for £23.50! Plus bus fares and keep! The dole isn't much less.

Some young women applied to YOP schemes rather than suffer the monotony of life on the dole.

CG: So what made you take the YOP place?
Marion: I was getting so bored with not finding a job, but not with being at home. It was doing the housework that was sending me round the bend (laugh).

They also hoped to get some training and work experience which would have some value in the 'real' job market. Five young women were WEEP trainees: Marion was an office junior at the city council; Liz and Jan were sewing machinists at Dalcourts; as were Babs and Monica at Lycetts (see Chapter 10). Sue and Wendy were trainees on the EITB junior operatives scheme (see Chapter 11).

These young women were all fortunate enough to be taken on as full-time employees after their time as WEEP trainees, and Sue and Wendy both found jobs with Ms Webb's help at the end of the EITB course. The MSC was notoriously secretive about the percentage of YOPS trainees who were kept on as permanent employees, but the figure for 1980 and 1981 was estimated to be around 60 per cent (A. Webb, 1980; Education Group, 1981). Dalcourts and Lycetts were using YOPS as a form of government-subsidised training, and they kept most of their WEEP trainees on permanently. Townsend Graphics usually had one or two WEEP trainees at any one time, but they did the most menial unskilled jobs, and were only taken on to the firm's payroll if there was a suitable vacancy.[8]

The Youth Opportunities Programme was introduced as a temporary measure by Jim Callaghan's Labour government in 1978, and launched under the aegis of the Manpower Services Commission, which had been created in 1964 to review the chaotic state of industrial training provision (Holland Report, 1977). Officially, YOPS was intended to improve further education and training for 'non-academic' school leavers at a time when there was a distinct lack of such provision and a decline in the youth labour market. YOPS was also a response to employers' complaints that post-war education was producing school leavers with 'unsuitable' attitudes to waged work. YOPS therefore placed equal emphasis on basic skills training, and on developing the 'generic' skills required of an adaptable, acquiescent and employable workforce.[9]

YOPS was launched some three years after the Equal Pay and Sex Discrimination Acts became law, and only two years after the 1976 Race Relations Act. The programme provided the Labour government with an ideal chance to put their equal opportunities legislation into practice, but this policy commitment never materialised (C. Griffin, 1983).

Although equal numbers of young women and men have moved through YOPS, traditional gender-based divisions of labour have continued to operate in most schemes (Brelsford et al., 1983). Whilst equal numbers of young women and men have gone into WEEP placements, proportionally more young women have moved through Community Service schemes, and far more young men through project-based and training schemes with a greater skill component (Bedeman and Courtney, 1983). Young black people have been disproportionately concentrated in college and workshop-based schemes which were less likely than WEEP placements to lead to permanent jobs (Smith, 1981; Cross et al., 1983).

Birmingham's MSC provision for unemployed youth followed this national pattern (Coffin, 1981). Only 10 per cent of those attending the city's Job Preparation Units were female, and traditional gender divisions operated, with young men involved in a wider range of activities than their female peers. On the twenty-one project-based schemes, six had no female trainees and seven had a tiny minority of young women. Only the EITB operatives scheme and the Smallheath JPU catered specifically for young women. In the voluntary sector, the four main community-based schemes all had traditional gender-based divisions of labour, and there was minimal provision for young women in Birmingham's Youth Service (see Thorpe, 1982).

Attempts at breaking down gender-based divisions in MSC schemes have so far been confined to the publications of working groups and research studies sponsored by the Special Programmes Division (e.g. 'Opportunities for Girls and Women', 1979; Brelsford et al., 1983). Putting these recommendations into practice was left to the discretion of individual project supervisors and MSC area development officers. As Sally Thorpe concluded in her study of local provision for unemployed young women: 'from the Birmingham example there is no indication that MSC has acted on it's own findings (let alone any others), and young women will continue to fare badly under YOP until it does so' (1982, p. 100).

Most YOPS supervisors were unaware that the MSC had an official equal opportunities policy (see Hilgendorf and Welchman, 1983). Only two of the supervisors I interviewed were at all concerned to implement this policy. One was Ms Webb (and her co-workers) on the EITB scheme, and the other was Ms Crawley, a JPU supervisor who liaised with employers, careers advisers and other YOPS schemes in the course of her work. Like Ms Webb, she saw women-only schemes as the best possible means of breaking down traditional gender-based divisions of labour, and supporting young women.

CG:	How have you found the other schemes?
Ms Crawley:	Oh, the YOP supervisors can be terrible. They're sponsored from industry and when the girls come in they set them to make the tea. They say 'why bother to train girls, what's the point?' With [male] supervisors like that, and the lads as well, it's vital to have all girls' schemes otherwise they won't have a go at woodwork and metalwork, not with boys there taking the mickey all the time. The division between girls and boys is *huge* though, we've had a couple of boys go into catering but not *one* girl has gone the other way. When you try to talk to supervisors about training girls in engineering or suchlike, they say 'it'll be taking jobs off the boys and they must come first'.

Some employers treated WEEP placements like normal vacancies, demanding academic qualifications and rejecting 'unsuitable' applications in direct contravention of MSC policy (see Hilgendorf and Welchman, 1983). Such practices only reinforced traditional divisions of labour.

CG:	So what type of schemes do young women go into?
Ms Crawley:	With Work Experience (WEEP) it's mainly sewing, clerical and catering. The type of factory work which girls do is not usually suitable for YOPS, because you do need a training component, even if they do end up making the tea. Girls' factory work is often unskilled. Some of these schemes are a bit of a fiddle to be honest, just six months training paid for by the government. They aren't all like that, the MSC do have some sort of control, and it's a bit loose, and it's open to abuse.

As youth unemployment levels rose from 1980 onwards, YOPS schemes changed from being treated as last resorts to being rejected altogether as young people saw through the hollow promise of permanent employment and valuable training (cf. Chapter 11). By 1982, unemployed young women and those involved in YOPS were viewing the future with considerable pessimism. Uncertainty about the proposed replacement for YOPS did little to allay these fears.

Ms Crawley: I can't see a way out, it's so huge. In the future things won't be the same again. *If* employment picks up then they'll have more money again, and first thing that companies will do is buy new technology in offices and shops. They just won't need young people any more. Particularly girls. I can't see that this new [Youth Training] scheme will be any different.

Conclusion: 1984 and beyond

Much has changed since these young women left school in 1979, and most of these changes have been for the worse. The election of Margaret Thatcher's Tory government in May of that year heralded a radical shift to the right in Britain's political climate, and the dawn of a new hard-line monetarist economic regime. The sharp rise in unemployment rates continued well into the 1980s, affecting young people, women, black people and those with few recognised skills or qualifications to a disproportionate extent (Friend and Metcalf, 1981).

The late 1970s and early 1980s saw the gradual decline of Britain's manufacturing industries, and a corresponding drop in the number of manual jobs available. There was a simultaneous expansion of the service industries and the non-manual employment sector, but this was not sufficient to compensate for the collapse of Britain's manufacturing base (A. Webb, 1980; Counter Information Services, 1981b). The introduction of new automated work processes in offices, shops and factories led to considerable job losses in most sectors of the labour market (Finn, 1981; Counter Information Services, 1979). This period also saw a radical restructuring of training provision for young people, and the rapid expansion of the MSC (Green, 1983; Education Group, 1981).

How have these changes affected the position of young working class women in the context of the main issues raised in this book? The most obvious change has been the phenomenal rise in youth unemployment, which was already having an impact on young women's employment prospects in 1980 (see Jones, 1983). Having a full-time job enhanced their position in the family, and this usually lessened the extent of their domestic commitments. Long-term unemployment tended to draw young women into the home, bringing added burdens of housework and childcare.

The part-time child labour market and informal job-finding networks played an important role in young women's entry to full-time employment. These were most prevalent in factory work and small family firms, and they operated to maintain traditional divisions of labour along race, age, class and gender lines. The use of such informal job-finding methods is unlikely to diminish as small companies struggle to survive and the hidden economy expands (Friend and Metcalf, 1981).

Sharp distinctions between women's and men's jobs pervaded Birmingham's labour market in 1979. Young women's position in full-time employment was expected to be temporary, in line with their primary role in the home as future wives and mothers. Their male peers were assumed to have a permanent place in the job market, and as the recession deepened, employers tended to guard any jobs 'for the boys'. Yet women were not thrown out of the labour market altogether as unemployment levels rose. As Friend and Metcalf have pointed out: 'where women can be exploited more effectively than men, they continue to be recruited — where they are in competition with men, they are likely to be expelled from the workforce' (1981, p. 63).

Racism was an equally pervasive influence on young women's lives. The personal racism of young white women and men was overlaid by the racist assumptions of white teachers, employers and careers advisers. Black cultures and family forms were seen as deviant and abnormal, and identified as one of the main causes of young black women's problems in school and the job market. White teachers and employers adopted a 'divide and rule' tactic which played young Asian women off against their Afro-Caribbean peers. The prevalence of such interpersonal racism and its central place in the leisure activities of white youth became all the more alarming as Britain moved into a new era of institutional racism with the implementation of harsher immigration legislation and increased police powers (Race and Politics Group, 1982; *Outwrite*, no. 19, November 1983; Sivanandan, 1976; *Race and Class*, 1981, nos. 2/3).

The YOPS programme had become an integral part of the youth labour market by 1980. The young women I spoke to had relatively positive experiences with YOPS, but employers were using the scheme as a form of subsidised training, and a means of easing their recruitment costs. By the launch of YTS in 1983, the traditional youth labour market had all but disappeared. Young people were soon voting with their feet, and rejecting YTS schemes in large numbers, despite the possibility of having their social security benefits cut.[1]

This book is full of examples where existing theories have been of limited value for understanding young women's experiences. These theories are not rendered completely invalid, it simply means that they cannot be applied to *all* young people in an indiscriminate manner. As Susan Griffin has pointed out: 'So little of real female experience has ever been expressed. We have no familiar images with which to speak of our lives or our identities, or through which to voice our feelings. . . . There is no educated nor any conventional way to describe real female experience' (1981, p. 245). It is difficult to articulate or theorise women's experiences when the words, the ideas and the research tradition are either completely absent, or only present in developing and fragmented forms (cf. Spender, 1980).

I have argued that research on youth cultures needs to shift away from the 'gang of lads' model, which is not appropriate for young women's smaller friendship groups (see Chapter 1). I have also identified particular female cultures in schools, leisure time and in specific workplaces, which were highly valued by the young women, who often felt ill at ease in predominantly male cultures or situations (see Chapters 5 and 11).

Studies of the so-called 'transition from school to work' have tended to oversimplify the whole process of getting a job, underestimating the importance of the child labour market, informal job-finding networks and young women's domestic commitments. Apart from moving from school into the full-time labour market, young working class women were also managing social and economic pressures to get a man. I have understood this in terms of their simultaneous positions in the sexual, marriage and labour markets (cf. Griffin, 1982b).

The sexual marketplace values women according to their perceived attractiveness to men, with youth at a particular premium. In leisure time this could be measured by young women's ability to get a boyfriend (or boyfriends). In the workplace it might refer to their fulfilment of the non-technical side of office or shop jobs: developing a particular mode of sexy service with a smile (see Chapter 9).

The marriage market covers pressures to get and *keep* a man, with the role of devoted wife and mother presented as women's primary function and biologically ordained destiny. Several studies have referred to marriage and motherhood as a sort of alternative 'career' for women, running parallel to the traditional waged labour market (e.g. Hamilton, 1981; Pollert, 1981). This was certainly true in a structural sense, and many employers and teachers expected young working class women to end up as 'supermums', but young women themselves did not always see their futures in these terms (see Chapter 4).

Marriage and motherhood seemed distant if inevitable events: most young women were more concerned with managing simultaneous pressures to get a job and a boyfriend. The latter process tied them into the marriage market, laying the foundations for their probable future isolation in the home as wives and mothers (cf. Hobson, 1978b). Our ideas on the 'transition from school to work' need to expand to include young people's relative positions in the sexual and marriage markets.[2]

The move from school to waged work involved a considerable shift in social status:

CG: What do you think is the main difference between school
         and work? Are there any?
Elaine: Oh yeh, definitely. I think work brings you to your senses.
         If you're not an adult, you're suddenly an adult when you go
         to work. At school you're just classed as a schoolchild, a
         little schoolgirl with pigtails (laugh).

An increasing proportion of young working class women (and men) are leaving school with little chance of finding a full-time job, and few alternatives apart from further education or a place on an MSC scheme. Most are soon caught in the social and psychological limbo of long-term unemployment. Despite my various criticisms of the transition from school to work model, it can still be relevant to a situation of high youth unemployment, providing that we avoid jumping to ill-informed conclusions about the experience of being on the dole in the 1980s.

Research on waged work and unemployment has tended to focus on men's experiences, so relatively little is known about the implications of unemployment for women. There is a widespread assumption that young working class women will deal with the prospect of long-term unemployment by turning to marriage or motherhood (cf. Chapter 12).

Ms Crawley: I sometimes feel that girls are trapped, especially the ones that have been out of work for a while. They get bored and end up pregnant, think they might as well get married, it'll happen some day. Then they really are trapped, there is just no future, no hope. Girls are trapped between work, unemployment, and the home, going from one to the other.

There is a real sense in which young women *are* trapped between the demands of the sexual, marriage and labour markets, but they do not *all* rush to 'get a man' in the absence of 'proper jobs' (cf. Breakwell, 1983; Presdee, 1982). Unemployed young women were more likely to stay at home with increased domestic commitments and no money. Pressures to get a man and a job operated at the same time, but they were not directly interchangeable: young women did not see marriage or motherhood as a substitute for full-time employment.

Pressures to get a man influenced young women's entry to the job market: office work was seen as a particularly 'good job for a girl' because it was expected to offer young working class women the chance to meet eligible men in high status white collar jobs (see Chapter 7). Conversely, pressures to get a job affected the process of getting a man: the full-time wage could give young women access to more expensive, exciting leisure activities and potential boyfriends (see Chapter 5).

Young women's experiences in particular jobs did not always conform to their expectations. Office work rarely matched up to the glamorous image of clean, interesting work which offered reasonable training and promotion prospects. 'Women's' factory jobs often entailed doing monotonous tasks in unpleasant working conditions, although some did offer the chance to learn a recognised skill (e.g. sewing). The least popular aspect of factory jobs was the pressures of meeting production deadlines, and the strict disciplines of working on piecework rates (see Chapter 10).

Office and factory work were associated with very different forms of feminine appearance and behaviour, which were race, age, class *and* gender-specific. The academic research tradition has tended to identify capitalism *or* patriarchy as the overriding social structure determining young women's position, with class *or* gender as the main influence on their lives.[3] This sets up a sort of hierarchy of oppressions, in which one factor has overwhelming importance. The experiences of the young women I spoke to suggest that the picture is far more complex. Gender was an ever-present influence which could not be ignored, but it interacted with social relations based on age, race and class in complicated and not always consistent ways. I have chosen to present these interactions in their full complexity, rather than focusing on a relatively narrow band of young women's experiences. So this book does not end with any clear or simple message about the links between gender, race and class, since there are no easy points to be made.

Typical Girls? demonstrates the importance of social and economic pressures to get a man for all young women, and young white working class women in particular. These pressures define heterosexuality as *the* normal form of sexuality for women and men. They operate at the ideological level through representations of love and romance (cf. McRobbie, 1978a), and at the material level through male demands for sex, and sexual harassment at work and in young women's leisure time. What has been termed the 'institution of compulsory heterosexuality' played an important part in shaping the mixture of excitement and anxiety with which young women viewed the prospect of getting a boyfriend (cf. Rich, 1981; Chapter 5).

This analysis has clear implications for the implementation of equal opportunities policies in education, training and the labour market, and for practical work with girls and young women in schools and youth clubs. There is a widespread assumption that now Britain has legislation against race and sex discrimination, the golden age of equality has arrived. Young women's experiences in traditionally female and male jobs demonstrated that this was far from the case.[4]

Equal opportunities policies have resulted in token female successes. In 'male' jobs like engineering, token women either remained invisible, passed as 'one of the lads', or were treated (and discounted) as 'special cases' (see Newton, 1983). The overwhelmingly masculine atmosphere of the shopfloor continued almost unchanged, since young women were incorporated into 'women's jobs' within engineering (see Chapter 11). The equal opportunities approach has failed to tackle some of the main barriers facing women in the labour market. It has had little impact on those occupations in which an unbroken pattern of full-time employment is required to gain promotion into the higher status and better-paid jobs (see Chapter 9; Barker and Allen, 1976).

Positive action programmes stand a better chance of improving women's position in the job market (Newton, 1983). The women-only EITB schemes were based on this principle; but their effectiveness was limited because they had to place one or two token women in engineering firms for work experience. The only example of positive change occurred at the launch of the EITB girls' technician scheme in the UM craft training centre, when there were enough female trainees to produce a sense of collective unity and confidence which undermined the predominantly male culture of the training centre (see Chapter 11).

Young women recognised the drawbacks of equal opportunities policies and the problems involved in being the token woman in a 'man's job'. Many preferred the support and 'laughs' of working with other young women in traditionally female jobs. This was not a mark of their conservative views, but a pragmatic decision made in a situation of limited available options: an affirmation of the value of female friendship groups.

CG: Do you think there is any difference between women's and men's jobs?
Tracey: Well, I think girls are more close, they stick together and talk more easily to each other. But blokes all like to show off in front of their mates, they don't like to look sissy. I wouldn't like being a fella (laugh), I like being a girl, I'm glad I'm a girl.

In this context, teachers and careers advisers who are concerned to develop anti-sexist practices would be unwise to try and force young women into non-traditional jobs. A more appropriate strategy would aim to develop students' understanding of *why* their choices are so limited (see McCabe, 1981). Attempts at breaking down assumptions about 'suitable' women's and men's work would be better directed at other teachers and careers advisers, as well as employers and YTS supervisors.

This analysis also demonstrates the particular value of single sex provision and women-only groups in youth work, education and training initiatives (cf. Thorpe, 1982). Such groups have the potential to strengthen female friendship groups and undermine pressures to get a boyfriend. Young women had a range of strategies for resisting these pressures; they had various ways of dealing with potentially 'troublesome' men in their leisure time, and defending female friendship groups against the dreaded 'deffing out' process (see Chapter 5).

Jeanette: We've known each other for years and we decided once
we left school we don't want to split. So we've kept in
touch, there's a group of us. We go out together, or sit in
here listening to records and drinking. We go to this private
social club mostly, it's local, they all know us, it's good.
We know two blokes there, and they buy us drinks, we buy
them drinks. They treat us like equals, it's different to
usual, we're friends.

Cathy: Yeh, we take blokes for a ride at discos though (laugh).
We're awful. We kid them on, last time we pretended we
was French, or Swedish was it? I got that from my sister.
You put on these accents, so you make out you don't
understand when they try something on. Then when they
ask what you want to drink, it's 'gin and tonic' quick as
a flash in a Brummy accent (laugh). . . . When you go
down some roads, men stop you and ask you out, then
ask you how much!

Jeanette: Yeh, and if you say you're a police cadet, then flash out
your travel-card, that soon gets rid of them (laugh).

Cathy: She's my protection, she's brawn, I'm brains. They don't
believe me when I say I'm a police cadet, I'm too small
(laugh).

Another strategy was designed to prevent one boyfriend from
totally dominating young women's lives. 'Two-timing', or going out
with two (or more) boyfriends at a time, was exciting, and it gave
young women the illusion of controlling young men's lives for a
change.

Tracey: Tim comes in from college at 8.00 pm, saying 'make me
something to eat?' I say 'get lost' (laugh). He's the only
person I know round here, but I'm seeing him less now,
'cos of his job, I don't mind, I'm seeing this other bloke
from work, but don't tell Tim (laugh).

Young women's resistances did not follow the white working class
male pattern of verbal and physical aggression (e.g. Robbins and Cohen,
1978; Corrigan, 1979). They had their own more subtle, but none
the less effective methods of managing and undermining pressures
to get a man and a 'good job for a girl'. As the recession deepened

and youth unemployment levels rose, young working class women developed their own analyses of the political situation which had little in common with the dominant image of silly and reactionary 'typical girls' (e.g. Hoggart, 1957).

Mandy: Now these Tories, they're terrible. They take from the poor and give to the rich. They make us working people spend money on the most expensive things, like fags, booze and petrol. We need a *woman's* revolution I think, to make them *all* see some sense.

Tables

TABLE A: Domestic responsibilities: who does the work?

| No. (%) of those with domestic responsibilities | Young women interviewed | | | | |
| | Fifth form students | | | Sixth form students | Total |
	White	Asian	Afro-Caribbean		
Self	24 (51.1)	2	14 (66.7)	7 (20.6)	47 (45.2)
Mother	39 (83)	2	12 (57)	24 (70.6)	77 (74)
Sister(s)	6 (12.8)	—	11 (52.1)	3 (8.8)	20 (19.2)
Father	2 (4.3)	—	2 (9.5)	4 (1.2)	8 (7.7)
Brother(s)	—	—	—	—	—
Grandparent(s)	—	—	1 (4.8)	—	1 (9.6)
Daily	—	—	—	2 (5.9)	2 (1.9)
Left home	2	—	—	—	1 (9.6)
Total of young women	47	2	21	34	104

Note: Table A gives the proportion of young women in each group (white, Asian, etc.) who said that particular people in their households (self, mother, etc.) had some responsibilities for housework or childcare. The percentages for each cell are given in brackets, and these do not add up to 100 per cent for each group because most young women named more than one individual in their household who did domestic work. Only those with regular commitments were

194

included: occasionally doing the washing up was not counted. In Tables A, B and C all the fifth formers were young working class women, and the sixth formers were all white and middle class.

TABLE B: Family structures

No. (%) of young women with	Fifth form students			Sixth form students	
	White	Asian	Afro-Caribbean		Total
Mother:					
in full-time employment	8 (17)	—	12 (57)	11 (32)	31 (29)
in part-time employment	19 (40)	1	5 (24)	9 (26)	34 (32)
unemployed/ at home	19 (40)	3	3 (14)	14 (42)	39 (37)
absent	1 (3)	—	1 (4)	—	2
Total	47 (100)	4	21 (100)	34 (100)	106 (100)
Father:					
in full-time employment	37 (78)	2	7 (33)	30 (88)	76 (72)
in part-time employment	—	—	—	—	—
unemployed/ at home	5 (11)	2	4 (19)	2 (6)	13 (12)
absent	5 (11)	—	10 (48)	2 (6)	17 (16)
Total	47 (100)	4	21 (100)	34 (100)	106 (100)

TABLE C: Young women's part-time employment

No. (%) of young women	Fifth form students			Sixth form students	
	White	Asian	Afro-Caribbean		Total
No part-time job	23 (50)	2	19 (80)	16 (56)	60 (60)
Part-time job(s)	23 (50)	1	2 (20)	13 (44)	39 (40)
Total	46 (100)	3	21 (100)	29 (100)	99 (100)

TABLE D: Young women: qualifications and first jobs

Young women	School	Date of leaving (1979)	Exams passed	First job	Job found via:	Weekly wages (£ gross)	Family background
Elaine	St Cath.	June	4 'O'	Bank	CO	40	Irish RC
Kim	St Cath.	June	4 'O'	Bank	CO	40	Eng. RC
Tracey	St Cath.	June	4 'O'	Trainee Sec.	CT	22.50	Spanish RC
Berni	St Martin's	June	2 CSE	Office	CO	34	Irish RC
Clare	St Martin's	June	3 CSE	Office (VDU)	CO	42	Eng. RC
Jane	St Martin's	June	2 CSE	Office	CO	30	Irish RC
Cathy	Lodgehill	June	3 CSE	Office	Ad	23	Irish Prot.
Jeanette	Lodgehill	June	3 CSE	Office	IC	39	Eng. C of E
Marion	Moorcroft	June	2 CSE	Office (YOPs)	CO	23.50	Eng. C of E
Sandra	St Martin's	June	2 CSE	Hair-dressing	CO	22	Irish RC
Mandy	St Martin's	June	2 CSE	Hair-dressing	Ad	22	Irish RC
Pippa	Moorcroft	June	None	Shop	Ad	32	Eng. C of E
Ann	Tildesley	June	None	Shop	Ad	26	Eng. C of E
Cheryl	St Martin's	June	2 CSE	Shop	Ad	33	Eng. RC
Shelly	St Martin's	May	None	Factory	IC	33	Irish RC
Jenny	St Martin's	June	2 CSE	Factory	Ad	35	Eng. RC
Ann-Marie	St Martin's	May	None	Factory	IC	33	Polish RC
Liz	Tildesley	June	2 CSE	Sewing Mach.	IC	23.50 (YOPs)	Eng. C of E
Monica	Lodgehill	May	None	Sewing	CO	23.50	Eng. C of E
Jan	Lodgehill	June	2 CSE	Sewing	IC	23.50	Eng. C of E
Babs	Shareshill	April	None	Sewing	Ad	23.50	Eng. C of E
Loz	Shareshill	June	4 CSE	Enginrg Apprent.	CO	45	Eng. C of E
Jill	Shareshill	June	2 'O' 2 CSE	EITB CTS	CT	35	Eng. C of E
Sue	Tildesley	April	None	EITB JOTC	Ad	23.50 (YOPs)	Eng. C of E
Wendy	Moorcroft	May	None	EITB JOTB	Ad	23.50 (YOPs)	Irish Prot.

KEY TO TABLE D

Job finding methods
CO   Careers centre or careers officer's advice in school
CT   Careers teacher's advice in school
Ad   Advert in local papers or on local radio
IC   Informal contacts with friends or relatives

First jobs

Sewing mach.	Sewing machinist
Enginrg apprent.	Engineering apprenticeship
EITB	Engineering Industry Training Board
CTS	Craft Training Scheme
JOTC	Junior Operatives Training Centre
YOPs	Youth Opportunities Programme (Work Experience: WEEP)

Family background

RC	Roman Catholic
Prot.	Protestant
C of E	Church of England
Eng.	English

NB. 'Weekly wages (gross)' refers to young women's starting pay.

Shareshill was a large mixed comprehensive with about 1800 students on the edges of the inner city. I did not have time to visit Shareshill before June 1979, when most of the fifth formers had left, so I contacted Babs, Loz and Jill through their workmates. This gave me a more extensive coverage of young women in engineering jobs.

TABLE E: Young people entering employment: distribution by industry (%)

Industries		Male school leavers		Female school leavers	
		Total	Apprentices	Total	Apprentices
I	Agriculture, fishing and forestry	4.3	1.9	0.9	0.8
II	Mining and quarrying	2.0	2.1	0.1	0.1
III	Manufacturing	37.4	41.6	35.1	9.5
IV	Construction	14.9	20.9	1.3	0.7
V	Gas, electricity and water	1.3	2.9	0.5	0.5
VI	Distributive trades	14.7	4.0	26.0	5.4
VII	Other services	22.0	22.8	33.3	82.4

NB. Tables E and F are based on the results of the Careers Service Survey of 1979's school leavers in England and Wales. These figures refer to the first job destinations of 16-year-old school leavers (see Careers Bulletin, Spring 1982).

TABLE F: Young people entering employment: distribution of occupation (%)

Occupational groups		Male school leavers		Female school leavers	
		Total	Apprentices	Total	Apprentices
I	General management	—	—	—	0.1
II	Professional and related management and administration	0.4	0.4	0.7	0.2
III	Management and admin. in health, education and welfare	0.2	0.3	0.9	1.2
IV	Literary, artistic and sports	0.5	0.5	0.5	1.4
V	Management in science	8.8	18.7	0.6	3.1
VI	Management (not general)	0.9	1.2	0.2	0.5
VII	Clerical and related	5.0	1.1	32.9	6.6
VIII	Selling	6.2	0.5	18.2	1.1
IX	Security and protected services	4.0	2.3	0.3	0.8
X	Catering, cleaning, hairdressing and personal services	3.4	1.8	12.5	74.2
XI	Farming, fishing, etc.	4.9	2.3	1.4	1.2
XII	Material processing (not metal)	4.0	2.0	2.8	1.3
XIII	Making and repairing (not metal and electrical)	9.3	11.5	13.1	1.9
XIV	Processing, making and repairing (metal and electrical)	24.3	43.6	1.6	2.9
XV	Painting, repetitive assembly work, inspection packaging, etc.	4.9	3.5	7.7	0.5
XVI	Construction, mining, etc.	8.2	6.1	0.2	0.3
XVII	Transport	6.1	0.8	0.5	—
XVIII	Miscellaneous	8.9	3.6	6.0	2.8
Total number of school leavers		19,286	7,395	13,897	1,018

TABLE G: First destination jobs for Birmingham's 1979 school and college leavers

Occupational	Female school and college leavers		Male school and college leavers	
	Total	Asian and Afro-Caribbean students	Total	Asian and Afro-Caribbean students
01: Working with Metal	257 (14.7%)	20 (14.6%)	1,346 (61.3%)	214 (74.6%)
02: Working with Wood	–	–	40 (1.8%)	11 (3.8%)
03: Working with other materials	158 (9.0%)	33 (24.1%)	86 (3.9%)	7 (2.4%)
04: Building and construction	–	–	214 (9.7%)	14 (4.8%)
06: Farming	10 (0.01%)	–	25 (0.11%)	–
07: Transport and communication	64 (3.7%)	8 (5.8%)	221 (10.1%)	15 (5.2%)
10: Medical and nursing	11 (0.01%)	–	1	–
11: Catering and personal service	162 (9.3%)	8 (5.8%)	40 (1.8%)	18 (6.3%)
12: Sales	470 (26.9%)	25 (18.3%)	152 (6.9%)	7 (2.4%)
15: Admin. and data processing	616 (35.2%)	43 (31.4%)	68 (3.1%)	1 (0.3%)
Total	1,748	137	2,193	287

NB. The above job categories refer to routine work ('X' level), and first destination statistics only give an indication of general tendencies. Categories 09 (Scientific services), and 13 (Arts and media) were excluded since there were only negligible numbers involved. Tables G and J were taken from the annual and triennial statistics gathered by Birmingham Careers Service. These gave the figures for 'ethnic minority' (i.e. Asian and Afro-Caribbean) young people separately, in addition to those for the total population of Birmingham school leavers.

TABLE H: Positions of Birmingham school leavers
(count in September after leaving school)

No. and %age of school students	Sept. 1979		Sept. 1978	
		%		%
Entered employment	7,394	35.0	7,140	34.2
Training courses (+ YOPs)	616	2.9	319	1.5
Stayed at school (SAS)	4,238	20.1	4,557	21.8
Other full-time FE	9,910	9.1	1,911	9.1
Still seeking work	3,493	16.6	4,076	19.5
Awaiting information	3,026	14.3	2,673	1.1
Others: not seeking work, left city	424	2.0	233	1.1
Total in count	21,101		20,909	

TABLE I: Birmingham school leavers, November 1979: first destination statistics

No. and %age of students	Female school students		Male school students	
	Total	Asian and Afro-Caribbean students	Total	Asian and Afro-Caribbean students
Stayed at school/Further education	4,932 47.0%	1,117 58.1%	3,753 33.4%	723 34.5%
Seeking work	2,881 27.4%	634 33.0%	2,996 26.6%	942 44.9%
Found job in first-choice occupn.	2,688 25.6%	172 8.9%	4,493 40.0%	432 20.6%
Total (100%)	10,501	1,923	11,242	2,097

TABLE J: Academic requirements and skill levels in first destination jobs of Birmingham's 1979 school and college leavers

Skill level of first dest. job	Female school and college leavers		Male school and college leavers	
	Total	Asian and Afro-Caribbean students	Total	Asian and Afro-Caribbean students
H/T (4 'O' levels-2 'A' levels)	209 (7.8%)	9 (5.2%)	484 (20.6%)	20 (4.6%)
C (2 Grade 3 CSE's and over)	727 (27.0%)	26 (15.1%)	1,801 (40.2%)	125 (29.0%)
X (routine work: on-job training)	1,753 (65.2%)	137 (79.7%)	2,208 (49.2%)	287 (66.4%)
Total	2,689	172	4,493	432

Notes

Introduction

1 I had three years' funding (plus a six-month extension) with which to look at the move from school to the job market for young women. Paul Willis's research in the same area with the 'lads' had six years' funding.
2 See Amos and Parmar (1981) and Lawrence (1981) for critiques of this tendency in academic research. Throughout the book I have referred to people of Asian and Afro-Caribbean origin or descent as black, because they are affected in similar (though not identical) ways by white racism.
3 C. Griffin, in press, gives a more detailed account of the qualitative research methods used in this study, and their advantages for studies of women's experiences. See also Stanley and Wise (1983).

Chapter 1

1 See Education Group (1981) for an analysis which puts the move towards comprehensive schooling in a wider political context.
2 All of the people and places referred to in this book have been given pseudonyms to maintain the confidentiality of the research.
3 Tildesley school was closed in 1983 as a result of government education cuts and falling rolls.
4 References to 'academic' and 'non-academic' students are in quote marks because they refer to young women's presumed levels of ability according to the academic yardstick of the education system. As Dan Finn has pointed out, 'What these formal examination entries reflect are degrees of performance at school — they say nothing about what particular pupils *can* do, only what he or she *will* do' (1981), Chapter 10, p. 4, original emphases).
5 I interviewed 'non-academic' fifth formers because I wanted to contact those

who would leave school at 16 to look for a job. I had to be careful how this was explained to some teachers in the more academic schools, since they resented the inference that *any* student would leave at 16. I usually asked to see those who were not taking any — or not many — exams.

6 Throughout the book I have used the term 'culture' to refer to 'shared principles of life, characteristics of particular classes, groups or social milieux. Cultures are produced as groups make sense of their social existence in the course of everyday experience' (Education Group, 1981, p. 27; see also Introduction to Hall *et al.*, 1980).

7 Chapter 2 gives a more detailed analysis of the contradictory messages of contemporary education, which urges students to work hard in order to 'get on', but also to be 'realistic' and fit into their appropriate places in the job market.

8 Lynne Davies (1979) had similar problems when she looked at the meanings of conformity and deviance for white working class girls in school. She preferred to identify the 'social scripts' available to the young women, rather than search in vain for pro- and anti-school cultures. See also Thomas, 1980.

9 Chapter 2 examines the view of Asian students' 'over-aspiration' and the 'under-achievement' of their Afro-Caribbean peers in more detail. See also Amos and Parmar (1981) and Stone (1981).

10 Jenny Shaw's work has shown that male students' 'nicking off' tends to be labelled as 'truancy', whilst girls are treated less seriously as 'non-attenders' because of their greater domestic responsibilities (Shaw, 1978).

11 Restrictions on the appearance of female students sometimes applied to teaching staff, as in one London school where women and girls were not allowed to wear trousers (Hemmings, 1982; Parmar and Mirza, 1981).

Chapter 2

1 A Department of Education and Science study of 'Careers Guidance in Secondary Schools' (HMSO, 1973) found that almost one-third of all schools devoted no time specifically to careers education, and that 75 per cent of third formers, 28 per cent of fourth years, and 52 per cent of fifth formers received no careers education whatsoever. The 1973 Act was introduced to enable the careers service to take on this work, but schools were to retain some responsibility for careers education.

2 Ms Morgan welcomed my presence in school as a representative of the 'outside world' for similar reasons.

3 Groups of Afro-Caribbean parents in a number of British cities have organised additional evening and weekend classes for their children, because they are unhappy with the quality of the education provided in State schools (see Stone, 1981).

4 Students wishing to apply to universities must complete an UCCA form giving their preferred choices of courses and colleges. These forms are sent to a central office for England and Wales which sends them on to the appro-

priate university departments, and co-ordinates students' applications and eventual placements.

Chapter 3

1 Women's domestic work has a long history. The English upper and middle classes were using working class women as servants until well into this century. These women received paltry wages and their board and lodging in exchange for working hard, long hours (Johnson, in Clarke *et al.*, 1979). Black women and men from all over the British Empire were also used as slave labour in the homes of the aristocracy and the gentry. See Carby in Race and Politics Group (1982) and Lewenhak (1980) for a broad-ranging historical account of women's work.

2 Due to equipment failure, there is insufficient information on the distribution of domestic work in Asian students' households to permit a detailed analysis. The batteries in my cassette recorder failed during all the interviews with Asian students (this also applies to Table B and C).

3 See Holly (1982) for a feminist critique of this literature, and its implications for motherhood — and fatherhood.

4 This group of young men had asked if they could be interviewed out of curiosity, and because they wanted to avoid part of a careers lesson.

5 See Dyhouse (1977) for an historical account of the inclusion of domestic skills in the school curriculum for girls.

Chapter 4

1 A pamphlet from the Conservative Political Centre in 1981 expressed concern at the decline of 'the family', and called for the introduction of a Minister for the Family. Mrs Thatcher later convened a Family Policy group to present proposals for wide-ranging policy recommendations (see *Outwrite*, March 1983; and the *Guardian*, 26 February 1983).

2 Although I talked to Asian students about their families, equipment failure meant that I was unable to include this information in the quantitative analysis. The figures for black working class students therefore refer primarily to the responses of the young Afro-Caribbean women. The information given in Table B is relatively limited, since the main purpose of the interviews was not to compile detailed quantitative information. I was primarily interested in the way that particular family forms were seen as deviant, and treated as the main cause of students' 'problems' by teachers and other students.

3 Concentrated into Irish Catholic students' nervous or defiant laughter about the size of their families was a whole history of religious and political struggles in the far from 'United Kingdom'. This is still with us in the form of anti-Irish jokes; the attempt to withdraw the right to vote from the half a million people with Irish citizenship living in 'mainland' Britain in 1983; and the British army's occupation of the North of Ireland (cf. Ullah, 1983).

Irish people have played an important part in the development of the English working class, but this has not always been reflected in historical studies (e.g. Thompson, 1963).

4 For more detailed accounts of homelessness amongst young and/or single women, see *Spare Rib*, June 1983; and Austerberg and Watson, 1983.

5 The first annual report of the Birmingham Rape Crisis Centre 1980 found that young women aged 16-25 were the most likely victims of the rapes reported to them. Fifteen per cent were under 15, whilst half of the rapists were relatives or acquaintances of the women concerned.

6 Gayle Rubin (1975) has developed a sophisticated analysis of women's status as objects of exchange in a wide range of cultures and across a diverse group of marital practices. Roberta Hamilton (1978) gives a historical account of the shift from feudalism to capitalism, and from Catholicism to Protestantism as the dominant religions in Britain. This links the development of the contemporary notions of romantic heterosexual love to women's position in marriage and family life.

Chapter 5

1 Thompson (1967), gives a marxist analysis of the development of manufacturing capitalism and its effect on work, leisure and time discipline.

2 Rapoport and Rapoport (1975) do acknowledge the importance of women's domestic work. See Griffin *et al.* (1980) for a feminist critique of mainstream leisure studies.

3 Such friendship groups amonst young white working class women have been termed 'teenybopper fan cultures', and compared to the male-dominated youth cultures of mods, punks or skins (McRobbie and Garber, 1975). Some of the young women I interviewed were fans of Adam Ant and other pop groups, but this 'fandom' was not the main focus of their leisure activities.

4 Some reports have suggested that up to one in ten students at some schools may be sniffing glue on a regular basis (Central News, regional ITV programme, July 1982).

5 *Jackie* and similar magazines aimed at young women sell around one million copies per week in Britain. They reach an estimated three million readers each week. These figures were quoted by John Saunders of IPC (International Publishing Corporation, who publish several of these magazines) on 'The Editors', BBC 2, in August 1981 (see McRobbie, 1978a; and Connell, 1981).

6 Considerable press attention was devoted to the activities of the so-called 'Yorkshire Ripper' (Peter Sutcliffe) throughout the research period (see Merck, 1981; and Hollway, 1981, for analyses of press coverage of Sutcliffe's trial). Young women viewed these events with a mixture of morbid fascination and horror.

> *El:* I dunno why he did it, this Ripper bloke, he had a wife himself, he could have done it to her.

> *Cathy:* But why should he have to do it to *anyone*, his wife or any-
> one? They're all loonies, they ought to be locked up — hanged
> — no they ought to be castrated, (all laugh).

> (ex-Tildesley students, white fifth formers)

7 Doc Marten's are heavy, lace-up boots, part of the skinhead style. APL
  refers to 'Anti-Paki League', NF is the National Front and BM is the British
  Movement. The latter are organised white racist and fascist groups, which
  were expanding their mainly white male working class membership during
  the early 1980s (Billig and Cochrane, 1983).

Chapter 6

1 Oakley (1972) gives basic definitions of sex and gender. Social psychological analyses have usually concentrated on sex-role stereotypes or the
  personality characteristics associated with being female or male (see Bem,
  1974; Spence and Helmreich, 1978). Kessler and McKenna (1978) and
  Breakwell (1979) are interesting exceptions to this tendency. More 'sociological' studies have focused on gender-based divisions of labour (see Barrett,
  1980; Chetwynd and Hartnett, 1978).
2 I have put quote marks around 'women's work' here because this can be
  both a prescriptive and a descriptive term. It is descriptive in that more
  women than men *are* employed in particular jobs (Counter Information
  Services, 1981a). It is prescriptive to the extent that this is taken as evidence of women's supposedly 'natural' abilities, and of what women *should*
  do.
3 Assumptions about 'female' and 'male' school subjects and jobs were specific
  to contemporary Western society. Many women work on building sites in
  India doing poorly paid jobs as brick and rubble carriers, for example,
  but Britain's building trade is an almost exclusively male occupation.
4 Jane's father worked at a local motor manufacturer's as a maintainence
  engineer.

Chapter 7

1 I asked students if they had ever done any part-time jobs, and Dan Finn
  asked how many fifth formers were currently in casual employment, and
  how many had previously had part-time jobs. He found that 64 per cent
  of 'academic' students (taking four or more 'O' levels), and 83 per cent of
  'non-academics' (taking fewer than four 'O' levels) had done casual jobs
  at some stage, with 50 per cent of the 'academic' girls and 72 per cent of
  their 'non-academic' sisters being in part-time jobs when he spoke to them.
  McLennan's study confirmed that at least 50 per cent of young people
  under 16 were in casual employment.
2 The latter case caused some consternation when one young woman dis-

covered that she was making cricket teas for nothing whilst her friend
was paid for doing the same work.

3 Dan Finn found that 'academic' boys earned an average of £1.03 an hour;
'academic' girls 77p an hour; 'non-academic' boys just over 70p, and their
female peers 68p an hour.

4 Government-sponsored youth training schemes (YOPs and YTS) have also
been fulfilling this role (see Chapter 12).

5 Dan Finn has quoted evidence given at a seminar on child employment in
1979 (see Forester, 1979), of a massive increase in child labour in the
Birmingham area. *Registered* child employment rose from 4,683 in 1963
to 7,821 in 1971, and to 13,336 in 1978. These figures are lower than the
true levels, but the increases can only partly be accounted for by improved
registration methods. Another 3,000 children are estimated to be employed
illegally in 'building sites, industrial cleaning, street trading, coal delivery,
fairgrounds and rag trade sweatshops' (Finn, 1981, Chapter 10, p. 20). Dan
Finn suggested that rising unemployment was the main cause of this rise in
child labour (cf. Chapter 12).

6 See chapter 3 for a full account of what those 'other ideas' were: Sandra's
mother wanted her to stay at home and look after her elder sister's daughter.

7 The 5,000 Youth Training Schemes places proposed for the Armed Forces
in 1983 started at 16, and most of these went to young men.

8 This is confirmed by Finn (1981), and by Beynon and Blackburn's (1972)
research with older women workers.

9 This distinction between 'clean' and 'dirty' jobs reflected an extremely
pervasive cultural symbolism, which has played a central role in racist
attitudes and sexual taboos (see Douglas, 1966).

Chapter 8

1 Of the 800,000 young people who reached school leaving age in 1979 in
England and Wales, about 50 per cent continued into full-time education
or training. Just over 45 per cent had entered their first full-time job by
the end of 1979, when the rest were still unemployed. About 40 per cent
of 16-year-old male school leavers found full-time jobs in 1979, compared
to 30 per cent of their female peers (Careers Service Survey, quoted in
Careers Bulletin, spring 1982).

2 I obviously had no control over which jobs (if any) these young women
would be moving into when I asked if they would take part in the research
when they were still at school. The ten workplaces I visited were not intended to be representative of all young women's employment but they do
cover a relatively broad range.

3 Kapp Howe (1977) looks at women's work in the so-called 'pink collar
jobs' in hairdressing, shop work and waitressing in North America. See
Counter Information Services, 1981a, for details of women's employment
in similar jobs in Britain.

4 Every time that I taped an interview I would first ask the respondent's
permission, and explain that the material was completely confidential.

Chapter 9

1   Cathy's job as an office junior at a city centre solicitors' (Courtfields) was advertised as a 'Person Friday': presumably as a token gesture of deference to the Sex Discrimination Act, which would not allow them to advertise for a 'Girl Friday'. I did not have time to visit Cathy at Courtfields: she soon left to start work at Gaskells, where I visited her in July 1980.

2   The promised promotion never materialised. In 1982 Clare was still working in a similar job, although her pay had increased in line with her age, and she had learnt to deal with more specialist orders.

3   The manager of Kim's branch would not allow me to visit her there, because he felt that my presence would disrupt the work of such a busy and crowded bank. His refusal was interesting since Kim was very unhappy with her job at that time.

4   At the city centre headquarters of the bank for whom Kim and Elaine worked, there was a male-only bar which was mainly used by top management. Women had to drink in the smaller 'mixed lounge'. So women were excluded from the informal discussions of the male banking hierarchy (cf. Imray and Middleton, 1982).

5   Hazel Downing argued that the higher status secretarial jobs were differentiated from lower-paid jobs in the typing pool when working class women followed their middle class sisters into the office during the early twentieth century. These higher status jobs developed a semblance of a career structure which seemed to offer a route into sales or management.

6   Employers also tried to protect young women from the swearing found in the 'heaviest' male cultures in engineering (see Chapter 11).

7   After the course finished in May 1980, Tracey did not move straight into such a high status job. She joined UM's pool of temporary relief staff for four months, still on the training allowance. She then found a permanent job as a secretary in a small firm of carburettor manufacturers which had been taken over by UM. The job started at £35 a week, and had been advertised through UM's internal appointments system.

8   The technical part of the course was based on RSA (Royal Society of Arts) standards, which were also used in most school and college courses.

9   Hazel Downing (1981) has suggested that a 'nice' genteel feminine appearance and manner developed as an ideal for female office staff because white middle class women entered office work before their working class sisters.

10   The Alfred Marks Bureau is a staff agency for office workers, and the report is entitled 'Prejudice at work: a report on the personal attitudes of employers to their secretaries' (see Downing, 1981).

11   Braverman's (1974) influential study of deskilling had little to say about women's work in the office. See Downing (1981) for a critical analysis of this research, and Cockburn (1983) for an interesting study of the introduction of word processors into the male-dominated printing industry.

12   When these machines were first introduced, employees could outwit the monitoring system by repeatedly pressing the pause key to increase their rates. Most systems now count the number of pause depressions.

Chapter 10

1   See Pinchbeck (1930), Dayus (1982), and Hall in Whitelegg *et al*. (1982)
    for historical accounts of women's employment which include a detailed
    look at women's work in Birmingham.

2   Birmingham careers service statistics estimate skill level by the academic
    requirements of school leavers' first jobs, which might not always correspond
    exactly with the skill levels involved in those jobs. See Lee *et al*. (1982), who
    suggested that the extent of racial segregation in Birmingham's female youth
    labour market was minimal compared to that found in the male job market,
    which does not match with the careers service figures.

3   Dalcourts recruited between three and six young women twice a year,
    although they were not all YOPs trainees. About ten of their one hundred
    machinists were trainees in 1979. By 1981, this had dropped to six out of
    eighty machinists, since Dalcourts and Lycetts had both cut their recruit-
    ment rates by half.

4   The design staff at Lycetts and Dalcourts were mainly graduates of design
    diploma courses. Most colleges demanded 'O' levels or good CSEs in art,
    English and maths as the basic academic requirements for these courses.
    Dalcourts' design team included four young women who had moved up
    from the assembly lines, after Mr Appleby had recruited them with this
    promotion in mind. They were all white and middle class.

5   These assumptions treated all people of Asian (or Afro-Caribbean) origin
    or descent as one uniform group, but Asian culture is not a monolithic
    social system. Asia covers a vast area, and an enormous range of cultural,
    religious and ethnic groups (see Wilson, 1978; and Race and Politics Group,
    1982, pp. 135-6).

6   Ms Granby was speaking in November 1980, during a prolonged conflict
    between the management and workforce at BL's nearby Longbridge plant
    (see Chapter 11). Mr Stockton was referring to local firms run by Asian
    people, many of whom had come to Birmingham from India, Pakistan and
    other parts of the New Commonwealth in the 1950s and 1960s.

7   Sue had completed the EITB's junior operatives engineering course (see
    Chapter 11), but she was employed in a traditionally female manufacturing
    job, so her work experience has been covered in this chapter.

8   Finch (1983) gives a comprehensive analysis of the vital (though seldom
    paid or acknowledged) role that the wives of professional men play in
    the latter's business lives.

Chapter 11

1   Most copies of the *EOC News*, the Equal Opportunities Commission's
    paper, include several items along these lines (cf. Blackstone and Weinreich-
    Haste, 1980).

2   The Technician Education Council (TEC) certificate replaced the old City
    and Guilds qualifications system (see Bennett and Carter, 1983).

3   Mr Wright visibly warmed towards me when he discovered that my father

was also a mechanical engineer who had started like him, 'at the bottom', working in a foundry.

4   Cynthia Cockburn (1983) has suggested that men object so strongly to women swearing, and to swearing themselves in women's presence, because of the particular significance of swearing in some male cultures. The everyday conversations of white working class men are peppered with swear words which are mainly derogatory references to women or parts of the female body. There is no equivalent vocabulary of negative terms which refer to men and the male body (cf. Spender, 1980).

5   TASS is the Technical Administrative and Supervisory Section of the Amalgamated Union of Engineering Workers: the AUEW. Most of the female employees at UM, as in the rest of the engineering industry, worked as operatives in the lighter semi- and unskilled assembly jobs, or as office staff.

6   In early 1980, BL was in the middle of the most severe crisis since Sir Michael Edwardes became chairman in October 1977. The so-called 'Edwardes Plan' for recovery included a massive reduction in the workforce, and the removal of 'militant shop stewards', who 'riddled the Company' and 'had seized effective control' (Edwardes, 1983). The BL workforce dropped by 18,000 in 1978 and 1979, and a total of 90,000 people had left the payroll by Edwardes's departure in mid-1982. The media gave these disputes considerable attention, showing a definite bias in favour of the management.

7   Women in a wide range of 'men's jobs' and other skilled trades have formed Women and Manual Trades (WAMT). This national network is based around numerous regional groups and projects, and holds an annual national conference.

8   The TSA is the Training Services Agency, which later became the Training Services Division (TSD) of the Manpower Services Commission (MSC).

9   Lin Farley's analysis of sexual harassment in North America argued that 'the function of sexual harassment in non-traditional jobs is to keep women out; its function in the traditional female job sector is to keep women down' (1978, p. 90).

10   Peggy Newton (1980) looked at the first groups of EITB technicians in Birmingham and Croydon, in a study based mainly on quantitative methods. She found that their fathers and boyfriends were fairly supportive, whilst female relatives and friends tended to be jealous or discouraging. The 1979-80 trainees that I interviewed did not all follow this pattern. Some had received most support from their mothers, and others had found fathers or boyfriends unsympathetic.

11   Whilst a French-accented English would be quite acceptable, even glamorous to most white people, the accents of Asian and Afro-Caribbean students tended to be taken as evidence of 'low ability' (Carby, 1980; Groocock, 1983).

12   Large multinational companies with manufacturing bases in parts of the Third World have used these notions to justify their use of local black women as cheap labour in the production of micro-electronic 'chips' (Thitsa, 1981; *Outwrite*, January, 1983).

Chapter 12

1 Department of Employment figures quoted by Birmingham city council's Economy Topic Group. The figure of 2.3 per cent represented a 3.2 per cent *drop* in male unemployment and a 0.5 per cent *rise* in female unemployment.

2 Department of Employment figures. The Counter Information Services pamphlet *Women in the Eighties*, 1981a, gives a clear review of women's position in the job market, including their under-representation in the official unemployment statistics. Thorpe (1982) quotes Birmingham's unemployment figures in detail.

3 Several researchers have suggested that similar reasoning lies behind contemporary government provision for unemployed young people (e.g. Green, 1983; Finn, 1981; Cohen, 1982).

4 The college was about five miles from Mandy's home, in an upmarket residential area, with a predominantly white and middle class student population.

5 Kapp Howe (1977) has analysed the health hazards of similar 'pink collar jobs' in North America. In Britain, trade unions have been slow to recognise and support women workers' complaints about the health hazards of working as hairdressers, cooks, and microprocessor operatives (see *Women's Voice* pamphlet, 1979).

6 Billig and Cochrane, (1983) and Breakwell (1983) have looked at young people's attribution of their own and other people's unemployment to a mixture of personal and external political and economic factors.

7 This is one example of the so-called 'hidden economy', which was forced to expand during this period of crisis in the mainstream economy. There are no exact figures on the extent of the hidden economy, but see Finn (1981) and Friend and Metcalf, (1981) for studies which have looked at this area.

8 During my visits to Townsend Graphics, two young white women were working as WEEP trainees, but they were not taken on full-time at the end of the YOP scheme.

9 See Finn (1981), Education Group (1981) and Green (1983) for more detailed analyses of the role of YOPS and the MSC.

Conclusion

1 One in four of those who took up the first YTS places in the autumn of 1983 dropped out within the first six months. In the first three months of 1984, 4,826 young people had their social security benefits cut by 40 per cent because they left the schemes of their own accord (*Guardian*, 4 April 1984).

2 Young men are also involved in these sexual and marriage markets, but they usually occupy quite different positions to their female peers. Young women tend to be judged according to their relative attractiveness to men: young men are more likely to be making the judgments, and marriage

and parenthood have very different connotations for women and men (cf. Chapter 4; Leonard, 1980).

3 See for example Hartmann (1979), Rowbotham *et al*. (1979) and Delphy (1977). See Race and Politics Group (1982) for analyses which cover the relative influence of race, racism and imperialism.

4 The gap between women's and men's average hourly pay gradually decreased after 1975, with the introduction of equal pay and sex discrimination legislation. After 1977, the gap began to widen once again (Snell, 1979; Coussins, 1980). The government had to widen the scope of Britain's Equal Pay Act from January 1984 to bring it into line with other Common Market countries. A woman can now claim equal pay for work which is of 'equal value' to a man's in terms of the effort, skill and decision-making required (*Guardian*, 7 July 1983).

Bibliography

Amos, V. and Parmar, P. (1981), 'Resistances and responses: the experiences of Black girls in Britain', in A. McRobbie and T. McCabe (eds), *Feminism for Girls: An Adventure Story*, London, Routledge & Kegan Paul.

Ariés, P. (1962), *Centuries of Childhood*, London, Penguin.

Ashton, D. and Field, D. (1976), *Young Workers*, London, Hutchinson.

Ashton, D.N., MacGuire, M. and Garland, V. (1982), 'Youth in the labour market', Department of Employment research paper, no. 34.

Austerberg, H. and Watson, S. (1983), *Women on the Margins: A Study of Single Women's Housing Problems*, London, Housing Research Group, City University.

Backhouse, C. and Cohen, L. (1978), *The Secret Oppression: Sexual Harassment of Working Women*, Toronto, Macmillan.

Barker, D.L. and Allen, S. (1976), *Sexual Division and Society: Process and Change*, London, Tavistock.

Barrett, M. (1980), *Women's Oppression Today: Problems in Marxist Feminist Analysis*, London, New Left Books.

Barrett, M. and McIntosh, M. (1982), *The Anti-Social Family*, London, Verso.

Barry, K. (1979), *Female Sexual Slavery*, Englewood Cliffs, New Jersey, Prentice Hall.

Bedeman, T. and Courtney, G. (1983), '"One in Three": 2nd national survey of people on YOP: summer 1980 – spring 1982', MSC Research and Development series, no. 13.

Bem, S. (1974), 'The measurement of psychological androgyny', *Journal of Consulting and Clinical Psychology*, vol. 42, no. 2, pp. 155-62.

Benett, Y. and Carter, D. (1983), 'Day release for girls: an investigation into why so few girls receive time off work for part-time study', Equal Opportunities Commission pamphlet.

Beynon, H. and Blackburn, R. (1972), *Perceptions of Work: Variations within a Factory*, Cambridge University Press.

Billig, M. and Cochrane, R. (1983), 'Political identification amongst adolescents',

212

paper given at symposium on SSRC 'Young People in Society' initiative, British Psychological Society conference, York.

Binney, V. et al. (1981), Leaving Violent Men: A Study of Refuges and Housing for Battered Women, London, Women's Aid Federation.

Birmingham Rape Crisis Centre (1980), 'First Annual Report', Birmingham RCC.

Blackstone, T. and Weinreich-Haste, H. (1980), 'Why are there so few women scientists and engineers?' New Society, 21 February, p. 383.

Boston, S. (1980), Women Workers and the Trade Union Movement, London, Davis-Poynter.

Brah, A. and Golding, P. (1983), 'The transition from school to work among young Asians in Leicester', Centre for Mass Communication Research, University of Leicester.

Brannen, P. (ed.) (1975), Entering the World of Work: Some Sociological Perspectives, London, HMSO. Department of Employment.

Braverman, H. (1974), Labor and Monopoly Capital: The Degradation of Work in the 20th Century, New York, Monthly Review Press.

Breakwell, G. (1979), 'Women: group and identity', Women's Studies International Quarterly, vol. 2, pp. 9-17.

Breakwell, G. (1983), 'Young people in and out of work', paper given at symposium on SSRC 'Young People in Society' initiative, British Psychological Society conference, York.

Brelsford, P., Smith, G. and Rix, A. (1983), 'Give us a break: opportunities for young women within YOPS/YTS', MSC Research and Development series, no. 11.

Brent Community Health Council (1981), 'Black people and the Health Service', Brent CHC pamphlet.

Brooks, D. and Singh, K. (1978), 'Aspirations versus opportunities: Asian and white school leavers in the Midlands', Walsall Community Relations Council, Leicester Community Relations Council, Commission for Racial Equality.

Bruegel, I. (1979), 'Women as a reserve army of labour', Feminist Review, vol. 3, pp. 12-23.

Bryne, E. (1978), Women in Education, London, Tavistock.

Carby, H. (1980), 'Multicultural fictions', stencilled paper no. 58, Centre for Contemporary Cultural Studies, Birmingham University; also in Screen Education, no. 34.

Carby, H. (1982), 'White women listen: black feminism and the boundaries of sisterhood', in Race and Politics Group (eds), The Empire Strikes Back; Race and Racism in '70s Britain, London, Hutchinson.

Careers Service Survey (1982), 'First employment of young people: 1979', Careers Bulletin, spring, pp. 14-17.

Carpenter, V. (1980), 'Working with girls', Spare Rib, no. 94, pp. 30-4.

Carter, M. (1962), Home, School and Work: A Study of the Education and Employment of Young People in Britain, London, Pergamon Press.

Carter, M.P. (1966), Into Work, London, Penguin.

Casburn, M. (1979), 'Girls will be girls: sexism and juvenile justice in a London borough', London, Women's Research and Resources Centre pamphlet, no. 6.

Chetwynd, J. and Hartnett, O. (eds) (1978), The Sex-Role System: Psychological and Sociological Perspectives, London, Routledge & Kegan Paul.

Clarke, J., Critcher, C. and Johnson, R. (eds) (1979), *Working Class Culture: Studies in History and Theory*, London, Hutchinson.

Clarke, L. (1980), 'The transition from school to work: a critical review of research in the UK', London, HMSO.

Cockburn, C. (1983), *Brothers: Technology and Trade Unionism in Printing*, London, Pluto Press.

Cockram, L. and Beloff, H. (1978), 'Rehearsing to be adults: the personal development and needs of adolescents: a review of research considered in relation to the Youth and Community Service', National Youth Bureau pamphlet, Leicester, NYB.

Coffin, G. (1981), 'Girls and the Youth Opportunities Programme', working paper from Birmingham YOPS evaluation study, for Department of Social and Administrative Studies, Oxford University.

Cohen, P. (1982), 'Schooling for the dole', *New Socialist*, January/February, p. 43.

Commission for Racial Equality (1976), 'Between two cultures: a study of relationships in the Asian community', London, CRE pamphlet.

Commission for Racial Equality (1979), 'Youth in a multi-racial society: the urgent need for new policies: The Fire Next Time', London, CRE.

Connell, M. (1981), 'Reading Romance', unpublished MA thesis, CCCS, Birmingham University.

Conservative Political Centre (1981), 'The future of marriage', London, CPC pamphlet.

Coote, A. and Kellner, P. (1980), 'Hear this brother: women workers and union power', *New Statesman* pamphlet.

Corrigan, P. (1979), *Schooling the Smash Street Kids*, London, Macmillan.

Counter Information Services (1979), 'The new technology', London, CIS report.

Counter Information Services (1981a), 'Women in the eighties', London, CIS report.

Counter Information Services (1981b), 'Anti-Report', London, CIS report.

Coussins, J. (1980), 'Equality for women: have the laws worked?' *Marxism Today*, 6-10 January.

Coussins, J. and Coote, A. (1981), 'The family in the firing line: a discussion document on family policy', London, joint National Council for Civil Liberties/Child Poverty Action Group pamphlet.

Cowie, C. and Lees, S. (1981), 'Slags or drags', *Feminist Review*, no. 9, pp. 17-31.

Coyle, A. (1982), 'Sex and skill in the organisation of the clothing industry', in J. West (ed.), *Work, Women and the Labour Market*, London, Routledge & Kegan Paul.

Cross, M., Edmonds, J. and Sargeant, R. (1983), 'Ethnic miniorities: their experience on YOP', MSC special occasional paper, no. 5.

Dale, R. (1974), *Mixed or Single Sex School: Attainment, Attitudes and Overview*, vol. 3, London, Routledge & Kegan Paul.

Davies, L. (1979), 'Deadlier than the male? Girls' conformity and deviance in school', in L. Barton and R. Meighan (eds), *Schools, Pupils and Deviance*, London, Nafferton Books.

Davies, P. (1983), 'Trapped: unmarried West Indian mothers in Handsworth', Birmingham, Westhill College, Department of Youth and Community Work.

Dayus, K. (1982), *Her People: A Working Class Edwardian Childhood*, London, Virago.

Deem, R. (1978), *Women and Schooling*, London, Routledge & Kegan Paul.

Deem, R. (ed.) (1980), *Schooling for Women's Work*, London, Routledge & Kegan Paul.

Delamont, S. (1980), *Sex roles and the School*, London, Methuen.

Delphy, C. (1977), 'The main enemy: a materialist feminist analysis of women's oppression', London, Women's Research and Resources Centre pamphlet.

Dobash, R. and Dobash, R. (1980), *Violence Against Wives*, London, Open Books Publishing.

Douglas, M. (1966), *Purity and Danger: An Analysis of the Concepts of Pollution and Taboo*, London, Routledge & Kegan Paul.

Downing, H. (1981), 'Developments in secretarial labour: resistance, office automation and the transformation of patriarchal relations of control', unpublished PhD thesis, CCCS, University of Birmingham.

Dworkin, A. (1981), *Pornography: Men Possessing Women*, London, The Women's Press.

Dyhouse, C. (1977), 'Good wives and little mothers; social anxieties and the schoolgirls' curriculum: 1890-1920', *Oxford Review of Education*, vol. III, no. 1, pp. 297-311.

Education Group, CCCS (eds) (1981), *Unpopular Education: Schooling and Social Democracy in England since 1944*, London, Hutchinson.

Edwardes, M. (1983), *Back from the Brink*, London, Collins.

Faderman, L. (1981), *Surpassing the Love of Men: Romantic Friendship and Love Between Women from the Renaissance to the Present*, New York, Junction Books.

Farley, L. (1978), *Sexual Shakedown: The Sexual Harassment of Women on the Job*, New York, McGraw Hill.

Finch, J. (1983), *Married to the Job*, London, Allen & Unwin.

Finn, D. (1981), 'New deals and broken promises', unpublished PhD thesis, CCCS, University of Birmingham.

Fletcher, C. (1962), *Britain in the Sixties: Family and Marriage*, London, Penguin; revised in 1966.

Foner, N. (1978), *Jamaica Farewell: Jamaican Migrants in London*, London, Routledge & Kegan Paul.

Forester, T. (1979), 'Children at Work', *New Society*, 1 January, p. 259.

Foucault, M. (1978), *The History of Sexuality*, vol. 1, London, Penguin.

Friend, A. and Metcalf, A. (1981), *Slump City: The Politics of Mass Unemployment*, London, Pluto Press.

Gardiner, J. (1976), 'The political economy of domestic labour in capitalist society', in D.L. Barker and S. Allen (eds), *Dependence and Exploitation in Work and Marriage*, London, Longman.

Gilroy, P. (1981), 'You can't fool the youths: race and class formation in the 1980s', *Race and Class*, vol. 23, nos 2-3.

Green, A. (1983), 'Education and training: under new masters', in A.-M. Wolpe and J. Donald (eds), *Is there anyone here from Education?*, London, Pluto Press.

Griffin, C. (1982a), 'Cultures of femininity: romance revisited', stencilled paper,

CCCS, Birmingham University.

Griffin, C. (1982b), 'The good, the bad and the ugly: images of young women in the labour market', stencilled paper, CCCS, Birmingham University.

Griffin, C. (1983), 'Women's work, men's work — the great divide: education, training and gender', in A.-M. Wolpe and J. Donald (eds), *Is there anyone here from Education?*, London, Pluto Press.

Griffin, C. (1984), 'Young women and work: the transition from school to the labour market for young working class women', stencilled paper, CCCS, Birmingham University.

Griffin, C. (in press), 'Qualitative methods and cultural analysis', in R. Burgess (ed.), *Field Methods in the Study of Education: Issues and Problems*, London, Falmer Press.

Griffin, C., Hobson, D., McIntosh, S. and McCabe, T. (1980), 'Women and leisure', paper given at Leisure and Social Control conference, CCCS, Birmingham; also in J. Hargreaves (ed.), *Sport, Culture and Ideology*, London, Routledge & Kegan Paul, 1982.

Griffin, S. (1981), *Pornography and Silence: Culture's Revenge Against Nature*, London, The Women's Press.

Groocock, V. (1983), 'Cutting the tongue ties: report on a pluralist approach to language teaching', *Education Guardian*, 15 February.

Guillamin, C. (1972), *L'Idéologie raciste: genèse et langage actuel*, Paris, Mouton.

Hall, S. (1978), 'Race and "moral panics" in post-war Britain', British Sociological Association lecture.

Hall, S., Critcher, C., Jefferson, T., Clarke, J. and Roberts, B. (1978), *Policing the Crisis: Mugging, the State and Law and Order*, London, Macmillan.

Hall, S. and Jefferson, T. (eds) (1975), *Resistance Through Rituals: Youth Subcultures in Post-war Britain*, London, Hutchinson.

Hall, S., Hobson, D., Lowe, A. and Willis, P. (eds) (1980), *Culture, Media, Language*, London, Hutchinson.

Halsey, A., Heath, A.F. and Ridge, J.M. (1980), *Origins and Destinations: Family, Class and Education in Modern Britain*, Oxford, Clarendon Press.

Hamilton, C. (1981), *Marriage as a Trade*, London, The Women's Press (first published 1909).

Hamilton, R. (1978), *The Liberation of Women*, London, Allen & Unwin.

Hanmer, J. (1964), 'Girls and leisure', London Union of Youth Clubs.

Harrison, B. (1978), *Separate Spheres: The Opposition to Women's Suffrage*, London, Croom Helm.

Hartmann, H. (1979), 'The unhappy marriage of marxism and feminism', *Capital and Class*, summer, pp. 1-33.

Hartnett, O. (1979), 'What sex is science?', in O. Hartnett, G. Boden and M. Fuller (eds), *Sex-Role Stereotyping*, London, Tavistock.

Hayes, J. and Hopson, B. (1971), *Careers Guidance*, London, Heinemann.

Hebdige, D. (1979), *Subcultures: The Meaning of Style*, London, Methuen.

Hemmings, S. (1982), *Girls are Powerful: Young Women's Writings from Spare Rib*, London, Sheba Press.

Hilgendorf, L. and Welchman, R. (1983), 'Young women and youth training in the UK', paper given at seminar on 'Young, Female and Unemployed', at the Australian Studies Centre, London.

Hobson, D. (1978a), 'A study of working class women at home: femininity, domesticity and maternity', unpublished PhD thesis, CCCS, Birmingham University.

Hobson, D. (1978b), 'Housewives: isolation as oppression', in Women's Studies Group, CCCS (eds), *Women Take Issue: Aspects of Women's Subordination*, London, Hutchinson.

Hoel, B. (1982), 'Contemporary clothing "sweatshops": Asian female labour and collective organisation', in J. West (ed.), *Work, Women and the Labour Market*, London, Routledge & Kegan Paul.

Hoggart, R. (1957), *The Uses of Literacy*, London, Chatto & Windus.

Holland Report (1977), 'Young people and work', Manpower Services Commission, London.

Hollway, W. (1981), '"I just wanted to kill a woman": Why? The Ripper and male sexuality', *Feminist Review*, vol. 9, pp. 33-40.

Holly, L. (1982), 'A new image for fathers — or new gloss on the old man?', *Spare Rib*, no. 122, pp. 52-3.

Humphries, J. (1977), 'Class struggle and the persistence of the working class family', *Cambridge Journal of Economics*, September.

Imray, L. and Middleton, A. (1982), 'Public and private: marking the boundaries', paper given at British Sociological Society conference.

Institute of Race Relations (1982), 'Roots of racism', and 'Patterns of racism', London, IRR pamphlets.

Jamdagni, L. (1981), 'Hamari rangily zindagi (Our colourful lives)', research report, Leicester, National Association of Youth Clubs.

Jones, P. (1983), 'Effects of rising unemployment on school leavers', *Employment Gazette*, January, pp. 13-16.

Kapp Howe, L. (1977), *Pink Collar Workers: Inside the World of Women's Work*, New York, Avon Books.

Kelly, A. (1978), *Girls and Science: An International Study of Sex Differences in School Science Achievement*, Stockholm, Almqvist & Wiksell.

Kessler, S. and McKenna, W. (1978), *Gender: An Ethnomethodological Approach*, New York, Wiley.

Khan, V. (1976), 'Purdah in the British situation', in D.L. Barker and S. Allen (eds), *Dependence and Exploitation in Work and Marriage*, London, Longman.

Knasel, E.G., Watts, A.G. and Kidd, J. (1982), 'Guidance and support in YOP schemes: implications for the Careers Service', *Careers Bulletin*, spring, pp. 2-7.

Lavigneur, J. (1980), 'Coeducation and the tradition of separate needs', in D. Spender and E. Sarah (eds), *Learning to Lose: Sexism in Education*, London, The Women's Press.

Lawrence, E. (1981), 'Common sense, racism and the sociology of race relations', stencilled paper no. 66, CCCS, Birmingham University.

Lee, G., Sykes, P. and Wrench, J. (1982), 'Jobs for white girls; jobs for black girls?', paper presented at British Sociological Association conference.

Leonard, D. (1980), *Sex and Generation: A Study of Courtship and Weddings*, London, Tavistock.

Lewenhak, S. (1980), *Women and Work*, London, Fontana.

McCabe, T. (1981), 'Schools and careers: for girls who *do* want to wear the trousers', in A. McRobbie and T. McCabe (eds), *Feminism for Girls: An*

Adventure Story, London, Routledge & Kegan Paul.

MacKinnon, C. (1979), *Sexual Harassment of Working Women*, New Haven, Yale University Press.

McLennan, E. (1980), 'Working children', London, Low Pay Unit pamphlet.

McNally, F. (1979), *Women for Hire: A Study of the Female Office Worker*, London, Macmillan.

McRobbie, A. (1978a), '*Jackie*: an ideology of adolescent femininity', stencilled paper, CCCS, Birmingham University.

McRobbie, A. (1978b), 'Working class girls and the culture of femininity', in Women's Studies Group, CCCS (eds), *Women Take Issue: Aspects of Women's Subordination*, London, Hutchinson.

McRobbie, A. (1980), 'Settling accounts with subcultures: a feminist critique', *Screen Education*, vol. 34, pp. 37-49.

McRobbie, A. (1982), 'The politics of feminist research: between talk, text and action', *Feminist Review*, no. 12, pp. 46-57.

McRobbie, A. and Garber, J. (1975), 'Girls and subcultures: an exploration', in S. Hall and T. Jefferson (eds), *Resistance Through Rituals: Youth Subcultures in Post-war Britain*, London, Hutchinson.

Maizels, J. (1970), *Adolescent Needs and the Transition from School to Work*, Athlone Press.

Malcolm, P. (1980), 'The anatomy of youth unemployment', *Careers Bulletin*, summer.

Manpower Services Commission, Special Programmes Division (1979), 'Opportunities for girls and women in the MSC Special Programmes for the unemployed', MSC SPD working party report.

Marks, P. (1976), 'Femininity in the classroom: an account of changing attitudes', in J. Mitchell and A. Oakley (eds), *The Rights and Wrongs of Women*, Harmondsworth, Penguin.

Merck, M. (1981), 'Sutcliffe: what the papers said', *Spare Rib*, no. 108.

Millman, M. (1975), 'She did it all for love: a feminist view of the sociology of deviance', in M. Millman and R. Kantor (eds), *Another Voice: Feminist Perspectives on Social Life and Social Science*, New York, Anchor Press.

Network Training Group (1983), 'Training and the state: responses to the MSC', Manchester, Network Training Group.

Newson, J. and Newson, E. (1965), *Patterns of Infant Care*, London, Penguin.

Newton, P. (1980), '"Women's work" in engineering', paper given at Social Psychology and Social Policy workshop at the University of Kent at Canterbury.

Newton, P. (1983), 'Only one or two? Social and psychological implications of some research on female engineers', paper presented at British Psychological Society conference, Sheffield.

Oakley, A. (1972), *Sex and Gender in Society*, London, Temple Smith.

Oakley, A. (1974), *Housewife*, Harmondsworth, Allen Lane.

Oakley, A. (1981), 'Interviewing women: a contradiction in terms', in H. Roberts (ed.), *Doing Feminist Research*, London, Routledge & Kegan Paul.

Parker, S. (1971), *The Future of Work and Leisure*, London, Longman.

Parker, S. (1976), *The Sociology of Leisure*, London, Allen & Unwin.

Parmar, P. and Mirza, N. (1981), 'Growing angry, growing strong', *Spare Rib*, no. 111.

Pinchbeck, I. (1930), *Women Workers and the Industrial Revolution: 1750-1850*, London, Virago (republished 1981).

Pollert, A. (1981), *Girls, Wives, Factory Lives*, London, Macmillan.

Powell, R. and Clarke, J. (1975), 'A note on marginality', in S. Hall and T. Jefferson, (eds), *Resistance Through Rituals: Youth Subcultures in Post-war Britain*, London, Hutchinson.

Prendergast, S. and Prout, A. (1980), 'What will I do? Teenage girls and the construction of motherhood', *Sociological Review*, vol. 28, no. 3, pp. 517-35.

Presdee, M. (1982), 'Invisible girls: a study of unemployed working class young women', paper given at seminar on 'Young, Female and Unemployed' at the Australian Studies Centre, London; also in *New Society*, 1981.

Pryce, K. (1979), *Endless Pressure*, Harmondsworth, Penguin.

Race and Class (1981), double issue on 'Rebellion and repression: Britain '81', vol. 23, nos. 2-3.

Race and Politics Group, CCCS (1982), *The Empire Strikes Back: Race and Racism in '70s Britain*, London, Hutchinson.

Rampton Committee (1981), 'West Indian children in our schools: interim report of the committee of inquiry into the education of children from ethnic minority groups', London, HMSO, Department of Education and Science.

Rapoport, R. and Rapoport, R. (1975), *Leisure and the Family Life Cycle*, London, Routledge & Kegan Paul.

Rapoport, R. and Rapoport, R. (1976), *Dual Career Families Re-examined: New Integrations of Work and Family*, Oxford, Martin Robertson.

Rauta, I. and Hunt, A. (1975), 'Fifth form girls: their hopes for the future', London, HMSO, Census Office.

Read, S. (1982), *Sexual Harassment*, London, Hamlyn.

Rich, A. (1981), 'Compulsory heterosexuality and lesbian existence', London, Onlywomen Press pamphlet.

Robbins, D. and Cohen, P. (1978), *Knuckle Sandwich*, Harmondsworth, Penguin.

Roberts, H. and Sharpe, M. (1982), 'After sixteen: what happened to the girls', Manchester, Equal Opportunities Commission pamphlet.

Roberts, K. (1970), *Leisure*, London, Longman.

Roberts, K. (1972), *From School to Work: A Study of the Youth Employment Service*, London, David & Charles.

Roberts, K. (1976), 'Where is the Careers Service heading?', *Careers Bulletin*, autumn.

Roberts, K. (1978), *Contemporary Society and the Growth of Leisure*, London, Longman.

Roberts, K. (1980), 'Occupational choice: an historical romance', *Youth in Society*, vol. 89, pp. 16-18.

Rowbotham, S., Segal, L. and Wainwright, H. (1979), 'Beyond the fragments: feminism and the making of socialism', Newcastle Socialist Centre and Islington Community Press.

Rubin, G. (1975), 'The traffic in women: notes on the political economy of sex', in R. Reiter (ed.), *Towards an Anthropology of Women*, New York, Monthly Review Press.

Saadawi, El, N. (1980), *The Hidden Face of Eve: Women in the Arab World*,

London, Zed Press.

Seccombe, W. (1974), 'The housewife and her labour under capitalism', *New Left Review*, no. 83.

Sharpe, S. (1976), *Just Like a Girl: How Girls Learn to be Women*, Harmondsworth, Penguin.

Shaw, J. (1976), 'Finishing school: some implications of sex-segregated education', in D.L. Barker and S. Allen (eds), *Sexual Division and Society: Process and Change*, London, Tavistock.

Shaw, J. (1978), 'School attendance: some notes on a further feature of sexual division', paper given at conference on 'Patriarchy, Capitalism and Educational Policy' at the London Institute of Education.

Shaw, J. (1980), 'Education and the individual: schooling for girls, or mixed schooling – a mixed blessing?', in R. Deem (ed.), *Schooling for Women's Work*, London, Routledge & Kegan Paul.

Sivanandan, A. (1976), 'Race, class and the state: the Black experience in Britain', *Race and Class*, vol. 17, no. 4; also *Race and Class* pamphlet, no. 1.

Smith, D. (1976), *The Facts of Racial Disadvantage: A National Study*, PEP, London, Policy Studies Institute.

Smith, D. (1981), 'Unemployment and racial minorities', report, London, Policy Studies Institute.

Snell, M. (1979), 'The Equal Pay and Sex Discrimination Acts: their impact on the workplace', *Feminist Review*, vol. 1, pp. 37-58.

Spence, J. and Helmreich, R. (1978), *Masculinity and Femininity: Their Psychological Dimensions, Correlates and Antecedents*, University of Texas Press.

Spender, D. (1980), *Man Made Language*, London, Routledge & Kegal Paul.

Spender, D. (1982), *Invisible Women: The Schooling Scandal*, London, Writers and Readers Collective.

Spender, D. and Sarah, E. (eds) (1980), *Learning to Lose: Sexism in Education*, London, The Women's Press.

Stanley, L. and Wise, S. (1983), *Breaking Out: Feminist Consciousness and Feminist Research*, London, Routledge & Kegan Paul.

Stanworth, M. (1983), 'Gender and schooling: a study of sexual divisions in the classroom', London, Hutchinson.

Stone, M. (1981), *The Education of the Black Child: The Myth of Multiracial Education*, London, Fontana Original.

Tajfel, H. (1978), 'The social psychology of minority groups', Minority Rights Group pamphlet.

Thitsa, K. (1981), 'Tourist Thailand: women for sale', *Spare Rib*, no. 103.

Thomas, C. (1980), 'Girls and counter-school cultures', in D. McCallum and V. Ozolins (eds), *Melbourne Working Papers*, University of Melbourne, Australia.

Thompson, E.P. (1963), *The Making of the English Working Class*, London, Gollancz.

Thompson, E.P. (1967), 'Time, work-discipline and industrial capitalism', *Past and Present*, vol. 38, pp. 56-97.

Thorpe, S. (1982), 'Young women's unemployment: a survey of Birmingham', unpublished BSc dissertation, University of Aston in Birmingham.

Tolson, A. (1977), *The Limits of Masculinity*, London, Tavistock.

Ullah, P. (1983), 'Pride and prejudice: an ethnographic study of ethnic identity in second generation Irish adolescents', paper presented at British Psychological Society conference, Sheffield.

Walden, R. and Walkerdine, V. (1982), 'Girls and mathematics: the early years', University of London Institute of Education, Bedford Way papers, no. 8.

Wallsgrave, R. (1983), 'Girls and maths — summing it up', *Spare Rib*, no. 127, p. 31.

Watson, J. (1977), *Between Two Cultures: Migrants and Minorities in Britain*, Oxford, Blackwell.

Webb, A. (1980), 'The transition from school to work: an economic analysis', paper given at National Youth Bureau/Social Science Research Council workshop on 'The School to Work Transition', Leicester.

Webb, C. (1980), 'Birmingham: the city is still a workshop', *The Times*, 11 August.

Whitelegg, E. *et al*., (1982), *The Changing Experience of Women*, London, Open University Press.

Whitfield, R. (1980), *Education for Family Life: Some New Policies for Child Care*, London, Hodder & Stoughton.

Willis, P. (1977), *Learning to Labour: How Working Class Kids get Working Class Jobs*, London, Saxon House.

Willis, P. (1979), 'Shop floor culture, masculinity and the wage form', in J. Clarke, C. Critcher and R. Johnson (eds), *Working Class Culture*, London, Hutchinson.

Willis, P. (1980), 'Notes on method', in S. Hall, D. Hobson, A. Lowe and P. Willis (eds), *Culture, Media, Language*, London, Hutchinson.

Wilson, A. (1978), *Finding a Voice: Asian Women in Britain*, London, Virago.

Winship, J. (1980), 'Sexuality for sale', in S. Hall *et al*., (eds), *Culture, Media, Language*, London, Hutchinson.

Women's Voice, (1979), 'Jobs massacre at the office', *Women's Voice* pamphlet.

Young, M. and Willmott, P. (1973), *The Symmetrical Family*, London, Routledge & Kegan Paul.

Index